57.50
80u

D1711202

Crimes by the Capitalist State

SUNY Series in Radical Social and Political Theory

Roger S. Gottlieb, Editor

Crimes by the Capitalist State

An Introduction to State Criminality

Edited by

Gregg Barak

State University of New York Press

Published by
State University of New York Press, Albany

© 1991 State University of New York
All rights reserved

Printed in the United States of America

For information, address State University of New York
Press, State University Plaza, Albany, N.Y., 12246

Production by M. R. Mulholland
Marketing Dana E. Yanulavich

Library of Congress Cataloging-in-Publication Data

Crimes by the capitalist state: an introduction to state criminality
/ edited by Gregg Barak.
    p.   cm. — (SUNY series in radical social and political
theory)
    Includes bibliographical references and index.
    ISBN 0-7914-0584-2 (alk. paper). — ISBN 0-7914-0585-0 (pbk. :
alk. paper)
    1. Criminology.   2. Corruption (in politics)   I. Barak, Gregg.
II. Series.
HV6030.C744   1991
364.1'32—dc20

90-9889
CIP

In any society, the dominant groups are the ones with the most to hide about how a society works. Very often, therefore, truthful analyses are bound to have a critical ring, to seem like postures rather than objective statements.

Barrington Moore

The problems researched, the way in which the research is conducted, and the strategies devised to reach a solution tend either to support and reinforce society's status quo or undermine it. In this sense, social research is inescapably political, although usually (and ironically) only the research aimed at changing the system is so labelled.

Emilio Viano

Does not utopian mean merely: what acknowledges other values as relevant and possibly even sovereign? But in truth, are not those who in the name of realism act like crackpots, are they not the utopians? Are we not now in a situation in which the only practical, realistic down-to-earth thinking and acting is just what these crackpot realists call "utopian"?

C. Wright Mills

Contents

Preface

STATE AND CRIME was the theme of the 40th Annual Meeting of the American Society of Criminology held at the Marriott Hotel in Chicago, November 9–12, 1988. As a member of the Program Committee, I was responsible for the topical sessions on "Crimes By and Against the State." About two-thirds of the papers submitted to me addressed the topic of crimes by the state. The fact that at least twenty-five criminologists in attendance at these meetings were already engaged in the study of state criminality suggested to me that criminology had finally evolved to the point where the field was ready to devote attention to the very serious problem of crimes by the state. Moreover, criminology had reached that critical point where it was ripe for the scholarly production of texts on this subject. This anthology is the result of an attempt to produce the first scholarly book on the subject of state criminality.

With the possible exception of *The Lawless State: The Crimes of the U.S. Intelligence Agencies* (1976), written some fifteen years ago, this reader becomes the first book to exclusively focus on the subject of state criminality. While there is some overlap in these two works, the differences are quite obvious. *The Lawless State* was basically the first documented report on the crimes of the Central Intelligence Agency, the Federal Bureau of Investigation, the Internal Revenue Service, the National Security Agency, and other U.S. intelligence agencies. *Crimes by the Capitalist State* is basically the first analytically developed overview of the broad range of state criminality. More important, perhaps, this collection includes states from North America, Latin America, Europe, and Australia. My intention initially was to produce a book of readings on crimes by the state. As it turned out, the book became more specific because all of the contributions revolved around crimes committed or omitted by capitalist states. Therefore, I decided to name the anthology *Crimes by the Capitalist State*.

This is not to suggest that only capitalist states and Western democracies have some kind of monopoly over or inside track on state criminality. On the contrary, it appears that state criminality (or its pre-state equivalent) knows no economic, ideological, or geographical boundaries. State criminality has existed under other modes of production (e.g., feudal, socialist), both in the past and the present. And it can be found in the Eastern and Southern as well as the Western and Northern Hemispheres.

However, the nature, patterns, or seriousness of state crime will not necessarily be the same for all types of state formation. In fact, a structural and dialectical analysis of state criminality, such as the one presented here, would predict that crimes by the state would vary according to the changing interaction between a particular state formation and the developing worldwide political economy. It is assumed that a fully developed criminology of state criminality would have to incorporate the full array of state crimes committed by the varying kinds of state formations; hence the subtitle of this anthology, *An Introduction to State Criminality* — which recognizes that this work is fundamentally only a prerequisite for the study of state criminality.

Crimes by the Capitalist State is not meant to be comprehensive, but it does attempt to provide a broad overview of state criminality. In the process, it provides not only rich and detailed case studies of the various forms of crimes by the state, but also highly developed analyses of state crimes grounded in politically, economically, and ideologically informed discussions. I hope the reader finds these essays as interesting and as valuable as I have, but more importantly, I hope the book will move criminologists and others to participate in the demanding study and reduction of state criminality.

Gregg Barak

I
Prologue

Toward a Criminology of State Criminality

Gregg Barak

Most discussions of crime and victimization emphasize traditional offenses such as homicide, rape, robbery, assault, and burglary committed by feuding family members, sexual deviates, drug addicts, or members of the marginal underclasses. The victims of these crimes are usually abused wives, battered children, the elderly, or other vulnerable populations (Christie, 1986). The victimization caused by these 'crimes against the state' is both direct and immediate: victims are all quite tangible and in close proximity to the source of their victimization.

In addition to these traditional crimes against the state, most scholars and students of crime acknowledge less conventional (though not less frequent) forms of criminality involving white-collar abuses and corporate injuries which may or may not be legally defined as crimes against the state. The victims of socially and physically harmful actions such as pollution of the environment, production of hazardous substances, and manufacture and sale of unsafe products are less tangible than the victims of traditional criminal acts. And while the pain and suffering caused by white-collar and corporate crime is greater in both economic and physical terms than that caused by street crime (Reiman, 1984), the graphic portrayals and discussions of these 'crimes by the powerful' are dwarfed by those mediated themes involving the 'crimes of the powerless' (Barak, 1988). In other words, although the victims of white-collar and corporate misbehavior — business as usual — are no less real, their victimization does not fit with the historical, ideological, and structural construction of the ideal victim. In fact, real victims of these upper-world crimes number in the millions each year. For the most part, however, the victims of these business and corporate dealings go unreported, and these offenses are typically not prosecuted.

Other types of crime committed by government agencies or caused by public policies create additional groupings of victims and forms of victimization that are traditionally overlooked or downplayed: victims of social, political, and economic injustice; victims of racial, sexual, and cultural discrimination; and victims of abuse of political and/or economic power. In an effort to turn attention to such crimes and victims, this book examines state criminality and asks criminologists and others to join forces with those who already recognize the need to study and reduce the various forms and institutionalization of 'crimes by the state.'

Often, crimes by the state are either ignored totally or defended totally. Either way, the political situation for state-crime victims is significantly more precarious than the political situation for victims of traditional street or suite crime. Because the victims of state criminality typically lack any means of judicial redress, they usually have very little, if any, political recourse against the perpetrators of their abuse. Generally, justice is not rendered to victims of state crimes without some kind of international intervention, and any international intervention naturally becomes both the object and subject of the geopolitical realities of worldwide state power. In other words, nations with the most state power vis-à-vis other nations or their own citizens are most likely to 'get away with murder' (or any other crime, for that matter).

The mass beatings, murders, and arrests carried out by the Chinese military and the paramilitary People's Armed Police against Chinese student demonstrators in June 1989 were obvious and overt examples of state criminality. Most people, especially those outside China, found it difficult not to label China's latest governmental crackdown, its "reign of terror" (to use a *Newsweek* cover story phrase) aimed at those student dissidents and others who Chinese state authorities accused of "committing crimes of counterrevolutionary propaganda and instigation," as anything less than criminal (*Newsweek*, 1989:14). Most folks rejected the official Chinese line that the hundreds (probably thousands) of detainees were actually "looters, vagrants, rumormongers, individual entrepreneurs and recidivist criminals who had not reformed properly." One foreign diplomat who observed a governmental roundup commented that "their victims were on a list" (*Newsweek*, 1989:14).

Crimes by the state—capitalist, socialist, or otherwise—are usually far more subtle and covert, however. For example, truly counterrevolutionary attacks or forms of repression such as censuring of the media in China, South Africa, and Israel are means or crimes of last resort. Moreover, while state crimes may include obvious and subtle acts and omissions, they may also include crimes of a political or nonpolitical nature. Nonpolitical state crimes are usually identified with and committed by individuals employed by the government who take advantage of their positions to engage in crime for personal and/or monetary gain. Unlike political state crimes, these crimes are not motivated by a desire to maintain the status quo or curtail change, and they are not committed by agents working 'from the top down.'

The study of state criminality is by definition a political enterprise. It involves, among other things, the study of power, ideology, law, and public and foreign policy. As such, the study of state criminality is part and parcel of the emotionally charged landscape of a changing political economy. It is often noted that one person's terrorist is another person's freedom fighter. To develop a criminology of state criminality, therefore, we must go well beyond the media imagery and political discourse concerning crimes by the state. Moreover, it is important for criminologists, legal scholars, political scientists, and others to develop conceptual frameworks regarding state criminality which not only incorporate the full array of state crimes, but which can aid in understanding the relative harm and injury caused by the behaviors and/or policies of nation-states.

Take the state crimes of Libya and the United States, for example. Official agencies of the Libyan state have certainly sponsored acts of terrorism, but Libya's Western critics have exploited the weaknesses and stigma of Moammar Qadhafi, thereby distorting the true seriousness of his nation's crimes. The actual frequency and systematic nature of Libya's state crimes are far less than suggested by the Western media (Jenkins 1988).

The United States engages in systematic counterrevolutionary warfare, proinsurgency, and interventionism which, for the most part, remain secret from both the American people and the mainstream media. This *low-intensity conflict* or *warfare* is "designed not only to defend the U.S. empire against rising challenges from the poor but also to conceal from U.S. citizens the unpleasant consequences of empire." The activities of this kind of warfare involve "an unprecedented degree of coordination among the White House, the National Security Council, the Central Intelligence Agency, the State Department, the Agency for International Development, conservative private aid groups, and a shady semiprivate network of drug runners, arms merchants, and assassins" (Nelson-Pallmeyer, 1989:2 – 3). This so-called secret does not escape world opinion and accounts not only for conflicts over U.S. foreign policy (both inside and outside the United States) but for the relative insignificance given to the general policy of low-intensity global warfare by both the mass media and the ruling politicos. The policies of low-intensity conflict engaged in by both Western and Eastern countries seek to integrate traditional military aspects of warfare with modern, technological aspects of mass communications, private consumption, and social control, on the one hand, and with the political, economic, and psychological aspects of warfare, on the other. As contemporary data and analyses reveal, these and other crimes by the state are more lethal and destructive than more traditional crimes committed against the state. (Herman, 1982; Nelson-Pallmeyer, 1989).

State Criminality and the Need for a Criminology of States

To study state criminality (both domestic and international) means confronting the fundamental and irreconcilable conflict between empire and social justice. Countries under the influence of the Soviet and U.S. empires have experienced exploitative relationships. Of course, neither country readily admits to its respective state crimes, and each (through various propaganda and disinformation efforts) attempts to put a noble or heroic label on the seamy and contradictory side of its professed ideals. Pragmatically, this translates into holding nation-states accountable to the principles of international law, satisfying universal human rights, and supporting global treaties, declarations, and other efforts aimed at achieving self-determinism and independent development for the worldwide family of nations.

The study of state criminality is complicated by the differences between proactive state criminality and crimes of omission. Examples of the former include the activities of the Iran-Contra affair and the subsequent behaviors of both the Contras and the Sandinistas. Examples of the latter include the denial of sufficient and adequate housing to the homeless and the informal economy and the traditional forms of criminal activity it produces. There has been very little systematic or analytic study of either proactive or omissive crimes by the state. Even less ground has been broken toward developing a theoretical understanding of the criminality of states.

Although students of comparative crime and criminal justice have paid some attention to political crimes committed against the state, they have seriously neglected the political crimes committed by the state. This neglect is not new.

More than a decade ago one observer of the crime problem made the critical point that criminologists neglected the study of large-scale, primarily economically motivated, international criminal networks, some of which included drug trafficking and arms trafficking among their activities. . . . At about the same time Manuel Lopez-Rey . . . complained about the neglect by criminology and criminal justice of "non-conventional" crime, including law violations for patriotic, ideological, and revolutionary reasons, including terrorism against the state and state-sponsored terrorism (Martin et al., 1988:1).

In short, criminology has failed to formulate any theories about terrorism, espionage, and drug and arms trafficking. In fact, the international crime patterns involved in these four types of crimes are rarely even mentioned in the criminology literature.

Like the study of corporate crime, the study of state crime involves examining behaviors and processes committed by agents and organizations that are both socially acceptable and politically powerful (Clinard and Yeager, 1980; Ermann and Lundman, 1982). Although both corporate and state criminality can potentially undermine the very stability of the system the corporate state strives for, crimes by the state pose the greater threat to the system as a whole. State criminality, in other words, creates inherent contradictions which simultaneously threaten the legitimacy of the prevailing political order yet accommodate the very same behavior in the name of common interests or national security. The political repression of and crimes committed against the Chinese demonstrators in 1989 provides an excellent example of this point.

The impact of state criminality is enormous. Like struggles for global emancipation and so-called wars against various forms of antidemocratic repression, state criminality deserves the utmost attention by students of criminological inquiry. Whether conducting detailed investigations of agents or organizations violating the rights of their own citizenry or exploring the patterns of interstate terrorism, criminologists and others must recognize "that it is futile and hypocritical selfdeception to suppose that we can use the word *terrorism* to establish a double standard pertaining to the use of political violence. Unless we are consistent and self-critical in our use of language we invite the very violence we deplore" (Falk, 1988:xiv). As syndicated columnist David Broder noted about the connection between Oliver North and Manuel Noriega, shortly after the general and his people stole the results of the Panamanian election in May, 1989, the lesson to be learned was: "when the executive branch of the U.S. government evades the laws passed by Congress, when it brushes aside the verdict of the World Court on its illegal mining of Nicaraguan harbors, then it cannot be surprised when

the head of a client government decides to ignore the election returns"
(Broder, 1989:2b).

The criminological journey toward a 'criminality of states' will not
be accomplished overnight. To begin with, criminology must overcome
its tendency to treat political violence and state criminality one-dimen-
sionally, as though they involved the behavior only of 'bad guys' and not
'good guys' as well. Moreover, there is much work to be done — theoretically, strategically, and ideologically. As Ross (1988:1) informs us
about the case of terrorism:

> Over the last two-and-a-half decades there has been an increasing
> number of studies of political terrorism in advanced industrial de-
> mocracies. Unquestionably, the majority of studies on terrorism
> have tended to be descriptive and normative, have conceptual and
> methodological problems, and are marked by theoretical general-
> izations without any basis in empirical data.

For the most part, academic interest in this area has focused on selective
terrorist acts — selective not only in terms of countries emphasized and
neglected, but also in terms of the various forms of terrorism committed. Typically discussed are 'retail' terrorist acts, acts committed by
groups or individuals against agents or symbolic representatives of an
enemy state. Typically ignored are 'wholesale' acts of terrorism, those
waged by state-supported networks against independence or national
revolutionary movements (Chomsky and Herman, 1979; Herman,
1982).

Ross's indictment of the study of terrorism is even more relevant
to the overall study of state criminality. The study of state criminality is
problematic because the concept itself is controversial, in part because
of a debate over whether one should define crime in terms other than
the law codes of individual nations. Some argue that if a state obeys its
own laws, it should be judged by no other higher criterion — religious,
philosophical, or political. Others argue that there are definitions of
'crimes against humanity' which transcend nation-state definitions of
illegality. Consistent with this latter view is the fundamental belief underlying this anthology — namely, that higher criteria for establishing
state criminality exist in various international treaties and laws. Criminologists and others should not be limited to or circumscribed by law
codes of individual nations. Similarly, investigators of state criminality
should not be deterred by the failure of the state to adjudicate itself or
its agents as criminals. Just because states have historically ignored
their own criminality, does not mean that criminologists and others
should do so too.

As early as the fifth century A.D., for example, it was noted and understood that pirate bands shared the essential qualities and abilities of states and empires: both pirates and empires had the capacity to seize property by violence. The primary differences between the two were the scale of their endeavors and the success of states at imposing a rhetoric and ideology to justify their thefts of land, property, and people.

A brief glance at the history of the United States also reveals the patterned actions of state criminality. The U.S. government and its agents violated the fundamental human rights of native and African Americans during the eighteenth and nineteenth centuries and the legal and civil rights of workers, minorities, and other dissidents during the twentieth century. For the most part, these crimes were not accidental or due to negligence, but rather the outcome of premeditated and intentional acts on behalf of the state and its political-economic policies. Furthermore, patterns of U.S. state criminality have always been both domestic and international, recognizing no absolute boundaries of national sovereignty. Quite often, these crimes against humanity have been in full compliance with the law (i.e., slavery).

In light of these facts, students of state criminality should also recognize that the FBI has been not only a crime-fighting institution but a political police apparatus as well. The Palmer Raids and Red Scare of 1919, the McCarthyism of the early 1950s, and the counterinsurgency campaigns of the late 1960s and early 1970s used against citizens protesting U.S. involvement in the war in Vietnam — all of these reveal a domestic history of significant political repression and state criminality against citizens who have seriously challenged the status quo (Glick, 1989). Such covert and overt activities are not limited to domestic enemies but include international enemies as well. The CIA has a long record of supporting dictators in countries such as Cuba, Iran, the Philippines, Nicaragua, Brazil, South Korea, and Argentina and of overthrowing or destabilizing democratically elected governments in Guatemala, Chile, Jamaica, Nicaragua, and other countries (Bodenheimer and Gould, 1989).

What these domestic and international state crimes have in common are ongoing series of illegal clandestine operations used against politically-defined enemies. The FBI's infamous counterintelligence programs (COINTELPRO) aimed at the Black Panther Party, the antiwar movement, and the American Indian Movement in the 1960s and 1970s included a variety of illegal and unconstitutional techniques for deligitimatizing and criminalizing otherwise lawful organizations (Churchill and Wall, 1988). These state crimes included everyday activities such as illegal surveillance, burglary, and mail tampering, as well as more exotic state crimes such as using propaganda to smear progressive organizations and using agents provocateurs as disruptive forces within various progressive groups.

Distinguishing between the various motives for these kinds of state-organized crimes is by no means a simple task even though these crimes revolve essentially around money, power, and politics. Analysis of state criminality is further complicated because it involves the overlapping activities of criminal and noncriminal organizations making use of each others' resources. Alan Block has summarized the situation by saying that traditionally organized crime and state-organized crime are inseparable in many cases: "Organized crime has been and continues to be inextricably linked to transnational political movements and to that segment of the American political establishment known as the espionage community or more aptly, the transnational police force" (Block 1986:59). He concludes that this kind of interplay between organized and state criminality results in a situation where "it may very well be the case that certain political assassinations or other intelligence moves may be done not in the interests of foreign policy carried out by hired goons and thugs, but rather in the interest of drug smugglers and international gamblers carried out by their clients in the intelligence services" (Block, 1986:76).

However, such state-organized crimes and violence — as well as the political policing and repression associated with the Iran-Contra scandal or the corruption and enforced disappearances in Latin America — remain state-organized secrets as well. In other words, the structural and etiological roots of state criminality in both the United States and Latin America are related to the fundamental fact that the bourgeoisies or ruling elites in all of these countries are responding to the same set of geopolitical forces. The stateless crimes of U.S. workers and Latin American peasants, the client-state crimes of terrorist proportions in the Middle East, and the legalized state terrorism of South African apartheid — all of these raise fundamental questions concerning power and its relationship to the disparity between the de facto status quo and the de jure status quo (Dieterich, 1986).

The study of state-supported corruption and violence, therefore, can never really be separated from individual acts of criminality and terrorism because both are related to the inequitable relationships between economic wealth and political-juridical privileges. Heinz Dieterich has argued that the material debasement of "the majority of the Latin American peoples is an inevitable consequence of the current capitalist accumulation model" and the physical and psychological submission of these peoples "into a state of apathy and fear is a functional prerequisite for that accumulation model" (Dieterich, 1986:50). Enforced disappearances in Latin America and other parts of the Third World will not disappear until the underlying causes have been removed — in other words, not until a socioeconomic system is established to provide decent existences for peoples of all developing countries. Historically, the role of the United States in inhibiting such development is well known. On the subject of client-state terrorism in the Americas, Shank has concluded that:

> Washington has become the organizational center for a variety of institutions, agencies, and training programs which provide the expertise, financing, and technology to service client-state terrorist institutions. Since 1970s, this expertise has been supplemented by private services run by former intelligence and military officers (Shank, 1987:xiii).

The time for putting a stop to this kind of state intervention into the political affairs of other countries is long overdue. One step toward reducing such intervention is to recognize both its criminal content and its potential for criminalizing a host of other behaviors. This objective is one of the underlying thrusts of this anthology.

Crimes by the Capitalist State

The perspective on state criminality adopted in this volume is based on recent developments in critical criminology. In particular, the implicit and explicit assumptions underlying the analyses developed in each chapter are compatible with the philosophies and practices of the emerging schools of 'new left realism' and 'peacemaking' criminology.[1] In brief, the new left realists have stressed victimization, the deromanticizing of crime, and the policies of the capitalist state. The peacemaking criminologists, on the other hand, have stressed the necessity of transforming the human being with regard to the mutual dependence of criminals and victims, the need for a reduction of hierarchical structures, and the promotion of communities of caring people (Schwartz, 1989). These schools of critical criminology share a common appreciation of contradictory relationships in human affairs, a negative assessment of the status quo, and a belief in the need for fundamental change in productive and social relations (including the decentralizing and democratizing of government while emphasizing cooperative rather than competitive forms of socio-economic interaction). In different ways, both of these critical schools attempt to transform the contemporary

consumptive culture of myths, stereotypes, and ideologies which reproduce the exploitative materialism of a world grounded in gross inequality and privilege.

This study of state criminality is part of the development in radical
political and social thought which has characterized an emerging tradition in North American academia over the past two decades. As part
of this radical enterprise, *Crimes By the Capitalist State* departs from the
positivism, correctionalism, and conservatism of mainstream criminology. In the place of legalism, state definitions of crime problems, and
narrowly focused concerns on individual offenders and punishment,
this book focuses on the structural and organizational nature of governmental abuse. Attention is also given to the relationship between the
changing global political economy and the reproduction of class and social injustice worldwide.

Accordingly, contributions to this anthology have been grouped
into three parts: "Classical Forms of State Crime," "On the Dialectical
Nature of State Crimes," and "Crimes of State Omission." We believe
that this type of theoretical and methodological framework is absolutely
essential for developing an integrative, descriptive, and explanatory
analysis of state criminality.

In Part I, "Classical Forms of State Crime," two illustrations are
provided — the first from Australia and the second from the United
States — in order to expose the reader to a broad overview of the classic
expressions of state criminality. Specifically examined are state crimes
involving surveillance, harassment, homicide, suicide, propaganda,
ideology, imprisonment, the First and Fourth Amendments, adjudication, colonialism/imperialism, and racism.

In Part II, "On the Dialectical Nature of State Crimes," the four illustrations provide detailed political and economic analyses of how law
and order is as often a question of law *versus* order. In view of these contradictions, the reader can begin to appreciate the important role that
ideology plays in the dialectical and contradictory relationship between
rule of law and the rule of force. Specifically examined are state crimes
involving drug and arms trafficking, air piracy, terrorism, kidnapping,
murder, foreign policy, due process, international relations, national-
ism, struggles for independence, disinformation, and general abuse of
state powers. Contributions in Part II turn their attention to such places
as Latin America, Peru, Israel, and the United States.

In Part III, "Crimes of State Omission," the four illustrations provide interesting and critical examples of how the omission of public and
private policies addressing both nonstate and state forms of criminality
is at the root of the injury, suffering, and victimization experienced by

hundreds of millions of people worldwide. Generally addressed are economic, cultural, feminist, and political issues revolving around various legislative, enforcement, and reformative dimensions associated with intelligence gathering, policing, rape reduction, and the illegal opportunities for engaging in traditional street criminality. Although the contributions focus on experiences in Canada and the United States, they are generically valuable in understanding the fundamental processes involved in state criminality.

Finally, in the Epilogue, I underscore the value of studying state criminality and its relevance or importance to the field of criminology. I also attempt to explain the role that criminologists can play in the developing struggles to reduce both state and non-state crime.

Note

1. For samples of the new realist perspective, see Taylor, 1981; Platt, 1982; Hunt, 1982; Boehringer et al., 1983; Michalowski, 1983; Lea and Young, 1984; Young, 1986. For samples of the more recent peacemaking perspective, see Pepinsky, 1986; 1988; Quinney, 1988; 1989; Lozoff and Braswell, 1989. For an example that employs both of these perspectives, see Barak and Bohm, 1989.

References

Barak, Gregg
1988 Newsmaking Criminology: Reflections on the Media, Intellectuals, and Crime. *Justice Quarterly.* Vol. 5, No. 4. 565–587.

Barak, Gregg and Robert M. Bohm
1989 The Crimes of the Homeless or The Crime of Homelessness? On the Dialectics of Criminalization, Decriminalization and Victimization. *Contemporary Crises: Law, Crime and Social Policy.* Vol. 13, No. 4. 275–288.

Block, Alan A.
1986 A Modern Marriage of Convenience: A Collaboration Between Organized Crime and U.S. Intelligence. In *Organized Crime: A Global Perspective.* Ed. by Robert J. Kelly. Totowa, NJ: Rowman & Littlefield.

Bodenheimer, Thomas and Robert Gould
1989 *Rollback! Right-wing Power in U.S. Foreign Policy.* Boston: South End Press.

Boehringer, G., D. Brown, B. Edgeworth, R. Hogg, and I. Ramsay
1983 'Law and Order' for Progressives?: An Australian Response. *Crime and Social Justice,* No. 19.2–12.

Broder, David
1989 Lawlessness At Home invites Defiance. *The Montgomery Advertiser and The Alabama Journal*. Sunday, May 14.

Christie, Nils
1986 The Ideal Victim. In *From Crime Policy to Victim Policy: Reorienting the Justice System*, ed. by Ezzaat A. Fattah. New York: St. Martin's Press.

Chomsky, Noam and Edward S. Herman
1979 *The Washington Connection and Third Word Fascism*. Boston: South End Press.

Churchill, Ward and Jim Vander Wall
1988 *Agents of Repression: The FBI's Secret Wars Against The Black Panther Party & The American Indian Movement*. Boston: South End Press.

Clinard, Marshall B. and Peter C. Yeager
1980 *Corporate Crime*. New York: The Free Press.

Dieterich, Heinz
1986 Enforced Disappearances and Corruption in Latin America. *Crime and Social Justice*. No. 25. 40–54.

Ermann, David and Richard J. Lundman
1982 *Corporate and Governmental Deviance: Problems of Organizational Behavior in Contemporary Society*. New York: Oxford University Press.

Falk, Richard
1988 *Revolutionaries and Functionaries: The Dual Face of Terrorism*. New York: E. P. Dutton.

Glick, Brian
1989 *War At Home: Covert Action Against U.S. Activists and What We Can Do About It*. Boston: South End Press.

Herman, Edward S.
1982 *The Real Terror Network: Terrorism in Fact and Propaganda*. Boston: South End Press.

Hunt, Alan
1982 Law, Order, and Socialism: A Response to Ian Taylor. *Crime and Social Justice*. No. 18. 16–22.

Jenkins, Philip
1988 Whose Terrorists? Libya and State Criminality. *Contemporary Crises: Law, Crime and Social Policy*. No. 12. 1–11.

Lee, J. and Jock Young
1984 *What is to be Done about Law and Order*. Middlesex, England: Penguin Books.

Lozoff, Bo and Michael Braswell
1989   *Inner Corrections: Finding Peace and Peace Making.* Cincinnati: Anderson Publishing Company.

Mack, John A.
1986   *The Crime Industry.* Lexington, MA: Lexington Books.

Martin, John. M., Anne T. Romano, and James F. Haran
1988   International Crime Patterns: Challenges to Traditional Criminological Theory and Research. *Criminal Justice Research Bulletin.* Vol. 4, No. 2. 1–12.

Michalowski, Raymond J.
1983   Crime Control in the 1980s: A Progressive Agenda. *Crime and Social Justice,* No. 19. 13–23.

Nelson-Pallmeyer, Jack
1989   *War Against the Poor: Low-Intensity Conflict and Christian Faith.* Maryknoll, NY: Orbis Books.

Newsweek
1989   Reign of Terror (Cover Story). June 19.

Pepinsky, Harold E.
1988   Violence as Unresponsiveness: Toward A New Conception of Crime. *Justice Quarterly.* Vol. 5, No. 4. 539–564.
1986   This Can't Be Peace: A Pessimist Looks at Punishment. In *Punishment and Privilege,* ed. by W. Byron Groves and Graeme Newman. New York: Harrow and Heston.

Platt, Tony
1982   Crime and Punishment in the United States: Immediate and Long-term Reforms from a Marxist Perspective. *Crime and Social Justice.* No. 18. 38–45.

Quinney, Richard
1989   Foreword. In *Inner Corrections: Finding Peace and Peace Making,* Bo Lozoff and Michael Braswell. Cincinnati: Anderson Publishing Company.
1988   The Theory and Practice of Peacemaking in the Development of Radical Criminology. Paper presented at the annual meeting of the American Society of Criminology, Chicago.

Reiman, Jeffrey
1984   *The Rich Get Richer and the Poor Get Prison: Ideology, Class, and Criminal Justice.* New York: Wiley.

Ross, Jeffrey Ian
1988   Attributes of Domestic Political Terrorism in Canada, 1960–1985. *Terrorism: An International Journal.* Vol. 11, No. 3. 213–233.

Schwartz, Martin D.
1989   The Undercutting Edge of Criminology. *The Critical Criminologist.* Vol. 1, No. 2 (Spring).

Shank, Gregory
1987　Contragate and Counterterrorism: An Overview. *Crime and Social Justice.*
　　　Nos. 27–28. i–xxvii.
Taylor, Ian
1981　*Law and Order: Arguments for Socialism.* London: Macmillan.

Young, Jock
1986　The Failure of Criminology: The Need for a Radical Realism. In *Confront-
　　　ing Crime,* ed. by R. Mathews and J. Young. London: Sage Publications.

II

Classical Forms of State Crime

Overview

In the first contribution to this Part, "Passion and Policy: Aboriginal Deaths in Custody in Australia 1980–1989," Kayleen Hazlehurst examines the relationship between the crimes by and against the Aboriginal peoples and the role of the state and its various agencies, especially those involved in law enforcement, adjudication, and incarceration. In a historical and neocolonial context, Hazlehurst explores the events, activities, and protests that led to establishing the Royal Commission into Aboriginal Deaths in Custody. She discusses the commission's findings and how the inquiry itself obscured the fact that too many aboriginals are in prison who should not be there in the first place. Hazlehurst goes on to specifically define the treatment of the aboriginal peoples within the context of international human rights in general and specifically within the context of the International Covenant on Civil and Political Rights, of which Australia is a consignatory nation. Finally, Hazlehurst explores such issues as racism, genocide, and psychological terrorism. Among her summary statements are two which capture both the complexity and two-sided nature of state criminality:

> Aboriginal people are dying prematurely from ill health, imprisonment, despair and defeat. For many years, they have asserted that acts of oppression and neglect by authorities have continued in the face of legislation which should outlaw such acts. Evidence of this is now emerging from national and international inquiries.

> Daily intervention by police, abuse and neglect of basic community needs, cruel and degrading treatment of aboriginal prisoners, intimidation of witnesses to national inquiries, and unashamed attempts by state agencies to terminate the Royal Commission into Aboriginal Deaths in Custody — all of these raise the question of whether the domestic situation in Australia warrants international intervention.

In the next contribution, "Subcultures as Crime: The Theft of Legitimacy of Dissent in the United States," Susan Caulfield examines "the dialectical processes involved in state activities which create criminals by violating rather than protecting citizen's fundamental rights as guaranteed in the Constitution and other laws." Analyzing the state's role in creating politically subversive or criminal subcultures, Caulfield focuses attention on two contemporary groups, the Committee in Solidarity with the People of El Salvador and the CoMadres of El Salvador. In a theoretically informed discussion of subcultural formation, she explores the relationship between First Amendment dissent and subjection to government harrassment, break-ins, illegal monitoring, and so on, as well as the "state-created illusion of legitimate intervention (stopping crime) as a cover for the political criminality of state agents." Caulfield argues that the state's use of "subcultural methodology" results in vast and serious harms—ranging from "the theft of basic constitutional rights to the infliction of monetary hardship on U.S. citizens, and monetary and physical hardship, including death, on citizens in Central America and elsewhere." Caulfield further points out that it is important for criminologists and other social scientists to seek ways to transcend the use of methodologies that contribute to such harms.

1

Passion and Policy: Aboriginal Deaths in Custody in Australia 1980–1989

*Kayleen M. Hazlehurst**

Dispossession and Its Consequences

In the United States, indigenous people have special sovereign status vis-à-vis domestic governments. The American Supreme Court has recognized the inalienable, indigenous rights of native Americans as distinguished from other American citizens. In Canada, colonial (and later federal) governments recognized the inherent land rights of native Canadians. Where indigenous title had not been extinguished by treaty, large-scale settlements have been made through the return of land, monetary compensation, or legislative enactment. Both the United States and Canada have treated with their indigenous nations and have, with some qualification, recognized native ownership of certain renewable and nonrenewable resources.

In 1840, the British Crown treated with the Maori chiefs of New Zealand to facilitate peaceful foreign settlement. The Treaty of Waitangi is now revered as the cornerstone of New Zealand nationhood, and since the 1970s it has been increasingly recognized in law and government policy. Over the past fifty years, major land settlements and arrangements concerning fisheries, forestry, and land development have brought greater economic prosperity to the Maori people.

Australia is the only British settlement which, in the words of Nettheim, "completely terminated by the act of annexation" all aspects of indigenous sovereignty and rights to land, and which has since had no constitutional acknowledgement of indigenous rights of prior ownership (1987a: 292; Keon-Cohen, 1981a:253–4).

Australia's history of carnage, dispossession, and discrimination is closer to present-day policy and practice than many Australians care to admit. For 150 years, conflict and repression accompanied white settlement over two-thirds of the area of the continent, leaving Australia with a legacy of racism, bitterness, and distrust.

More than 20,000 aboriginals are now thought to have died in fierce clashes over land with early European settlers. Until recently, history books ignored the aboriginals' resistance to white settlement. But memories—of the pitched battles which extinguished whole aboriginal clans, the expropriation of lands coveted by the settlers, the poisoning of water and flour, the relocation of whole groups to mission reserves, and the abduction and enforced labor of aboriginal children—are still fresh in the minds of present-generation aboriginals (Nettheim, 1987b; Reynolds, 1981, 1987; Butlin, 1983; Miller, 1986; Mattingley and Hampton, 1988).[1]

The injustices of Australia's colonial past and paternalistic present have had a profound effect upon aboriginal peoples and Europeans alike. A widespread assumption has existed among white Australian officials that their exercise of authority over every aspect of indigenous peoples' lives is not only legitimate but essential to the 'civilizing' process of a 'backward' people. Changing attitudes in this area has been slow, even for liberal-minded governments (Bird, 1987).

Aboriginals did not receive the right to vote and equal wages until the late 1960s. In spite of efforts, particularly by federal governments since the 1970s, to identify and remedy the current ills of aboriginal Australia, immeasurable losses of life, dignity, and liberty have continued. The suffering continues in more subtle, though equally pernicious, forms.

The greatest misfortune of Australian aboriginals is that they are a people who have lost their spirit. The social ills which beset them — poverty, alcoholism, poor health, and hopelessness — are ills of a defeated people. A large proportion of aboriginal families live in substandard, overcrowded housing or temporary shelters. Their average life expectancy is twenty years less than other Australians, and infant mortality is three times higher. The incidence of hepatitis B, typhus, trachoma, venereal disease, and early death related to chronic alcoholism, is significantly higher than in the general population. Unemployment among aboriginals is four to six times the national average.[2]

The neglect of roads, drinkable water, proper sanitation, and educational needs of aboriginal communities by local, state, and federal authorities was highlighted in 1988 in the Human Rights Commission's *Toomelah Report*, (which followed an inquiry into incidents of racist attacks and public disorder in New South Wales and Queensland border towns). Justice Marcus Einfeld reported that:

Their treatment by government at all levels has been insensitive and uncaring. Their human rights ignored. This situation has persisted for decades despite the fact that authoritative attention has often been drawn to it . . . The consequence has been high rates of preventable disease, neglect of treatable conditions, and retardation of the development of children (1988:61).[3]

At the root of contemporary study of human rights and racial tension in Australia is the fundamental yet unresolved question raised by European occupation of aboriginal land. Aboriginal sovereignty was usurped on the basis of the now widely rejected legal principle of *terra nullius*—land belonging to no-one.[4] Britain's original claim over the Australian continent was based on the premise that the land was occupied by no people with any recognizable system of government; it was acquired by 'settlement' rather than by conquest. In fact, tribally organized aboriginal groups—with routinized and widely understood systems of land use and traditional ownership—had occupied the territory for thousands of years. Aboriginal people never ceded their land to the colonizers, nor were they ever invited to submit their sovereignty to British rule.[5] As one Australian lawyer has put it:

As a matter of historical fact, the absurdity of this account has now been recognized. Australia was colonized by a slow process of occupation, often in the face of armed resistance from Aborigines— yet the constitutional doctrines denying Aboriginal sovereignty and title to land remain. These doctrines have been recently described by one High Court judge as a "convenient falsehood" (Keon-Cohen, 1981b:5).

Since the early 1980s, federal governments have flirted with the ideas of a national treaty or compact with the aboriginal people, constitutional amendments giving recognition of aboriginal prior ownership and traditional rights, or making restitution through the introduction of national land rights legislation. Their resolve has been shaken, however, by powerful opposition from state governments and pastoral and mining interests. Under its Constitution, the Australian federal government possesses the power to make a commitment which would be binding on the state governments of the country—and there are legal precedents for this—but this power has been used only sparingly in relation to aboriginal peoples.[6]

Without a viable land or resource base (as has been settled on the indigenous peoples of Canada and New Zealand), many aboriginal groups continue to be dependent upon the patronage and vagaries of the Australian welfare system. In areas where some transfer of land title has occurred, considerable improvements to aboriginal prospects have accompanied land development.[7]

Aboriginal Land Councils and Aboriginal Legal Services are progressively assembling evidence of a strong connection between the granting of land rights and the decline of aboriginal unemployment and imprisonment. Aboriginal organizations, however, have become deeply concerned over the growth of racist campaigns — particularly the campaign against land rights conducted by extreme right-wing organizations and sections of the Liberal and National Parties. Aboriginals have been unable to overcome the opposition mounted by the Queensland and Western Australian governments against federal government efforts to protect or entrench these rights in government policy and legislation.

The impoverishment of the general aboriginal population has had its effect on race relations. Social exchange between white and black residents of small rural townships, suburbs, or inner-city areas — where aboriginals migrate in search of work and a better life—are stressed by the realities of poverty. Racial tensions have increased in recent years, and incidents of street violence and riot have led to pronouncements of public and political concern. Tensions between aboriginals and police have been particularly acute.

Aboriginals have claimed that the historic domination and neglect by so-called responsible authorities has been followed in recent times by overzealous attention to duty by law enforcers, inequitable treatment in the administration of justice, maltreatment in custody, and a continuing saga of subjugation covertly condoned by the State.

Aboriginals and the Criminal Justice System

In theory, aboriginal people are subject to the same obligations and protection under Australian law as other citizens. In practice, they are grossly overrepresented as defendants under criminal law and as complainants under antidiscrimination law (Hanks and Keon-Cohen, 1984; Hazlehurst, 1987a).

Aboriginal offenses are typically conspicuous—vagrancy, drunk and disorderly, petty theft, street and domestic assault, and resisting arrest. Poor aboriginals attract the attention of the police because their habit of socializing outdoors makes them vulnerable targets for authorities wishing to 'clean up the streets.' Police readily find certain kinds of offenses among aboriginals because that is what they routinely look for. Aboriginal street offenders fill the jails. Aboriginals are at least ten times overrepresented in Australian prisons.[8]

Research over the last five years has shown that aboriginals are overrepresented at every level of the criminal justice system and that this overrepresention increases with the age of the offender. In some areas, aboriginals' lack of English-language skills gives rise to special problems in police interrogation and court hearings. There are disturbing indications that the problems disadvantaging aboriginals have become institutionalized into the structure and processes of the Australian criminal justice system (Bailey-Harris and Wundersitz, 1985:11–27; Gale and Wundersitz, 1985:209–214; 1987a:118-13; 1987b:78–94; Wundersitz and Gale, 1988:348–358).

Aboriginals account for a low proportion of white-collar and drug-related crime, but they:

> . . . were imprisoned more frequently for offences Against the person (33.0% for Aboriginals and 24.2% for non-Aboriginals); and non-Aboriginals more frequently for offences Against Property (29.8% for Aboriginals and 33.1% for non-Aboriginals). For Aboriginals, Against Good Order (11.8%) and Traffic/Vehicle-related offences (16.0%) were relatively high compared to non-Aboriginals (7.0% and 6.16% respectively). On the other hand, Robbery/Extortion (7.6%) and drug-related offences (1.5%) were relatively low in comparison to non-Aboriginals (15.8% and 13.6% respectively) (Hazlehurst and Dunn, 1988).

Aboriginal crime statistics provide a picture of a severely impoverished, depressed, and demoralized society—a society more likely to turn against its own members in frustration or rage. Bar and street brawls, disorderly conduct, rape, child abuse, domestic violence, and unpremeditated murder typify aboriginal offences against the person. It is largely the uncalculating criminality characteristic of underprivilege and social disaffection. For this reason, aboriginal organizations see aboriginal criminality as a social disorder which is potentially changeable through the restoration of dignity to the human condition.

Protest and Response

In 1983, five Western Australian police officers were charged with the manslaughter of a young aboriginal detainee, John Pat. Pat had suffered multiple contusions, his head and body had been kicked and thrown against concrete, and an autopsy revealed that he died with a fractured skull, a hemorrhaged brain, two broken ribs, and a torn artery to the heart. Although aboriginal witnesses testified that he had been severely beaten by police officers, the officers were acquitted when the prosecution evidence was skillfully dismantled by the defense. To aboriginals and sympathetic nonaboriginals, this case represented a blatant denial of justice (Grabosky, 1988:87–94).

In 1986, during an eight-week tour of aboriginal communities throughout the country, the National Aboriginal and Islander Legal Services Secretariat, Dr. Julian Burger (of the London-based Anti-Slavery Society) reported extensive allegations of physical and psychological abuse of aboriginal people, including women and children. Burger's report, *Aborigines Today: Land and Justice*, presented to the Australian government and the United Nations in 1988, noted that aboriginals had been "oppressed to the point where they are now outcasts in their own land, unemployed, uneducated, unhealthy, impoverished and possibly the most imprisoned people on earth" (Burger, 1988).

In 1987, news of aboriginal protest at what appeared to be a spate of aboriginal deaths in prison or police custody reached the press. A media probe revealed similar occurrences throughout the country. A small group of bereaved family members and their supporters toured the country giving public talks and speaking to government authorities. In New South Wales, spokesmen for an action group, the Committee to Defend Black Rights, urged a national inquiry into black deaths in custody. The inquiry, they said, should include a thorough investigation of the conduct of police and prison custodians.

A disturbing picture of individual tragedies resulting in a large number of aboriginal deaths in custody was emerging. Although some aboriginals in custody were dying from illness or misadventure, most deaths were officially recorded as suicides. Coroner's reports were frequently scrappy and inadequate, and autopsy reports always supported police or prison officer accounts.

Aboriginal prisoners were apparently hanging themselves with socks, shoe strings, and torn bed sheets or blankets strung from light fittings, bars, and ceiling or wall protrusions in cells. Some deaths occurred from a lack of medical attention to prisoners who were clearly demonstrating signs of distress. Others occurred during violent struggles with police or prison wardens — sometimes by heart attacks induced by choke holds or other restraining techniques used by the officers. Most deaths occurred in younger men within the first six hours of incarceration.

The official view held that depression set in following imprisonment of intoxicated aboriginals, particularly those placed in solitary confinement. Questions were raised about the degree of responsible supervision aboriginal prisoners were receiving. It was asked whether suicide was induced by degrading physical or psychological abuse by officers which further impaired prisoners' mental state, and led to self-mutilation or death. As one aboriginal ex-prisoner described it: "It's the way the screws treat you—God, it makes you so depressed. They inflict this mental torment that drives you crazy." And another: "When you go to jail it breaks your heart . . . breaks your spirit."[9]

On August 15, 1987, more than 150 aboriginals rioted for five hours in the main street of Brewarrina in New South Wales.

> They armed themselves with rocks, bottles, and iron bars, attacking the ambulance and police vehicles, smashing headlights, windows, and doors with their bars, and hurled missiles at police, Aboriginal liaison officers, and bystanders.

> Two officers were taken to hospital from the fighting — one sustaining a broken leg, the other serious facial injuries. Several Aboriginals received baton wounds and an Aboriginal woman was also taken to hospital. Every window in the hotel has been broken. Glass and debris littered the main street (Hazlehurst, 1988:8).

The Brewarrina riot came after the funeral of a local aboriginal, Lloyd Boney, who had been found hanging by his socks in a police cell. Aboriginal deaths in custody had become the center of considerable aboriginal distress and public controversy. At the time, Boney was the forty-fourth aboriginal known to have died in custody since 1980. His death and the public outcry it caused prompted the federal government to set up a Royal Commission into Aboriginal Deaths in Custody under Justice James Henry Muirhead.

The Royal Commission into Aboriginal Deaths in Custody

The Commission's task was to review the causes of aboriginal deaths while in police custody, prison, or any other place of detention which had occurred since January 1, 1980; and any subsequent actions to be taken regarding the conduct of coroners, police, or prison authorities (Hazlehurst and Hazlehurst, 1989).

The inquiry was to be completed in twelve months, but it was soon realized that this would be impossible. The retrieval of documents and identification of witnesses alone was a complicated and protracted process. When the inquiry got underway, the hearings proved immensely cumbersome, with one case resulting in almost five thousand pages of transcripts. In its call for submissions, the Commission's special research unit was literally confronted by truck loads of documents. To make matters worse, deaths in custody doubled in 1987, and three additional Commissioners had to be appointed to conduct the hearings. By February 2, 1989 there were 110 aboriginal deaths to investigate, and the Commission's deadline had been extended to the end of 1990.

In December 1988, Justice Muirhead released an Interim Report based on research conducted by the Commission on 434 total (aboriginal and nonaboriginal) deaths in custody since January 1980. Of all deaths, 92 (21%) were aboriginal (86 males and 6 females). The majority of aboriginal custodial deaths since 1980 (60%) had occurred in police custody, whereas the majority of nonaboriginal deaths (68%) had occurred in prisons.

The inquiry pointed out that, although the rate of aboriginal deaths in custody was similar to that of nonaboriginals, the high number of aboriginal deaths reflected a disturbing overrepresentation of aboriginal people in custody. The inquiry also found that the age distribution between aboriginal and nonaboriginal prisoners differed markedly. In the 16- to 19-year and 20- to 24-year age groups, there were proportionally larger numbers of aboriginal prisoners, with relatively fewer over the age of forty (Muirhead, 1988:89–95).

The most significant point of the Commission's findings, to some extent obscured by the subject of the inquiry itself, was that too many aboriginals were in prison. The real issue—the one which should itself be the subject of government inquiry—is the high rate of aboriginal imprisonment in Australia. Why are aboriginals incarcerated in such disproportionate numbers? Why do young aboriginal males seem to be the target of police activity? Large numbers of aboriginals are being imprisoned for drunkenness (which in some states has been decriminalized)[10] or fine default for normally nonimprisonable offenses.[11] It seems that many of these aboriginals should not be in prison at all.

To address these issues, Muirhead's recommendations included the national decriminalization of public drunkenness, the setting up of detoxification units to treat alcoholics, and the use of sentences which enforce imprisonment as a "sanction of last resort" (Muirhead, 1988:67).

Many times during the inquiry, it was asserted that the treatment of aboriginal people at the hands of the police has been consistently rough and discriminatory, particularly when younger males are concerned. This would account not only for higher rates of aboriginal males in prison, but also for many of the aboriginal deaths in police custody.

Among his fifty-six recommendations, Muirhead stressed that:

- All personnel of police, prison, social welfare or other departments whose work will bring them into contact with aboriginal people should receive appropriate training or retraining to ensure that they have an understanding and appreciation of aboriginal history, culture and social behavior and the abilities to effectively communicate and work with aboriginal people.
- Appropriate screening procedures should be implemented to ensure that potential officers who will have contact with aboriginal people in their duties are not recruited or retained by police and prison departments whilst holding racist views which cannot be eliminated by training or retraining programs.
- Restraint methods which involve constriction of air supply or carotid pressure such as "choke holds" or "head locks" should never be used (Muirhead, 1988:70).

On February 2, 1989, Muirhead released his findings in the four cases he had heard, those of Kingsley Dixon, Edward Murray, John Highford and Charles Michael. Although he could not find evidence of foul play, and stopped short of recommending that the states launch criminal investigations, he was critical of police and prison officers.

It was clear to Muirhead that some of the evidence was inaccurate or had been deliberately concealed by officers. He found it unlikely that Dixon and Murray had intentionally taken their own lives, but rather that their deaths had probably occurred while under the influence of drugs and antidepressants or in an angry response to mistreatment. He criticized the postdeath investigations for not being thorough, and was appalled that, in one large jail, no one had medical or first aid knowledge. Prisoners, he concluded, had not been treated with the care or observation required.

Aboriginal families were dismayed that the Muirhead recommendations established no clear grounds on which police and prison officers could be charged. Paul Coe, chairman of the National Aboriginal and Islander Legal Service, reproached the Commissioner for evading his responsibility to recommend criminal proceedings. These reports said, "There is no deterrent—police and prison officers have nothing to fear because the Commission has not made specific recommendations in relation to evidence which the Commissioner has not accepted."[12]

Alleged Harassment and Brutality

Theories abound on why aboriginals have been 'suiciding' in custody. They include beliefs that heavily intoxicated aboriginals suffer from symptoms of withdrawal and depression following incarceration, that an epidemic of copycat suicides had been started, and that aboriginals were despairing about their life situations. None of these theories, however, absolves police or prison officials of their custodial responsibility for the physical and psychological well-being of their charges, nor — as is suspected in a significant number of cases— of their culpability.

Aboriginal legal services throughout the country confirmed widespread accounts of systematic provocation, beatings, and maltreatment of aboriginal children and youth—which were seldom reported, never properly investigated, and generally dismissed for lack of evidence. At the root of aboriginal disillusionment with the Australian justice system is the inadequacy of investigatory and disciplinary measures taken against police or prison officers who abuse their authority or offend against their prisoners.

In his report to the Anti-Slavery Society, Burger warned that there was growing evidence in rural towns of physical abuse, provocation, victimization, and the "increasingly extra-judicial" role which police appeared to be taking with aboriginal people, particularly minors. He detected a "prevailing attitude" among the authorities "that Aboriginal people are all criminals or potential criminals." That view, he said, "is probably the most harmful of all to any improvement in police and Aboriginal relations" (1988: 50, 60).

A study in the Pilbara, Western Australia traced the source of negative relations between police and aboriginal people to a collection of hostile and stereotypical on-the-street behaviors. There were reports of physical and verbal abuse between the two occasionally erupting into violence. Following the John Pat case, relations between police and the aboriginal community were particularly hostile. In the report of the Pilbara study, it was argued that relations were likely to deteriorate when interaction was characterized by (a) physical violence (fights or use of force); (b) verbal violence (name calling, abusive language, or ridicule); or (c) social violence (ostracism, offensive gestures, or other nonverbal slights).

Relations could also break down if members of one group believed that members of the other were prejudiced against them—for example, if one felt that the other;

- "falsely accused" or unfairly "labelled" them.
- intimated racial or cultural superiority.
- "abuse[d] its power in situations where there [was] a conflict of interest.
- "offended, abused or exploited" its women.
  (Roberts, Chadbourne and Rose, 1986; see also Lyons, 1983).

Whether or not individual police officers were prejudiced, in small towns like Bourke, Brewarrina, Goondiwindi, or Moree, they often inherited a chronic state of racial tension. Investigating violence which injured nine people and damaged hotels and shops in January 1987 at Goondiwindi, Justice Einfeld found extensive socioeconomic disparities between white and black communities (1988).

In a report on the disturbances of August 1986 in the Bourke, New South Wales, it was found that "a wall of suspicion divides most blacks and whites in Bourke. . . . " The report pointed out that to station too many police in a small center—especially young, enthusiastic officers —would make aboriginal residents feel harassed by an "army of occupation. . . . Such an enforced role would guarantee the continuation of a state of hostility between Aborigines and police and would ensure regular breakdowns of public order" (New South Wales Ministry of Aboriginal Affairs, 1987).

In their study of northwest New South Wales, Cunneen and Robb showed that increasing the number of police in a community has been singularly unsuccessful in improving race relations or in bringing a greater feeling of security. Historically, the researchers said, police have practiced a level of intrusion into aboriginal lives that extends beyond criminal law and would be totally unacceptable to other groups. This experience of intrusion remains a reality of contemporary aboriginal social experience, and the authors have interpreted aboriginal drunkenness and unrest as signs of emotional and political protest against years of excessive supervision (Cunneen and Robb, 1987:190–192, 197, 207).

Young people in particular bear the brunt of policing excesses in major cities and country towns alike, Aboriginal parents have become alarmed at the numerous petty charges (such as swearing in the streets) laid against their young people. In Adelaide, South Australia, aboriginal welfare and social service workers have expressed their concern for aboriginal juveniles, complaining that groups were frequently approached on the street, even when they were merely talking and socializing. Where aboriginals were concerned, there seemed to be little leniency or good-natured tolerance of youthful bravado or indiscretion (Hazlehurst, 1988:21–22; McNeil, 1987).

In the course of their duties among aboriginals, welfare workers (and, according to some reports, even priests and doctors) have been threatened with arrest when they were felt to be impinging on police work. That the diversionary and crisis intervention value of these workers seemed so little understood or appreciated by law enforcers suggests the need for a massive human relations re-education program for Australian authorities. Both nonaboriginals and aboriginals who had taken steps to address the Royal Commission into Aboriginal Deaths in

Custody repeatedly alleged that witnesses to the inquiry had to protect themselves from police intimidation. Others did not come forward at all for fear of reprisals against themselves or members of their family.

Although requests by the federal government to immediately put in place the interim recommendations of the inquiry for policing and prison reform—particularly in the handling of aboriginal prisoners, the improvement of medical services, and the alteration of prison architecture to minimize the risk of cell deaths—were welcomed in some states, in others they were given a cool reception. Correction administrators complained of the expense these reforms would incur.

The interim recommendation by Justice Muirhead that racists be weeded out of police and custodial forces was met with hostility by Queensland and Western Australian authorities, and there were threats of a state-wide strike by Western Australian prison officers. The Western Australian Police Union and the Western Australian Prison Officers' Union — with the financial backing of the Western Australian government — instituted a legal challenge to the validity of the Commission's proceedings in Western Australia.

In Western Australia, the Royal Commission inquiry was halted following a Western Australian Supreme Court injunction late in 1988, and there were fears that the entire Commission would be brought down if this challenge was successful. The Committee to Defend Black Rights, which represented the families of aboriginals who had died in custody, accused the West Australian government of running a campaign against aboriginals to win conservative votes in forthcoming state elections. A Full Bench of the Federal Court overturned the injunction in February 1989.[13]

A political test of strength between federal and state governments in Australia over this issue seems inevitable. The federal government certainly has the authority and power to insist on these changes, but noncooperation of state authorities could slow their introduction. The depth of federal commitment to human rights issues regarding aboriginal prisoners remains to be demonstrated.

International Human Rights

Australia must face international criticism of its long and continuing history of physical and cultural assaults upon its original inhabitants. For more than two centuries, these assaults have been perpetrated by migratory Europeans throughout the continent and include attacks upon the land-based economy, family life, social order, and persons of aboriginals. These continued attacks have taken a severe toll on the demographic fortunes, psychological and physical well-being, and social and economic opportunities of an entire population. It seems inevitable that in the 1990s there will still be significant political purpose and economic motive to continue the campaign against aboriginal interests and paltry mechanisms or deterrents in place to shield aboriginals from it.

In a report on her visit to Australia in 1987 and 1988, Professor Erica Irene Daes, chairman of the U.N. Working Group on Indigenous Populations, wrote:

> On my visits to Aboriginal territory and the Torres Strait Islanders, I found situations which, when compared with the general non-indigenous living standards in the same areas, cannot but lead to the conclusion that Australia stands in violation of her international human rights obligations relating to non-discrimination and unequal treatment in general and to the provision of certain minimum services in particular (1988:12).

Land rights and self-determination are central to contemporary indigenous rights. It is only a matter of time before the drafting of international standards on indigenous rights by the U.N. Working Group on Indigenous Populations will be complete (Cristescu, 1981; Cobo, 1983; Thompson, 1986; Gray, 1987). As a member nation, Australia has pledged commitment to a number of U.N. treaties, covenants, and conventions which protect the economic, political, and cultural rights of indigenous people. Further, the Australian federal government has both the constitutional and legislative power to see that these commitments are honored by state government and criminal justice authorities.[14]

The *International Covenant on Civil and Political Rights,* of which Australia is a cosignatory nation, holds that:

> All peoples have the right of self-determination. By virtue of that right they freely determine their political status and freely pursue their economic, social and cultural development.

> Where not already provided for by existing legislative or other measure, each State Party to the present Covenant undertakes to take the necessary steps, in accordance with its constitutional processes and with the provisions of the present Covenant, to adopt such legislative or other measures as may be necessary to give effect to the rights recognized in the present Covenant.[15]

Discriminatory state government legislation and practices, breaches of human rights standards, and incidents of official discrimination could be overridden by federal legislation. The problems, Nettheim pointed out, are in securing acceptance of international human rights conventions at the state government level and in seeing that antidiscrimination principles are implemented.[16] In practice, this may involve examining all state and federal legislation for inconsistencies with international standards. To enforce these standards, federal legal and political means may have to be resorted to when state governments are uncooperative in removing discriminatory legislation and systems.

Over the past fifteen years, Australian aboriginal people have — by treaty, constitutional amendment, or legislation—sought formal recognition of:

1. aboriginal prior ownership of Australia.
2. security of ownership, in perpetuity, of vacant Crown Land in traditional areas.
3. protection and preservation of culture, language and sacred sites.
4. rights to pursue traditional fishing, hunting and gathering activities in these areas.
5. control of public, industrial, or commercial access to this land.
6. control of, and benefits from, resources on or below the surface of their land.
7. positive discrimination in all areas of government aid, which will promote aboriginal community development and self-management.
8. negotiation on all matters concerning aboriginals, with increasing measures towards self-determination in all areas of social welfare and service delivery.
9. fair and equitable treatment under Australian law, with increasing avenues for local autonomy in areas of social control and justice administration.

These demands have much in common with those put forward by indigenous people in other countries. There are, however, many unresolved issues regarding aboriginal title and rights to land in Australia, and relatively little legal precedent or constitutional protection of special indigenous rights.

The Motives for Genocide

In 1983, an Australian High Court Judge, the late Justice Lionel Murphy, made a remarkable statement:

The history of the Aboriginal people of Australia since European settlement is that they have been the subject of unprovoked aggression, conquest, pillage, rape, brutalization, attempted genocide and systematic and unsystematic destruction of their culture.[17]

There has been a resurgence of academic interest in some of the worst incidents of genocide in human history. At Macquarie University, New South Wales, a new course on the politics of genocide has been designed by Professor Colin Tatz. The course includes a study of the treatment of Australian aboriginals which, Tatz contends, has amounted on occasion to genocide in Australia's not too distant past.[18]

In his two formidable works, *Genocide: Its Political Use in the Twentieth Century* (1982) and *The Prevention of Genocide* (1985), American sociologist Leo Kuper discusses contemporary theories and motives of genocide. In this context, the activities which have been perpetrated against aboriginals are instantly recognizable. Kuper draws attention to Charny's location of the source of human destructiveness in a "fear of death and nonaliveness." The projection of this fear can lead "nearly every one of us" to acts of genocide.

Driven by nameless, overwhelming fears, men turn to the primitive tools of self-protection, including the belief that they may spare themselves the terrible fate of death by sacrificing another instead of themselves (Charny and Rapaport, 1982:207).

Kuper alerts us to Charny's point that the "intervening mechanism in this process is the dehumanization of the victim as not deserving the protection due to members of our species" (Kuper, 1985:196).[19]

Reports of cases presented to the Royal Commission into Aboriginal Deaths in Custody read as a catalog of degradation. They can be epitomized in the case of the 29-year-old aboriginal actor and traditional dancer Paul Pryor—a man with professional success and respect—who committed suicide as a result of a number of humiliating incidents involving Queensland and Victoria police. According to family and friends, he had been denied the right to go to the toilet while in a police lock-up. Forced to defecate in his cell, he was then beaten and had his face rubbed in his own excreta by police. This experience so distressed Pryor that he was never able to regain his dignity, and six months later he took his own life.[20]

Many aboriginal families are convinced that official misconduct has led to some aboriginal deaths. Still-grieving families have experienced police harassment and midnight raids on their homes even while the inquiries into their sons' deaths were underway. Some families are convinced that their sons were murdered by officials; that prison officers or police assisted in their so-called suicides; or that they were driven to suicide by physical and psychological abuse. In all cases, they feel that the authorities should be held accountable. They are distrustful of a system that seems bent on covering up any official misconduct against aboriginals rather than exposing and punishing it.

The question of whether persons in positions of authority can be charged for the death of a prisoner as a result of psychological abuse raises new questions in law. Are these authorities responsible for the mental (as well medical and physical) well-being of their charges? Most police and prison authorities would say they are not, because custodial institutions 'inherit' the psychological state of a prisoner.

It could equally be argued, however, that a decline in the mental state of a prisoner as a result of abuse by officers could and should become a point of accountability. Until it does, there exists a very dangerous area in which official tyranny and harassment may reign free — with apparent public and legal consent. Physical and verbal abuse, denial of basic physical or medical needs, and cruel and degrading treatment of prisoners, are all causes enough to result in suicide or premature death. Such mistreatment clearly represent crimes against humanity under several U.N. conventions.[21]

Economic interests are also important factors in genocide, Kuper explains, and "racial or ethnic boundaries are usually not coterminous with class divisions. . . . Their role is most marked in the genocides of colonization, in the sacrifice of indigenous groups to economic development. . . . " (Kuper, 1985:197).

Mining and farming have traditionally offered the most employment to aboriginals in rural areas. Fellow workers in these industries, however, have not taken the side of aboriginals in their struggles for land rights. It is perhaps not without significance that Western Australia, the state which most strongly resisted federal efforts for national aboriginal land rights in 1983, is also the state which has the highest rates of aboriginal deaths in custody (Muirhead, 1988:84). During the Royal Commission on Aboriginal Deaths in Custody, racial hostility in this state has become raw and undisguised.

Not surprisingly, aboriginal people suspect a connection between official expressions of noncooperation with the Commission in certain states and the higher rates of aboriginal deaths in those regions. It is also significant that these states have been tardy in resource sharing, the promotion of aboriginal economic independence, and the introduction of criminal justice reforms for aboriginals.

No society benefits when one group languishes in poverty and subjugation. Unemployed, demoralized, and increasingly aliented populations threaten the peace and security of all. The savings to the taxpayer in unemployment benefits, medical care, policing and incarceration costs alone would justify increasing the economic well-being and self-sufficiency of indigenous peoples.

We cannot hope to reconstruct the human psyche overnight, but stern human rights legislation and constitutional safeguards could begin the process. Such undertakings would protect aboriginal people from immediate abuses and—with greater security and opportunities for self-determination—they would regain self-esteem through control over their lives. Through this process of improving conditions for aboriginal people, the basis for selfish and racist attitudes may be eroded (Williams, 1985, 1987, Hazlehurst, 1987b; Grabosky et al, 1988).

Summary

It is not universally understood that many Australian aboriginal people today live in Third World conditions. They live in conflict with and fear of state authorities, against whom they have conducted a long campaign of protest and passive resistance. Aboriginal people are dying prematurely from ill health, imprisonment, despair, and defeat. For many years, they have asserted that acts of oppression and neglect by local and state authorities have continued in the face of legislation which should outlaw such acts. Evidence of this is now emerging from national and international inquiries.

Daily intervention by police, abuse and neglect of basic community needs, cruel and degrading treatment of aboriginal prisoners, intimidation of witnesses to national inquiries, and unashamed attempts by state agencies to terminate the Royal Commission into Aboriginal Deaths in Custody—all of these raise the question of whether the domestic situation in Australia warrants international intervention. In such environments, aboriginal people must live in a constant state of siege. A day does not go by without seeing the paddy wagon or hearing of friends or family members being arrested. The widespread insecurity this breeds in aboriginal life is little acknowledged and generally denied by the dominant European society.

Aboriginal leaders warn of a new and alienated generation of youth, hardened by their experiences of growing up aboriginal. We now see rising rural and urban crime reates, increasing drunkenness, solvent and drug abuse, and an increase in incidents of racial confrontation. More radical aboriginal leaders have warned that, if state governments continue to oppose the human rights of aboriginals, revolutionary reaction from the aboriginal community may only be forestalled by the responsible employment of federal powers.

Nested in a history of colonialism and tutelage, even the most well-meaning welfare, judicial, or law enforcement agency cannot hope to act alone as a catalyst for constructive change. With the declining influence of traditional leadership and severely limited community-based mechanisms for social control, neither can the aboriginal community — at least not until it has a greater measure of autonomy and self-confidence.

Tampering with the existing criminal justice system can only produce limited change. Important though they are, the recommendations made in the Royal Commission's Interim Report are merely attending to problems (such as discriminatory processes and practices) which should not have existed in the first place. Not until there is a total reassessment of the allocation of economic and political resources will the so-called underlying aboriginal social issues begin to be resolved.

Few Australian aboriginals would question that their status in their own land after two hundred years of European rule is unconscionable. Continued crimes against aboriginal persons in modern times can be seen as the bitter fruit of the founding crime of dispossession.

Governments would ignore, at their peril, calls for a revolutionary solution. Invitations to Libya by radical aboriginals to give aid to an oppressed Australian minority have found some support in the aboriginal community. Even so, the predominantly moderate sector of aboriginal society continues to hope for a just and lasting solution and puts its faith in a democratic system of inquiry which it anticipates will begin a process of restitution and reform.

In 1983, the National Aboriginal and Islander Legal Services Secretariat attended the first conference of the U.N. Working Group on Indigenous Populations. In 1984, it obtained non-Governmental Organization status with the Economic and Social Council of the United Nations and has since become actively involved in U.N. endeavors to bring about the full protection of indigenous rights.

Although the worst violations of human rights are being resolved in law, the Einfeld and Muirhead national inquiries indisputably revealed policies and practices which have for many years resulted in neglect and discrimination against aboriginal peoples. As paternalistic administrations fail to provide adequate living standards, the arguments for aboriginal-run regional and community-based operations and independent economic enterprise become increasingly compelling.

Notes

*Research on the Aboriginal Deaths in Custody Inquiry was conducted by the author while acting as a consultant for the National Aboriginal and Islander Legal Services Secretariat, Sydney, on leave from the Australian Institute of Criminology, Canberra. The author wishes to thank both organizations for their support in this work.

1. The Yirrkala clans, on the Gove Peninsula, Northern Territory, were unaware of the arrival of Europeans until the years immediately prior to World War II. In the 1960s, when their lands came under threat by mining interests, the clans sought to reaffirm ownership through the Northern Territory Supreme Court. In the Gove Land Rights Case, (*Milirrpum v. Nabalco Pty Ltd* [1971] 17 F.L.R.), they were told by Justice Blackburn that the land had not been theirs since European arrival on January 26, 1788.

2. Only 4.1% of aboriginals gain postsecondary education or academic qualifications. Aboriginals who obtain work do so at a younger age (18% of working aboriginal males are 15–19 years old, compared to 9.5% of others). The median aboriginal family income is 54.4% of the median family income for all Australians. Only 18.9% of aboriginals work in white-collar occupations, compared to 44.4% of other Australians (Australian Bureau of Statistics, 1987; Department of Aboriginal Affairs, 1984).

3. The housing, health, welfare, economic, and interracial situation described by Justice Einfeld in the *Toomelah Report* is typical of the majority of country towns with significant aboriginal populations (1988:61).

4. In eighteenth-century British common law, a distinction between colonies acquired by conquest or cession from others with sovereign power and those acquired by settlement was made. Because the Australian continent was said to have been *terra nullius* — uninhabited, or at least "desert and uncultivated" — the Australian nation was said to have been founded by settlement. Aboriginal people argue against the assertion that their land was not acquired by conquest. Recent historical studies indicate that settlement was achieved only after extensive warfare and forced evacuations (Nettheim 1987b:9; also Reynolds 1981, 1987; Butlin, 1983; Miller, 1986; Mattingley and Hampton, 1988; Bird, 1987).

The soundness of the notion of *terra nullius* was challenged by the International Court of Justice in the Western Sahara case relating to the time of colonization by Spain. In the absence of cession or succession, *terra nullius* was employed in connection with the occupation of those territories. State practice of that period, however, demonstrated that the territories had been inhabited by tribes with unmistakable social and political organization. The court decided unanimously that, at the time of colonization, the Western Sahara was not an uninhabited territory (International Court of Justice, advisory opinion given on October 16, 1975 in response to the request of the General Assembly resolution 3292 (XXIX), December 13, 1974, UN doc. A/10300 of October 17, 1975:31–32).

5. Garth Nettheim, Professor of Law at the University of New South Wales, asked: "Need the infusion of English law mean that Aboriginal law ceased to operate, either of its own right or in terms of English law? Blackburn held that this was indeed the consequence of British settlement, so that the land in question did not belong to the Yirrkala clans." The Gove case is the only Australian judicial determination of the subject (see note 1) (Nettheim, 1987a: 292; McCorquodale 1987).

6. Under its external affairs power, conferred by s.51 (29) of the Constitution, the federal government can legitimately override state government powers and pass legislation implementing obligations arising under international conventions. In the *Koowarta v. Bjelke-Petersen* (1982) 56 A.L.J.R. 625 case, an aboriginal group, prevented from purchasing a Crown-leasehold pastoral property, brought an action in the Supreme Court of Queensland against the Queensland government. The complainant successfully claimed that the refusal of permission contravened the provisions of ss 9 and 12 of the federal *Racial Discrimination Act* (1975), which fulfilled international obligations under the *Under Nations International Convention on the Elimination of All Form of Racial Discrimination* (1965). In the Tasmanian Dams case, which involved a conflict between the federal and Tasmanian governments over the fate of native rainforests, an external obligation arising out of the UNESCO Convention for the *Protection of the World Cultural and Natural Heritage* was recognized by the High Court (*Commonwealth v. Tasmania* (1983) 625 A.L.J.R 143).

7. "In 1966," Nettheim noted, "no Aboriginal Australian owned land by virtue of being Aboriginal. By January 1986 some 643,079 sq.km representing 8.37% of the Australian land mass, were held by Aboriginals in freehold" (Nettheim 1987a:293). This had decreased slightly to 8.22% by mid-1987 (Department of Aboriginal Affairs, 1986/1988).

There has been an increasing public and bipartisan commitment to aboriginal claims since the late 1960s. "In 1975, a Labor government introduced path-breaking land rights legislation for the Northern Territory which a non-Labor Government saw through to enactment in 1976" (Nettheim 1987a:294). In 1983, the Labor federal government attempted to introduce a *National Aboriginal Land Rights Bill*. This undertaking failed in the face of heated state government and corporate opposition. In the last five years, some falling away of public and political support for aboriginal land rights in Australia has been noted (Evans, 1984:324–328; Kirby, 1988:186–188; Nettheim, 1987a:291–300; "Current Topic," 1982:381–383).

8. Prisoner overrepresentation estimates vary according to the base population chosen. Calculations which use the whole aboriginal population fall to just over 10 times (Hazlehurst and Dunn, 1988; Biles, 1988; Muirhead 1988:89); those which employ the imprisonable age (17–69 years) as the base population produce the startling figure of 23 times overrepresentation (Mukherjee and Scandia, 1988).

9. *The Australian,* August 5, 1987; *The Sydney Morning Herald,* August 3, 1987; *The Weekend Australian,* August 15–16, 1987; for a study on aboriginal self-mutilation and imprisonment, see Wilson (1988).

10. Public drunkenness has been decriminalized in the states of New South Wales, South Australia, and Tasmania, and in the Northern Territory and the Australian Capital Territory. It is still an offense in Victoria, Queensland, and Western Australia (on aboriginal drinking and crime see McCorquodale, 1984; Brady and Palmer, 1986; Hazlehurst, 1986; Hazlehurst and Dunn, 1988; Hunter, 1988).

11. On aboriginal crime default, see South Australian Cabinet (1987).

12. *The Sydney Morning Herald,* February 3, 1989; *The Canberra Times,* February 3, 1989; Muirhead, 1989. After the completion of his interim report, Justice Muirhead resigned from the Royal Commission on January 12, 1989 for "personal" and "health" reasons. He subsequently took up the post of Administrator of the Northern Territory (*The Age,* January 13, 1989).

13. *The Age,* November 24 and 25, December 22 and 29, 1988; *The Sydney Morning Herald,* December 24 and 30, 1988; *The Canberra Times,* December 29, 1988.

14. See United Nations conventions: *Convention on the Prevention and Punishment of the Crime of Genocide* (1948); *Universal Declaration of Human Rights* (1948); *Standard Minimum Rules for the Treatment of Prisoners* (1955/1977); *Declaration on the Protection of All Persons from Being Subjected to Torture and Other Cruel, Inhuman or Degrading Treatment or Punishment* (1975); *Code of Conduct for Law Enforcement Officials,* (1979).

15. Part 1: Articles 1 and 2 of the United Nations *International Covenant on Civil and Political Rights* (1966).

16. For some years, Nettheim has examined and written about civil, constitutional, and international law issues regarding Aboriginals. More than seven years, ago, Nettheim pointed out that, "Australia stands in breach of various of its obligations under international human rights conventions. . . . " In Queensland, for instance, he found that breaches have included: legislation and policy which have restricted the movement and residence of aboriginals; interfered with the family, social and political life of the community; affected the judicial process, aobriginal equality before the courts and legal rights; and discrimination against aboriginals in their rights to own property and receive equal rates of pay (Nettheim, 1981:150; see also Nettheim, 1983, 1985, 1987a, 1987b).

17. Justice Lionel Murply, (*Commonwealth v. Tasmania* (1983) 625 A.L.J.R. 737).

18. *The Australian,* January 16, 1989.

19. See also United Nations, *Convention on the Prevention and Punishment of the Crime of Genocide* (1948a).

20. *The Australian*, November 29, 1988; *The Age*, November 29, 1988.

21. For United Nations standards on the treatment of prisoners and the role of police and prison officers, see *Standard Minimum Rules for the Treatment of Prisoners; Declaration on the Protection of All Persons from Being Subjected to Torture and Other Cruel, Inhuman or Degrading Treatment or Punishment; Code of Conduct for Law Enforcement Officials;* and the *Universal Declaration of Human Rights.*

References

Australian Bureau of Statistics
1987   *Census of Population and Housing: 1981 and 1986*. Canberra: Australian Bureau of Statistics.

Australian Department of Aboriginal Affairs
1984   *Aboriginal Social Indicators*. Canberra: Australian Government Publishing Service.
1988   *Aboriginal Land Tenure and Population*. 2d ed. Canberra: Australian Department of Aboriginal Affairs.

Bailey, Rebecca
1984   A Comparison of Appearances by Aboriginal and non-Aboriginal Children before the Children's Court and Children's Aid Panels in South Australia. In *Aborigines and Criminal Justice*. Ed. by B. Swanton. Canberra: Australian Institute of Criminology: 43–78.

Bailey-Harris, Rebecca and Joy Wundersitz
1985   Over-Representation of Aboriginal Children in Care Proceedings Before the Children's Court of South Australia. *Australian Journal of Law and Society*. Vol. 2, No. 2: 11–27.

Benn, M. and K. Worpole
1986   *Death in the City: An Examination of Police Related Deaths in London*, London: Canary Press.

Biles, David
1988   "Research into Aboriginal Deaths in Custody." Sydney: paper presented at Fourth Annual Conference of the Australian and New Zealand Society of Criminology, 22–23 August.

Bird, Greta
1987   *"The Civilising Mission" Race and the Construction of Aboriginal Crime*, Monograph Series, Contemporary Legal Issues No. 4, Melbourne: Faculty of Law, Monash University.

Brady, Maggie and Kingsley Palmer
1986 *Alcohol in the Outback: Two studies of Drinking*, Darwin: Australian National University North Australia Research Unit.

Burger, Julian
1988 *Aborigines Today: Land and Justice*, London: Indigenous Peoples and Development Series, Report No. 5, Anti-Slavery Society.

Burman, Sandra and Barbara E. Harrel-Bond (eds.)
1979 "The Imposition of Law," in *Studies in Law and Social Control*, New York: *Academic Press*.

Butlin, Noel G.
1983 *Our Original Aggression, Aboriginal Populations of Southeastern Australia, 1788–1850*, Sydney: George Allen and Unwin.

Charny, Israel W. (ed.)
1982 *How can we Commit the Unthinkable? Genocide: The Human Cancer*, in collaboration with Chanan Rapaport, Boulder, Colorado: Westview Press.

Cobo, Jose Martinez
1983 *Study of the Problems of Discrimination against Indigenous Populations*, United Nations Economic and Social Council, (E7CN.4/Sub.2/1986/7/Add.1 – 5, Vols.I–V, 1986) New York: United Nations.

Cristescu, Aureliu
1981 *The Right to Self-Determination: Historical and Current Development on the Basis of United Nations Instruments*, (UN E/CN.4/Sub.2/404/Rev.1.) New York: United Nations.

Cunneen, Christopher and Tom Robb
1987 *Criminal Justice in North-West New South Wales*, Sydney: New South Wales Bureau of Crime Statistics and Research.

"Current Topics,"
1982 *Australian Law Journal*, vol. 56 no. 8 (August):381–383.

Daes, Irene Erica A.
1988 *Visit to Australia, 12 December 1987 – 22 January 1988*, Geneva: report by Chairman-Rapporteur of the United Nations Working Group on Indigenous Populations.

Einfeld, Justice Marucs
1988 *Toomelah Report: Report on the Problems and Needs of Aborigines living on the New South Wales-Queensland Border*, Sydney: Human Rights and Equal Opportunity Commission, (June).

Evans, Senator Gareth
1984 "Human Rights and International Law," *Australian Foreign Affairs Record*, vol. 55. no. 4, (April): 324–328.

Gale, Fay and Wundersitz, Joy
1985   "Variations in the Over-representation of Aboriginal Young Offenders in the Criminal Justice System," *Australian Journal of Social Issues*, vol. 20. no. 3, (August): 209–214.
1986   "Rural and Urban Crime Rates amongst Aboriginal Youth: Patterns of Different Locational Opportunity," *Australian Geographical Studies* 24, no. 2. (October).
1987a   "Aboriginal Youth and the Criminal Justice System in South Australia" in K. Hazlehurst (ed.) *Ivory Scales: Black Australia and the Law,* New South Wales University Press, Sydney: 188–135.
1987b   "Police and Black Minorities: A Case of Aboriginal Youth in South Australia," *Australian and New Zealand Journal of Criminology*, vol. 20. no. 2 (June): 78–94.

Grabosky, Peter N.
1988   "Aboriginal Deaths in Custody: the Case of John Pat," *Race and Class*, vol. 29, no. 3. (Winter): 87–94.

Grabosky, P., A. Scandia, et al., K. Hazlehurst, and P. Wilson.
1988   Aboriginal Deaths in Custody. *Trends and Issues in Crime and Criminal Justice*. No. 12, Canberra: Australian Institute of Criminology.

Gray, Andrew (compiler)
1987   *IWGIA Yearbook 1986: Indigenous Peoples and Human Rights,* Copenhagen: International Working Group for Indigenous Affairs.

Hanks, Peter and Bryan Keon-Cohen
1984   *Aborigines and the Law.* Sydney: George Allen & Unwin.

Hazlehurst, Kayleen M.
1986   Alcohol, Outstations and Autonomy: An Australian Aboriginal perspective. *Journal of Drug Issues*. Vol. 16, no. 2 (Spring): 109–220.

Hazlehurst, Kayleen M. (ed.)
1987a   *Ivory Scales: Black Australia and the Law.* Sydney: New South Wales University Press.

Hazlehurst, Kayleen M.
1987b   Widening the Middleground: the Development of Community-based Options. In K. M. Hazlehurst (ed.) *Ivory Scales: Black Australia and the Law.* Sydney: New South Wales University Press: 241–181.
1988   Racial Tension, Policing and Public Order: Australia in the Eighties. In I. Freckelton and H. Selby (eds.) *Police in Our Society.* Sydney: Butterworths.

Hazlehurst, Kayleen and Albert T. Dunn
1988   Aboriginal Criminal Justice. *Trends and Issues in Crime and Criminal Justice*. No. 13, Canberra: Australian Institute of Criminology.

Hazlehurst, Kayleen and Cameron Hazlehurst
1989   Race and the Australian Conscience: Investigating Aboriginal Deaths in Custody. *New Community: A Journal of Research and Policy on Ethnic Relations.* Warwick, Coventry: Centre for Research in Ethnic Relations, University of Warwick [October].

Hunter, Ernest M.
1988   On Gordian Knots and Nooses: Aboriginal Suicide in the Kimberley. *Australian and New Zealand Journal of Psychiatry:* 264–271.

International Working Group for Indigenous Affairs (IWGIA)
1987   *IWGIA Yearbook 1986: Indigenous Peoples and Human Rights.* (compiled by Andrew Gray), Copenhagen: International Working Group for Indigenous Affairs.

Keon-Cohen, Bryan
1981a   "Native Justice in Australia, Canada, and the USA: A Comparative Analysis." *Monash University Law Review.*
1981b   The Makarrata: A Treaty within Australia between Australians, Some Legal Issues. *Current Affairs Bulletin.* Vol. 57, No. 9 (February):4–19.

Kirby, Justice Michael
1988   Domestic application of International Human Rights Standards. *Australian Foreign Affairs Record.* Vol. 59, No. 5 (May):186–188.

Kuper, Leo
1981   *Genocide: Its Political Use in the Twentieth Century.* London: Penguin Books (also Yale University Press: New Haven 1982).
1985   *The Prevention of Genocide.* New Haven: Yale University Press.

Lyons, Gregory
1983   Aboriginal Perceptions of Courts and Police: A Victorian Study. *Australian Aboriginal Studies.* No. 2: 45–61.

Mattingley, Christobel and Hampton, Ken (eds)
1988   *Survival in Our Own Land: "Aboriginal" Experiences in "South Australia" Since 1836.* Adelaide: Wakefield Press.

McCorquodale, John
1984   Alcohol and Anomie: The Nature of Aboriginal Crime. In B. Swanton (ed.) *Aborigines and Criminal Justice,* Canberra: Australian Institute of Criminology: 17–42.
1987   *Aborigines and the Law: A Digest.* Canberra: Aboriginal Studies Press.

McNeil, E.
1987   *Inner City Kids.* Adelaide: Report to the Department for Community Welfare, (September).

Miller, James
1986   *Koori: A Will to Win: The Heroic Resistance, Survival and Triumph of Black Australia.* Sydney: Angus and Robertson.

Muirhead, Justice J. H.
1988   *Royal Commission into Aboriginal Deaths in Custody: Interim Report.* Canberra: Australian Government Publishing Service (December).
1989   *Report of the Inquiry into the Death of Edward James Murray; Kingsley Richard Dixon; John Clarence Highfold; Charles Sydney Michael,* (four reports), Royal Commission into Aboriginal Deaths in Custody, Canberra: Australian Government Publishing Service (January).

Mukherjee, S. and A. Scandia
1988   Aboriginal Imprisonment. *Crime Digest.* No. 88.1 (January).

Nettheim, Garth
1981   *Victims of the Law: Black Queenslanders Today.* Sydney: George Allen & Unwin.
1983   Justice and Indigenous Minorities: A New Province for International and National Law. In A.R. Blackshield (ed.) *Legal Change: Essays in Honour of Julius Stone.* Sydney: Butterworths.
1984   The Relevance of International Law. In P. Hanks and B. Keon-Cohen (eds.) *Aborigines and the Law.* Sydney: George Allen & Unwin: 50–73.
1987a   Indigenous Rights, Human Rights and Australia. *The Australian Law Journal.* Vol. 61 (June): 291–300.
1987b   Justice or Handouts? Aboriginals, Law and Policy. In K.M. Hazlehurst (ed.) *Ivory Scales: Black Australia and the Law.* Sydney: New South Wales University Press: 8–29.

New South Wales Ministry of Aboriginal Affairs
1987   *The Final Report of the Working Party on the Bourke Distrubances of August 1986.* Sydney: New South Wales Ministry of Aboriginal Affairs (May).

Reynolds, Henry
1981   *The Other Side of the Frontier: An Interpretation of the Aboriginal Response to the Invasion and Settlement of Australia.* Townsville, Queensland: James Cook University.
1987   *Frontier: Aborigines, Settlers and Land.* Sydney: Allen and Unwin.

Roberts, L., Chadbourne, R. and Rose, M.
1986   *Aboriginal/Police Relations in the Pilbara: A Study of Perceptions.* Perth: Special Cabinet Committee on Aboriginal/Police and Community Relations.

South Australian Cabinet, Aboriginal Task Force of the Justice and Consumer Affairs Committee
1987   *South Australian Aboriginal Fine Default Intervention Study 1986–1987.* Adelaide: South Australian Cabinet.

Thompson, Ruth (ed.)
1986   *The Rights of Indigenous Peoples in International Law: Workshop Report.* Regina: University of Saskatchewan Native Law Centre.

United Nations
1948a   *Convention on the Prevention and Punishment of the Crime of Genocide* (adopted by General Assembly resolution 260 A (III), 9 December).
1948b   *Universal Declaration of Human Rights* (adopted by General Assembly resolution 217 A (III), 10 December).
1955   *Standard Minimum Rules for the Treatment of Prisoners* (adopted by the First United Nations Congress on the Prevention of Crime and the Treatment of Offenders, also approved by the Economic and Social Council by its resolutions 663 C (XXIV) 1957 and 2076 (LXII) 1977)
1965   *International Convention on the Elimination of All Forms of Racial Discrimination* (adopted by General Assembly resolution 2106 A (XX), 21 December).
1966   *International Covenant on Civil and Political Rights* (adopted by General Assembly resolution 2200 A (XXI), (16 December).
1975   *Declaration on the Protection of All Persons from Being Subjected to Torture and Other Cruel, Inhuman or Degrading Treatment or Punishment* (adopted by General Assembly resolution 3452 (XXX), 9 December).
1979   *Code of Conduct for Law Enforcement Officials,* (adopted by General Assembly resolution 34/169, 17 December).

Walker, J. and D. Biles
1982 – 1986   *Australian Prisoners: Results of the National Prison Census 30 June.* Canberra: Australian Institute of Criminology.

Williams, Nancy M.
1985   On Aboriginal Decision-making. In D.E. Barwick (ed.) *Metaphor of Interpretation: Essays in Honour of W.E.H. Stanner.* Canberra: Australian National University Press.
1987   Local Autonomy and the Viability of Community Justice Mechanisms. In K.M. Hazlehurst (ed.) *Ivory Scales: Black Australia and the Law.* Canberra: New South Wales University Press, Sydney: 227–240.

Wilson, Paul
1988   *Black Death White Hands.* Sydney: Allen and Unwin/Winchester; Mass: Unwin Hyman Inc. (first ed. 1981).

Wundersitz, Joy and Fay Gale
1988   Disadvantage and Discretion: The Results of Aboriginal Youth in Relation to the Adjournment Decision. *Adelaide Law Review.* Vol. 11, No. 3 (June): 348–358.

2

Subcultures as Crime:
The Theft of Legitimacy of
Dissent in the United States

Susan L. Caulfield

> The notion that some ideas are "subversive" is dangerous for anyone who disagrees with an administration in power, or who may in the future. If the tag "subversive," and the harassment that follows, can be applied to some ideas today, they will be applied to *other* ideas tomorrow — that's been proven by many months of revelations of FBI abuses (Blackstock, 1975:viii).

In the United States, there is a constitutional right to freedom of speech. Specifically, the freedom to speak openly is a civil liberty, which means that it is protected from governmental action. Because speech is protected by the First Amendment, the Bill of Rights provides that people cannot be discriminated against for political action when such action only involves speech (Wasserman, 1988). Moreover, people who hold meetings to express concern with public policy issues are protected in that they have the right to convene and express dissent. Blackstock's analysis of the FBI's COINTELPRO program of Nixon's law-and-order era revealed, however, that when ideas became 'subversive,' apart from any criminal activity, they also became dangerous to the functioning of the state apparatus. Once they are viewed as dangerous, ideas are suppressed, often through illegal tactics employed by agents of the state. In addition, people, groups, and organizations associated with political dissent (i.e., dangerous ideas) are subject to efforts by agents of the state to delegitimate both them and their ideas.

This chapter examines the dialectical processes involved in state[1] activities which create criminals by violating rather than protecting citizens' fundamental rights as guaranteed in the Constitution and other laws. Analyzing the state's role in the creation of politically subversive or criminal subcultures, we focus attention on recent and contemporary groups—such as the Committee in Solidarity with the People of El Salvador (CISPES) and the CoMadres of El Salvador—who have openly engaged in First Amendment dissent and been subject to government harassment, break-ins, illegal monitoring, and other repressive activities. More specifically, this chapter explores the relationship between the state's creation of deviant or illegitimate subcultures and the state-created illusion of legitimate intervention (stopping crime) as a cover for the political criminality of state agents. Arguing that such state actions are criminal both in the legal and philosophical sense (they 'steal' the right to dissent), our discussion is also concerned with the role that criminologists play in producing and reproducing the subcultural methodology employed by the state in the suppression of dissent.

Identifying Groups as Criminal

Individuals tend to group together with like individuals—for purposes of survival, social interactions or protection of vested group interests. Such grouping takes various forms and occurs in adolescents and adults alike. Grouping itself is not considered problematic by agents of the state; only certain groups are targeted for state intervention.

The history of criminology is replete with tales and theories of conforming and nonconforming adolescents. Traditional explanations for male delinquency (and gang behavior in particular) are grounded in the identification of common needs or values. According to Miller (1958), adolescent males group together around certain focal concerns due to a chain of events that begins with an overabundance of female-headed households and leads to a need for these males to learn and develop the behaviors necessary for survival in the lower-class world. Cohen (1955) saw adolescents as reacting to status frustration and looking for a common solution to that frustration. For some boys, the gang provided an avenue they could pursue and excel in. Cloward and Ohlin (1960) saw all adolescent males as joining groups. Those who had both the desire for and access to legitimate opportunity structures were accepted into legitimate groups. However, males who did not have access to the legitimate opportunity structure entered illegitimate groups as drug dealers or runners for organized crime, depending on the availability of the illegitimate opportunity structures.

Although traditional delinquency theories stress the importance of belonging, they do so within an assumed normative consensus or legal order where only negative behavior is punished.[2] Accordingly, these theories view some boys as 'belonging' to legitimate groups and other as having 'fallen' into a life of delinquency or crime. When belonging is satisfied through delinquent acts, the group's association, apart from its criminality, is redefined as a deviant subculture (i.e., gang), calling for both public condemnation and state intervention. And whenever that subcultural grouping places a group in opposition to the power elite or prevailing order, that groups's ideas, values, and actions are subject to negative classification (Dahrendorf, 1959; Turk, 1969).

Although the subcultural school focuses on the behavior of adolescent males, the methodology can also be applied to adult group activity, especially legitimate political activity defined as deviant and moved against by rule-violating state agencies or agents. One recent subcultural group whose experience with such state intervention has been well documented is CISPES—a grass-roots organization which seeks to draw attention to the plight of the people of El Salvador, tries to bring some form of relief to these people, and demonstrates against U.S. involvement in the horrors of the Salvadoran war. CISPES's members have never been charged (or shown to be involved) in any criminal acts. On the contrary, CISPES actively demonstrates against not only what it views as criminal acts, but what the United Nations, World Court, and international law regard as violations of law and human rights (e.g., torture, genocide, and denial of self-determination)—namely, U.S. intervention in Central America (see Elias, 1986).

U.S. policy in Central America is a continuing display of long-term intervention in the name of democracy and anticommunism. Chomsky (1985a) has noted, however, that the United States is actually seeking global hegemony in order to preserve the fifth freedom—the freedom to rob and exploit. U.S. intervention in Central America, then, is not necessarily concerned with the freedom and safety of the people of Central America or the United States, instead, it may actually be designed to benefit those with political and economic power. Evidence of such a purpose goes beyond current practices in Central America. Similar activities have taken place in Chile, Guatemala, Vietnam, and elsewhere—often in response to the needs of multinational corporations with interests in those countries (Chomsky, 1988; Donner, 1980; Halperin et al., 1976; Herman, 1982).

Because of the long-held economic interests of multinationals in Central America, any action questioning the legitimacy of U.S. intervention becomes a cause of concern for those doing the original intervening. This concern translates into the pulling of political-economic strings and directing police action against groups who question U.S. policy. These groups are labeled subversive, a type of criminal subculture. As Chomsky states:

Separatism, *subcultures*, . . . acceptance without awareness of the doctrines of the state religion—these are among the many reflections of the enormous power of the Western system of fragmentation and ideological control. . . . (1985a:251; emphasis added).

The use of subcultural identification, then, serves the ideological role of separating the good guys from the bad guys and the practical role of advocating investigation and prosecution of the latter.

Another example of stealing the right to dissent, one involving the cooperation and support of the U.S. government with Duarte and the death squads in El Salvador, can be found with a group of women known as CoMadres—the Committee of Mothers and Relatives of Political Prisoners, Disappeared and Assassinated of El Salvador (Chomsky, 1988). These women document human rights abuses in El Salvador and make efforts both to stop the abuses and to inform people throughout the world of those abuses. Their efforts were recognized a few years ago when they were awarded the first Robert F. Kennedy Humanitarian Award. Unfortunately, CoMadres representatives were not allowed to accept the award in person because the U.S. State Department labeled them as a threat to U.S. policy and barred their entrance to the U.S. by invoking the McCarren-Walter Act (*Do Not Enter*, 1986; see also Grossman, 1987).

Similarly, the people of Nicaragua have been labeled as terrorists, in part because of their active resistance to U.S intervention in their country. The term *terrorist* conjures up images of killers and criminals, ignoring the chain of events that led to these people rising up against the right-wing forces that seek to put an end to self-determination. In Nicaragua, this chain of events includes more than forty years of intervention on the part of the United States to maintain the country as a subservient client-state of multinational capitalism (Chomsky, 1985a).

History shows us the effects of U.S. intervention in Central America and elsewhere. U.S. placement of puppet regimes or support of right-wing, military dictatorships not only aids economic and political ventures of the United States and others, but it also gives the resident regime nearly unbridled discretion to do as it pleases (Chomsky, 1988). Dictators—lacking the support and reciprocity of the popular masses and constantly threatened by political dissent—have a rich history of violating human rights, often maintaining death squads to suppress opposition. Regarding the recent human rights abuses in El Salvador and related, subsequent abuses by the FBI against CISPES in the United States, critics maintain:

Of course we're angry about the way the FBI's violated our constitutional rights. But look what they're doing in El Salvador. People working for democracy and human rights are arrested, tortured, and assassinated by Duarte's death squads. The harassment of CISPES shows that support for dictatorship abroad can only be maintained by repressing democracy at home. The counterinsurgency war is being fought against the people of El Salvador and against U.S. public opinion (Sanbrano, as quoted by Zielinski, 1988).

These are but a few examples of how subcultural methodology is used to identify one group as deviant or criminal in order to subordinate another group's criminal behavior against peoples' fundamental rights — in the name of free enterprise or anti-Communism. This process of deviant subcultural identification not only causes problems for CISPES members and their families, but it deflects attention from people or groups who are actually committing crimes and injuring people.

Subcultural Labels and the Dialectics of State Control

Hall and colleagues (1978) describe state use of moral panics to create a picture of crime and criminals so the populace will rise up and demand that something be done about the crime or criminals. Moral panics involve a lengthy process of events, including a spiral of signification in which events are portrayed as more and more threatening. Key to this signification is the identification of a subversive minority upon whom troubles can be blamed and punishments imposed. Moral panics, then, involve a lengthy process of directing attention to certain individuals, depicting events as either out of control or increasingly dangerous, and — coincidentally — outlining strategies for intervention.

Although it has been posited that subcultures do not exist in the United States because of the absence of a dominant culture, the state participates in manufacturing a "consensual/homogenized social reality" based on shared beliefs and cultural values in order to secure support for prevailing policies and practices of state intervention (Chomsky, 1985b). By promoting a dominant culture, state intervention tactics compete with a diversity of beliefs and values — specifically with opposition groups and ideologies. The state, in defending the current social structure and political-economic processes, resists ideas that challenge its authority and often finds itself caught up in contradictions between the dialectics of rule of law on the one hand, and legal repression and criminality on the other (Balbus, 1973). Accordingly, in order for the U.S. state political-economic structure to be maintained, various groups are targeted as unacceptable, too radical, and in need of being suppressed (or better yet, crushed altogether).

In order to maintain control over targeted group behaviors, such control must be viewed as necessary or legitimate by the majority of the population (or at least by those paying attention). Because overt coercion or naked force can be counterproductive and delegitimate state authority and power (see, e.g., Foucault, 1977), persuasion — accomplished by the mass-mediated themes of crime and justice — prevails (Barak, 1988). Using moral panics, the state sets the stage for citizens to demand that something be done about specifically identified criminals and selectively chosen crimes. The usual response has been intensification of state-mediated social control mechanisms.

The use of moral panics to further social control efforts is best seen in its application to groups primarily composed of adults — namely, people who protest the various policies of the state, either domestically or on a foreign basis. Through the use of moral panics and the identification of a subversive or criminal subculture, criminologists are in danger not only of becoming agents of this repression, but also of succumbing to the bastardization of a methodology that serves the dominant political and economic interests. For example, the subcultures of so-called terrorism portrayed by politicians, mass media, and criminologists are subject to widely differing interpretations (see Ratner, Georges-Abeyes and others in this anthology). Generally speaking, the U.S. government defines terrorism as the 'retail' activities of opponents of Western democracy. The 'wholesale' state terrorism of capitalist or socialist nations is not included in this definition (Herman, 1982).

The FBI's mandate to gather information on groups and individuals posing a threat to national security has existed since the days of the Palmer raids and the Red Scare. Buttressing this state mandate to protect domestic tranquility and national security is the belief that a link exists between domestic terrorism in the United States and worldwide expansion of terrorism in general (Donner, 1980). This alleged link creates support for the counterterrorism tactics employed by the U.S. in a previously neverending battle with the communist-backed terrorists of the cold war. The term *terrorist,* like *subversive,* has "acquired vague and sinister overtones, which recommend it for use in creating a climate favorable to the renewal of countersubversion" (Donner, 1980:456).

Implication of the Use of Subcultures by the State

Beliefs such as those described in the preceding section led to the formation of COINTELPRO (counter-intelligence program), the FBI's secret war against the political activity of citizens and organizations. According to Halperin and colleagues (1976:113), "The FBI used press contact to conduct campaigns to expose, discredit, and humiliate selected citizens. Derogatory information, arrest records, and other confidential bureau records were leaked to 'friendly media' to form the basis for stories that could harm the reputation of citizens."

Not only were individuals and organizations singled out for countersubversion when there was no real evidence of subversion, but FBI tactics were often in direct contradiction to law. The fact that the FBI broke the law, however, was not (and is not) in the forefront of most U.S. citizens' minds. Instead, many of the FBI's methods were viewed as necessary for ridding the United States of any Communist influence.

The FBI and others were relying on a cold-war ideology that pits the United States against communism. Because of this prevailing ideology, it has been relatively easy to convince the public that what the FBI is doing is legitimate. As a matter of fact, this belief structure is tautological. The public must be convinced that persons or groups critical of U.S. policy are Communist-backed and out to subvert or overthrow the U.S. government. If the belief structure is accepted and the connection can be made, then the state agency involved (e.g., the FBI) is able—by merely pointing a finger and identifying dissent as threatening national security—not only to employ illegal tactics (depriving dissenters of their rights), but also to escape punsihment, even when the wrongdoing comes to public attention.

The FBI, CIA, and other government agencies have been documented as employing illegal methods to further their goals. However, instead of being targeted for legal intervention, agencies are absolved of responsibility because they are clearly working to rid the United States of any truly criminal element. In other words, group activity on the part of the powerless—minorities, economically marginal people, political dissenters—is deemed as a legitimate target for state intervention, but activity on the part of state-organized groups is beyond reproach. The subcultural method, then, enables the state to strengthen social control tactics and to intervene in noncriminal affairs that are either not legitimate state concerns (e.g., political rallies regarding Central America) or state concerns but are singled out for intervention by selective or discriminatory strategies.

For example, internal disputes (self-originating or imported) in so-called Third World countries are presented to the public as matters of U.S. security, when the primary rationale for intervention is preservation of the fifth freedom, the freedom to rob and to exploit, or to deny universal human rights or self-determination. On the other hand, gang practices in the United States may very well be the concern of the state, but then so should the "gang activities" of the state be of fundamental concern. For example, the fact that the people who brought us the "Just Say No" antidrug campaign have for more than 20 years played a significant role in importing drugs to this country is evidence of contradictory legal and moral principles (Kennedy, 1970). It is also evidence of the manipulation of definitions that the state employs. By using the subcultural method, the state selectively punishes street dealers of crack and cocaine while international drug traffickers and cartels are ignored, (or even supported). It is a powerful methodology when the disparate results go essentially unquestioned by the majority of people.

The current attention paid to the U.S. drug problem is fertile ground for examining the use of subcultural methodology. Drug gangs, often centered around crack, are key targets for local and federal legislation. The current administration has even won the use of the death penalty for drug-related deaths. At the same time, although there is historical evidence of the medicalization of women through the use of tranquilizers (most notably Valium) and speed (Schur, 1984), these women are not referred to with a subculturel label. Instead, the state agrees that in some situations these women deserve help (if they can afford it). Not only are these women not subjected to a subculture label, but neither are the physicians who help to perpetuate the overreliance on such drugs, especially for women.

In addition, the CIA has been documented as playing a key role in transporting drugs into this and other countries (Moyers, 1988). But, of course, the subcultural label is not applied to the CIA, nor was the subcultural methodology applied to Manuel Noriega and other drug kingpins so long as their political interests or behavior was of use to U.S. foreign policy. This is evidence that there are a number of groups inside and outside this society who fit the general description of drug dealers and who should attract the derogatory subcultural label but do not.

Other evidence of the selective application of labels through the subcultural methodology includes youth gangs—primarily male, black, and lower-class—who commit certain criminal acts and are appropriately targeted for state intervention by various social control agents. At the same time, however, white-collar criminals (e.g., Florida bankers) are largely unregulated and do not fall prey to state intervention. They not only escape the negative label but more importantly they are allowed to make illegal profits in the billions. The criminal activities of the Iran-Contra affair, for example, have — at the time of this writing — resulted only in guilty findings for Poindexter and North; the rest of the Reagan gang got off scot-free. Likewise, criminal activities by U.S.-backed groups (e.g., the Contras, Duarte, death squads) are not subjected to the selective subcultural methodology that results in state intervention tactics.

Subcultural Methodology as a Crime by the State

The use, then, of subcultural methodology may result in criminal activity on the part of state agents. Even when it does not, using an established methodology of state intervention lends an air of legitimacy to the views and actions of the state. The very fact that officers of the state make the proclamations helps to reproduce the legitimacy of the methodology itself. State identification of certain groups not only targets those groups for intervention, but it turns attention away from other groups. Often the only crime that has been committed is that of dissent, a behavior supposedly viewed as a right, not a crime.

When a group is targeted for state intervention because of its political opposition, that group loses its right to dissent. Although the state would argue otherwise, because taking something that rightfully belongs to individuals and the group is a purposeful, premeditated act, this state behavior could be defined as criminal. Moreover, the use of subcultural methodology by the state should not only be viewed as evidence of a power-coercive tactic, but it should be regarded as a criminal activity and — because the state relies on punitive measures for crime — aptly punished. Such punishment would go far toward protecting democratic values and rule of law.

Not only can subcultural methodology result in the theft of a basic right, but the subsequent identification of groups by this methodology can result in numerous other, noncriminal harms. For example, many groups expressing dissent with U.S. foreign policy are grass-roots organizations without strong financial support. When their members are arrested, this results in additional harms to these individuals, thus making the state apparatus even more guilty. When peace groups are targeted for intervention tactics and this intervention is made public, the process promotes the premise that indiscriminate killing of people in other countries is legitimate. In other words, if it is wrong to protest the killing of people in Central America, then it follows that it is okay to perpetuate the killings.

Conclusion

Overall, the harms resulting from the state's use of subcultural methodology are vast and serious in nature. These harms range from the theft of basic constitutional rights to the infliction of monetary hardship on U.S. citizens, and monetary and physical hardship, including death, on citizens in Central America and elsewhere. It is important for criminologists to recognize the extent of these harms and seek ways to transcend the use of a methodology that contributes to such harms. As is implicitly and explicitly argued throughout this chapter, this methodology is harmful on both domestic and global levels. Criminologists must realize their role in reifying the subcultural methodology and developing alternatives for abating and resisting such harmful practices. As Schwendinger and Schwendinger (1970:138) pointed out two decades ago:

> It can be readily understood that, in the desire to examine and utilize apparently more precise categories, scholars might overlook the degree to which their own scientific behavior is determined by the same political conditions which gave rise to legal definitions in use. But this is insufficient for explaining why conventional political categories have succeeded in superseding all other ethical, as well as professional, criteria for defining the nature of crime. . . . These political standards are more than an encroachment on the autonomy of science. They are also in contradiction to the truly scientific and humanistic mandate that it is not the professional's function to be a mere technician who complies, wittingly or unwittingly, with established authorities. According to this mandate every professional is morally responsible for his own actions: this responsibility cannot be justifiably delegated to agents of the State.

In short, it is the responsibility of individual criminologists to ensure that the methods they employ are not harm-producing or crime-producing, even if the state desires to use such methods. It is important to demystify state intervention and remove the legitimate labels attached to such practices, especially when they involve breaking the law in the name of law and order.

Notes

1. The use of the term *state* should not be viewed as a reification of the state but, rather, should be understood as encompassing complex political-economic structures and processes. As Domhoff (1986:226) has noted:

> 'State' is a concept with three levels of meaning. At the most visible level, the state is a 'sovereign political territory.' It is a nation-state, such as the United States or France. However, the state as a sovereign political territory is maintained by a 'government system' or 'state apparatus.' This is the second meaning of 'state,' and it includes all aspects of the formal system of government—executive, legislative, judiciary, military, and police. Most important, however, the 'state' is a state of mind, and its essence involves a common will on the part of the people within a given territory to unite for the common defense of that territory. The 'state,' then, is ultimately defined by a common allegiance (patriotism), which is expressed in a willingness to accept the government system and to defend the common territory. The 'state' as government apparatus and as a state of mind are thus embodied in the definition of the state as a 'sovereign political territory.'

These comments demonstrate not the existence of a single entity, but rather the existence of various processes and structures through which people act for reasons of state.

2. Although these noncritical or conventional researchers (theorists) and others have tended to work within allegedly neutral or value-free, objective frameworks, most contemporary theorists recognize the presence of "domain assumptions" (Gouldner, 1970; Schwendinger and Schwendinger, 1974) which operate to affect all researchers and their research. Subcultural theorists based their work on official data. From the beginning, then, there was a reliance on state-defined acts, and the actors in the theory were defined based on their participation in such acts. While these subcultural theorists were, undoubtedly, seeking answers to the 'crime problem,' they inadvertently advanced methodology that could be used by the state to further its interests — interests which not only may have nothing to do with solving the crime problem, but which may, in fact, contribute to the crime problem.

References

Balbus, I.
1973 *The Dialectics of Legal Repression.* New York: Russell Sage Foundation.

Barak, G.
1988 Newsmaking Criminology: Reflections on the Media, Intellectuals, and Crime. *Justice Quarterly. Vol. 5, No. 4:565–587.*

Blackstock, N.
1975 *Cointelpro: The FBI's Secret War Against Political Freedom.* New York: Vintage Books.

Chomsky, N.
1985a *Turning the Tide.* Boston: South End Press.
1985b The Manufacture of Consent. *Our Generation. Vol.* 17, No. 1:85–106.
1988 *The Culture of Terrorism.* Boston: South End Press.

Cloward, R. A. and L. E. Ohlin
1960 *Delinquency and Opportunity.* New York: The Free Press.

Cohen, A. K.
1955 *Delinquent Boys: The Culture of the Gang.* New York: The Free Press.

Dahrendorf, R.
1959 *Class and Class Conflict in Industrial Society.* Stanford, CA: Stanford University Press.

Domhoff, G. W.
1986 The Ruling Class and the Problem of Power. In *Radical Perspectives on Social Problems: Readings in Critical Sociology,* 3d ed., ed. by F. Lindenfeld. Dix Hills, NY: General Hall, Inc.

Donner, F.
1980 *The Age of Surveillance: The Aims and Methods of America's Political Intelligence System.* New York: Vintage Books.

1986 *Do Not Enter: The Visa War against Ideas* New York: Righter Productions. Film for public television.

Elias, R.
1986 *The Politics of Victimization: Victims, Victimology and Human Rights.* New York: Oxford University Press.

Foucault, M.
1977 *Discipline and Punish: The Birth of the Prison.* New York: Vintage Books.

Gouldner, A. W.
1970 *The Coming Crisis of Western Sociology.* New York: Equinox Books.

Grossman, C. J.
1987 The McCarren-Walter Act: War Against Margaret Randall and the First Amendment. *Crime and Social Justice.* Vols. 27–28:220–233.

Hall, S., C. Crither, T. Jefferson, J. Clarke, and B. Roberts
1978 *Policing the Crisis: Mugging, the State, and Law and Order.* New York: MacMillan Press.

Halperin, M., J. Berman, R. Borosage, and C. Marwick
1976 *The Lawless State: The Crimes of the U.S. Intelligence Agencies.* Middlesex: Penguin Books.

Herman, E.
1982   *The Real Terror Network*. Boston: South End Press.

Kennedy, M.
1970   Beyond Incrimination: Some Neglected Facets on the Theory of Punishment. *Catalyst*. No. 5 (Summer): 1–37.

Miller, W. B.
1958   Lower-Class Culture as a Generating Milieu of Gang Delinquency. *Journal of Social Issues*. No. 14: 5–19.

Moyers, B.
1988   *The Secret Government: The Constitution in Crisis*. Cabin John, MD: Seven Locks Press.

Schur, E. M.
1984   *Labeling Women Deviant: Gender, Stigma, and Social Control*. New York: Random House.

Schwendinger, H. and J. Schwendinger
1970   Defenders of Order or Guardians of Human Rights? *Issues in Criminology*. Vol. 5, No. 2:123–157.
1974   *The Sociologists of the Chair: A Radical Analysis of the Formative Years of North American Sociology (1883–1922)*. New York: Basic Books.

Turk, A. T.
1969   *Criminality and the Legal Order*. Chicago: Rand McNally.

Wasserman, G.
1988   *The Basis of American Politics*. Chicago: Scott, Foresman, and Company.

Zielinski, M.
1988   FBI's Probe of CISPES Exposed. *The Guardian*. Feb. 3, 1988: 1, 9.

III

On the Dialectical Nature of State Crimes

Overview

In "The War on Drugs: Nothing Succeeds Like Failure," Johns and Borrero maintain that the real question about the war on drugs is "how to minimize the social costs of dangerous drug use, legal or illegal." They further argue that the current Reagan/Bush administration strategies of criminalization and eradication are counterproductive: they are neither stemming the importation of illegal drugs, nor are they cost-effective. In their detailed and thoroughly developed analysis, Johns and Borrero examine the complex relationships between the war on drugs, U.S. foreign policy in Central America, anticommunism, state criminality, and street criminality. Dialectically, they conclude that although drug decriminalization is called for as a rational alternative to the failed policies of criminalization and penalization, the war on drugs is, nevertheless, likely to escalate as the United States escalates both its rhetoric and its interventionism into Latin America. In the final analysis, Johns and Borrero contend that "the negative effects of the war on drugs are largely irrelevant. The battles are likely to go on and on, escalating the attendant crime and violence and increasing the exploitation and control of the periphery by the center. The war on drugs is, simply put, too useful a legitimation of state crime to abandon."

In the next contribution, "Multi-Tiered Terrorism in Peru," R. S. Ratner provides a sophisticated and dialectical analysis of the multiple dimensions of state and nonstate terrorism. In his attempt to explain the "symbiotic relationship between authoritarian and 'democratic' regimes," Ratner's analytical nets go well beyond the relatively one-dimensional perspectives put forth by the protagonists of moral order. Specifically, he locates the fields of terrorism (and terrorists) within the dynamics of protest and control at the level of superpower intervention on the one hand, and within the dynamics of a controlled and managed dialectic of transnational capital on the other. In his closing remarks about possible future scenarios for a poor and inflation-driven Peru (another military takeover vis-à-vis an expanding National Security State or, less likely, economic reorganization by international lending institutions), Ratner notes that, paradoxically, terrorism may in fact "represent Peru's only hope . . . but it may also ensure Peru's continued exploitation should liberation struggles merely rationalize increased authoritarianism."

In the next chapter, "Piracy, Air Piracy, and Recurrent U.S. and Israeli Civilian Aircraft Interceptions," Daniel Georges-Abeyie examines "piracy, air piracy, hostage taking with uniformed agents or representatives," of recognized nation-states. Exploring the concepts of terrorism and international law in general, Georges-Abeyie creatively addresses the specifics of Israeli and U.S. "interceptions" and "redirections" of civilian aircraft and seacraft. He argues that there is a need to revise the *jure gentium* definitions of piracy, air piracy, hijacking, and air hijacking. He further argues that "a new civil aviation security convention is needed to deter terror, (i.e., official, or state terrorism) via sea-, air-, or land-based military forces as well as via electronic interference (i.e., intervention) with the navigation system of noncombatant aircraft." In the course of his argument, Georges-Abeyie also provides a very interesting semantical discussion of terrorism and its relationship to international law.

Mark Hamm's contribution, "The Abandoned Ones: A History of the Oakdale and Atlanta Prison Riots," sets the record straight regarding the lives, activities, and events leading up to the Cuban detainee crisis and the longest siege in the history of American penology. Specifically, he explores the irony that "the most immediate impact of the U.S. political offensive against human rights abuses in Cuban prisons was to politicize Cubans locked up in U.S. prisons." Hamm also demystifies the extent to which not all of these Cuban detainees were hardcore criminals (less than one-half of one percent of the entire Freedom Flotilla was found to have serious criminal backgrounds). He further exposes the creation by the mainstream U.S. press of an untrue picture of the "Cuban Gulag" consistent with the Reagan Administration's diplomatic offensive against human rights abuses in Cuba's prisons. The pains of imprisonment suffered by the overwhelming majority of criminally innocent Cuban detainees, and the prison riots themselves, resulted primarily from what Hamm refers to as the "absurd existence" established by a political and social prison system operating "to deprive inmates of accurate information, good management, fundamental human rights, and an adversarial system of justice."

3

The War on Drugs: Nothing Succeeds Like Failure

Christina Jacqueline Johns and *Jose Maria Borrero N.*

Although the use of any dangerous drug carries with it social costs, in most societies people have and use one form or another of dangerous drug. Therefore, the real question is — or should be — how to minimize the social costs of dangerous drug use, legal or illegal.

The Reagan/Bush administration has consistently pursued a strategy which has escalated rather than minimized the social costs of using certain dangerous drugs. By pursuing a strategy of criminalization on the one hand and eradication on the other (of both drugs and people associated with them), the administration has guaranteed that the price society pays for the use of certain dangerous drugs is higher than it would have been had a policy of decriminalization, treatment, and education been pursued.

The negative consequences of an enforcement strategy are well known. The United States has had a great deal of experience with the problems caused by this strategy when it is used to deal with victimless (or, more accurately, complaintless) crimes. In the 1920s, attempts to enforce the 18th Amendment prohibiting the sale and use of alcohol brought about problems similar to those which characterize the present administration's "war on drugs."

The Domestic Effects of the War on Drugs

The criminalization and enforcement strategies which characterized the prohibition era, and now the "war on drugs" era, have never been effective in stopping the manufacture, use, and trafficking of illegal substances. A recent report from the American Bar Association (1988:6,44) notes that "police, prosecutors and judges told the committee that they have been unsuccessful in making a significant impact on the importation, sale and use of illegal drugs, despite devoting much of their resources to the arrest, prosecution and trial of drug offenders." The authors of the report conclude that the drug problem is "severe, growing worse, and . . . law enforcement has been unable to control it."

Even though government surveys indicated a decline in drug use among high school seniors in the 1980s, one out of two seniors had indicated that they had tried an illicit drug. And these figures did not include high-school dropouts, who were commonly thought to be more involved in illicit drug use. In some major metropolitan areas, the dropout rate is estimated to be as high as 50%. Even considering the figures only for those still in school, the war on drugs is evidently not having a significant impact on the availability of drugs. For example, 85% of high school seniors surveyed said marijuana would be easy to get, and 55% said cocaine would be easy to get (Criminal Justice Newsletter, 1989b).

The enforcement strategy pursued by the Reagan and Bush administrations has not only been ineffective in stopping the manufacture, use, and trafficking of drugs, it has also brought about additional social costs.

Enforcement Costs

The enforcement costs associated with criminalization are staggering. The Reagan administration conducted an eight-year, multibillion-dollar war against drugs. The federal government spent an estimated $3 billion to fight the war on drugs in 1988, with the largest share of that money, $962.2 million, allocated to interdiction. The Bush administration has asked Congress for $150 million in antidrug grants to state and local agencies alone. Lawmakers are seeking $275 million for fiscal year 1990. Under the Bush proposals, the Drug Enforcement Agency (DEA) would receive even more money ($551 million) than it received under the Reagan administration ($546 million), and an additional $68 million would go to DEA through a separate appropriation (Criminal Justice Newsletter, 1989a). In fiscal year 1988, New York City spent $500 million on drug-related enforcement, more than twice the money spent in 1986. According to New York State statistics, however, the number of regular cocaine abusers grew from an estimated 182,000 in 1986 to an estimated 600,000 in 1988 (Berke, 1989a).

The increased concentration of expenditure on enforcement is obvious when one compares the percentage of money devoted to treatment, education, and prvention in 1970 (55.9%) to the percentage devoted to these areas in 1987 (23.7%) (Drug Policy Letter, 1989). As Kadish (1971:63) noted nearly twenty years ago: "It seems fair to say that in few areas of the criminal law have we paid so much for so little."

Diversion of Police Time

The policing of complaintless crimes such as drug use and trafficking deflects police time and resources away from other, more serious crimes which are just as violent and arguably more destructive to the social fabric — white collar crimes, corporate crimes, environmental crimes, and political crimes (Reiman, 1984; Hills, 1987). For example, the House Subcommittee on Oversight and Investigation estimated that in 1976 unnecessary surgery cost the nation $3.5 billion and led to 12,000 deaths. The director of public health in California once argued that medical quackery kills more people than all crimes of violence taken together (Eitzen and Timmer, 1985:190,195).

Enforcement Primarily Affects Street Criminals

Enforcement tactics primarily affect lower-class individuals rather than middle- and upper-class dealers and users. Police officials use the same 'difficulty of enforcement' argument to explain this disparity as they do to explain the lack of enforcement of laws against white-collar crime. The police maintain that drug use and trafficking among the middle and upper classes is more difficult to detect because it does not commonly take place in the street (Jordan, 1988). The disproportionate impact on the lower class, however, cannot always be written off as an accident. In New York, enforcement tactics with regard to crack have purposefully been focused on street dealers rather than big-time suppliers.

Nearly twenty-five years ago, the President's Commission on Law Enforcement and the Administration of Justice (1967:103 – 104) noted that, "the application of these laws [against complaintless crimes] often tends to discriminate against the poor and subcultural groups in the population." The report concluded that, because of this differential enforcement, "poverty itself becomes a crime."

Profit Margin and Organized Crime

The criminalization of drugs invariably increases the profit margin associated with their production and distribution. For example, a former DEA agent charged in 1987 with laundering drug money paid $580,000 in cash for a new house (New York Times, 1988d). In the 1989 trial of Guillermo Tabraue, a Bay of Pigs veteran, federal prosecutors maintained that the single drug syndicate operated by Tabraue and his son earned $75 million between 1976 and 1987. Tabraue increased his profits by accepting $1,400 a month from the CIA to provide information about drug trafficking among Bay or Pigs veterans (Corn and Morley, 1989b).

The huge profits to be made from criminalized drugs guarantees organized crime involvement. The profits gleaned from liquor sales during Prohibition virtually established organized crime in the United States. Eddy and colleagues (1988:43) argue that the U.S. Mafia was the first to recognize the enormous potential of the cocaine market and the role that smugglers in Medellin could play as suppliers. Organized crime, in fact, is often dependent on new criminalizations for its profits.

Investment in the Legal Economy

Profits from illegal drug transactions are reinvested not only in other illegal activities, but in legal business activities as well, thereby further eroding the integrity of the social order and compromising the stability of the economy. For example, Max Mermelstein, a Miami drug-dealer-turned-FBI-informant, related stories of delivering cash to banks in duffel bags (Engelberg, 1989). In April of 1989, the Justice Department filed a civil suit seeking to seize $433.5 million in laundered drug money that had moved through the accounts of nine American banks and foreign banks with American branches (Wines, 1989b). Some of this money was invested in American real estate (Wines, 1989a).

Corruption

The clandestine nature and enormous profits in illegal drug trafficking inevitably lead to police corruption. Questionable, if not illegal, practices are characteristic of investigations of many complaintless crimes. The use of decoys, informants, bugging devices, wiretapping, and no-knock raids are commonplace. As Reiman (1979:53) has noted: "The use of such low visibility tactics increases the likelihood of corruption and arbitrariness in the enforcement of the law." The President's Commission on Law Enforcement and the Administration of Justice, (1967:103–104) also noted the negative consequences of such tactics of enforcement:

> The practical costs of this departure from principle are significant. One of its consequences is to communicate to the people who tend to be the object of these laws the idea that law enforcement is not a regularized, authoritative procedure, but largely a matter of arbitrary behavior by the authorities.

In 1987, the U.S. Attorney's office began investigating charges that Washington, D.C. police officers had routinely lied under oath to obtain search warrants of homes in vice cases. Investigators learned that, in some cases, the informants whose testimony was cited did not exist. In other cases, the informants were real, but the alleged drug transactions never took place. In response to this investigation, U.S. Attorney Joseph E. di Genova was forced to drop 300–400 drug cases (Walsh and Lewis, 1987).

The Miami police force was plagued by drug-related corruption scandals in the mid-1980s. In July 1987, a federal grand jury indicted twelve former Miami policemen on racketeering, drug, and civil rights charges. Six other former officers were indicted in another case involving the deaths of several drug smuggling suspects. They were charged with conspiracy; racketeering; possession and sale of cocaine, marijuana, and Quaaludes; tax evasion; and civil rights violations (Washington Post, 1987a).

The acquittal of a police officer in the beating death of a black businessman helped touch off the 1980 riots in Miami, riots which left 18 people dead and resulted in $80 million in property damage. In April 1989, this same police officer was arrested on drug charges along with a federal drug agent. The two men had offered to provide protection for someone working with an undercover sting operation who said he wanted to smuggle large quantities of cocaine into the United States from the Bahamas. For this protection, the two demanded a fee of $300,000. (Anchorage Daily News, 1989a).

The New York Police Department considers the problem of police involvement in illegal drug trafficking so serious that it has established a special undercover squad to try to control drug-related criminal activity among police officers. The special squad was initiated in response to findings in 1986 that officers had been systematically robbing drug dealers of cash, narcotics, and guns (Pitt, 1988a).

In 1988, three former DEA agents were charged with laundering more than $608,000 that they had apparently accumulated while dealing in drugs. The narcotics trafficking and money laundering of these three men went on both during and after their employment with the DEA (New York Times, 1988d).

As former U.S. Supreme Court Justice Earl Warren noted a decade ago: "The narcotics traffic of today . . . could never be as pervasive and open as it is unless there was connivance between authorities and criminals" (quoted in Eitzen and Timmer, 1985:233).

Secondary Crime

Criminalization creates a host of secondary criminal activity by creating an environment in which users must often resort to illegal means to get the money to buy drugs at prices inflated by criminalization. There is also violence associated with managing an illegal activity and disciplining an illegal work force, and law enforcement appears to exacerbate this violence. In a 1987 federal grand jury probe of police officers in the District of Columbia, sources reported that police connivance with certain drug dealers by arresting their rivals sparked violent battles between competing groups. Witnesses told authorities that officers protected some drug dealers from arrest and gave them advance notice of drug raids. Allegations that officers diverted to their own use police funds intended for paying informants and making undercover drug purchases were also being investigated. This investigation came at the end of an undercover FBI investigation into allegations that some of the officers were personally profiting from their work in drug enforcement (Anderson and Lewis, 1987).

Disrespect for the Law

With full enforcement virtually impossible, discriminatory enforcement common, and police tactics questionable or illegal, criminalization promotes a disrespect for the law and the legal system. In 1967, the President's Commission (1967: 103–104) noted:

> "It is costly for society when the law arouses the feelings associated with these laws in the ghetto — a sense of persecution and helplessness before official power and hostility to police and other authority that may tend to generate the very conditions of criminality society is seeking to extirpate."

An administration which presents itself as being concerned with preserving respect for law and order, must surely take note of a Bronx jury's recent decision to acquit Larry Davis on charges that Davis tried to kill nine police officers. Contrary to what the police maintained, the jury believed the defendant's argument that he had fired in self-defense. The police officers, Davis's lawyer maintained, had intended to kill Davis to silence him because of his knowledge of corruption and drug dealing in the local police precincts (Blair, 1988). After the trial, the jury forewoman stated, "[The police] wanted him dead so he couldn't squeal on them" (Pitt, 1988b).

Labelling

By criminalizing drug users, society labels as criminals a group of people who would not for any other reason be so labelled. In 1985, 45% of all arrests for drug law violations were for the possession of marijuana (Sourcebook of Criminal Justice Statistics, 1987:325). The deputy chief of New York's Tactical Narcotics Team admitted that the vast majority of arrests in New York have been of small-scale dealers and users (Marriott, 1989). These small-scale dealers and users then become labeled as criminals, and the discrimination they face in jobs and housing leads them further into criminal activity.

Health Problems

Criminalization makes dealing with the health problems associated with drug use more difficult to manage. In the United States, needle sharing among intravenous drug users is considered the primary link between Acquired Immunodeficiency Syndrome (AIDS) and the heterosexual population. The National Academy of Sciences recently recommended that needle exchange programs be permitted in order to help curb the AIDS problem. The Anti-Drug Abuse Act of 1988, however, prohibits the use of most federal treatment funds for any program providing drug users with clean needles, or even bleach to clean needles (Drug Policy Letter, 1989). Of the estimated 200,000 intravenous drug users in New York City, 120,000 (60%) are believed to carry the AIDS virus. Even so, the sale and possession of hypodermic needles in New York was, until recently, illegal, and Mayor Koch use to advocate prosecuting those who distribute free needles (Raspberry, 1988).

The International Effects of the War on Drugs

Just as it is not difficult to see the negative consequences of the war on drugs domestically, it is also not difficult to see the negative consequences of this 'war' internationally. Internationally, the war on drugs has been just as ineffective in stopping the flow of drugs into the country as has been the domestic war on drugs. The interdiction/eradication strategy has been so ineffective, in fact, that there is currently a cocaine glut (Lernoux, 1989:190). An estimated 265,000 pounds of cocaine are smuggled annually into this country from South America. Drug seizures are insignificant in relation to this traffic, and the street price of drugs has declined rather than increased. In 1983, for example, a street gram of 35% pure cocaine cost $110. In 1986, a 50% pure street gram cost $100 (Sourcebook of Criminal Justice Statistics, 1987). According to the Drug Policy Foundation (1989), the price of cocaine has dropped to one-third of the 1981 price.

After spending vast amounts of public monies on enforcement, more rather than less drugs are entering the country (Sourcebook of Criminal Justice Statistics, 1987). In March 1989, the State Department released a report detailing increases in arrests, seizures, and eradicated acreage, as well as the successful extradition of a small number of drug traffickers. The report, however, also acknowledged global increases in production and demand. It was estimated that, from 1987 to 1988, coca production increased 7.2% among Bolivia, Colombia, Peru, and Ecuador. Global crop increases were estimated at 22% for marijuana, 15% for opium, and 11% for hashish (Sciolino, 1989b).

In a New York Times article about the State Department report, Elaine Sciolino (1989b) noted: "The report was printed in a small quantity and will not be available to the public." Although this report was not available to the public, disinformation about drug seizures has been. In November 1988, the Justice Department agreed to review the DEA practice of allowing local police forces to publicize seizures of drugs brought into the U.S. in Federal undercover operations (New York Times, 1988e).

The Costs of Criminalization

The costs of international enforcement attempts are high. The Federal Government spent $900 million on interdiction in 1986 (Data Clearinghouse for Drugs and Crime, 1989). For fiscal year 1987, $1,369,300 was budgeted (GAO, 1988), and the Defense Authorization bill allocated $300 million for drug interdiction in 1989 (Berke, 1989a). The DEA plans to spend $50 million between 1988 and 1991 for eradication programs in Bolivia alone (Kerr, 1988). Mexico receives $14.5 million annually for drug eradication (Rohter, 1989).

The Deflection of Police Energy

Massive U.S. aid to the military and police in Latin American countries has been unsuccessful in decreasing — much less stopping — the production and distribution of drugs. In addition, although the U.S. provides funds for police and the military to fight the drug war, gross violations of human rights are commonplace in many Latin American countries, with a large number of these violations committed by the military and police. Joaquin Matallana, the former head of Colombia's state security agency, noted in 1988 that official corruption extended into the 1,800-member antinarcotics unit partially funded by the United States. The Colombian general staff has been accused of covering up human rights abuses by the military. An international human rights panel headed by Nobel Peace Prize recipient Adolfo Perez Esquivel concluded that some military officers were involved in death squad activity (Collett, 1988). But the United States is not fighting a 'war against human rights abuses'; in fact, the war on drugs is funding those abuses.

Effects on the Lower Rungs of Drug Trade

Even though there have been some notable successes in the prosecution of big-time drug traffickers, for the most part these individuals remain outside the criminal justice net. Senator Kerry's Congressional report documented in 1989 that the most powerful drug kingpins (such as Noriega) are often ignored. The prosecution of Carlos Lehder has been presented to the American people as a major law enforcement coup, but many argue that Lehder was caught and prosecuted only because the drug mafia itself wanted Lehder out of the way. Lehder's overtly aggressive political statements attracted too much attention and interfered with business.

Profit Margin

International efforts in the war on drugs have ensured that the profit margin on drugs is high — so high, in fact, that at one point the Colombian Mafia reportedly offered to pay off the Colombian National Debt. The personal fortune of Honduran drug trafficker Juan Ramon Matta is estimated at $1 billion (Rohter, 1988a). The economies of a number of the more important drug-producing and -trafficking countries depend on drug money. Eddy and colleagues (1988:48) detail the steps involved in processing and distributing cocaine and the profits at each step (based on a DEA report in 1979). The basic ingredients to produce a kilo of cocaine cost $625. Once coca leaves are turned into paste, then base, and finally one kilo of cocaine hydrochloride, the value in Colombia is $9,550. By the time this kilo reaches the United States, its value is $37,000. The distribution process increases the quantity of product. First the wholesaler cuts the cocaine to 50% purity and sells two kilos for $37,000 each. The distributor cuts it again and sells four kilos, and the street dealer after cutting sells eight kilos at $70 or more a gram. Coca leaves worth $625 are thereby turned into street cocaine worth $560,000. As Eddy and colleagues (1988:49) note, cocaine is "the most valuable commodity on earth."

Legal Reinvestment

Internationally, illegal profits do not remain outside the legitimate market. The banking industry, for example, is heavily implicated in money laundering. Robert Stankey, a former Treasury Department analyst who started compiling currency surplus figures in 1979, estimated that much of the $6.4 billion cash surplus of Southern Florida Banks in 1988 (compared to $3.3 billion in 1978) came from drug payments (Corn and Morley, 1989a). February 1989, thirty-three people were charged in

Los Angeles with laundering more than $500 million in Colombian cocaine profits destined for legal reinvestment. It was estimated that this operation alone had hidden the source of $1 billion in drug money over the previous two years and involved bank accounts in New York, Panama and, Uruguay (New York Times, 1989b). Juan Ramon Matta invested heavily in legitimate businesses in Honduras—including hotels, cattle ranches, factories, a tobacco plantation, and a processing plant that employs several hundred people (Rohter, 1988a). Lernoux (1989:190) estimates that $600 million of the $3 billion earned annually in Bolivia through drug trafficking is reinvested in the economy, with areas of investment including agriculture and construction.

Promotion of Corruption

Internationally, the war on drugs has had negative effects on police institutions by promoting questionable police tactics and even more widespread corruption than existed before the war on drugs. DEA agents are reportedly as afraid of the police they work with as of the drug traffickers they are supposed to arrest. In 1987, a State Department report criticized "endemic" corruption extending to the highest levels of the Mexican government (Sciolino, 1989b). The report characterized this corruption as the "single most important factor undermining meaningful narcotics cooperation" (Sciolino, 1989a). In large drug busts in Mexico, some of those arrested have been members of the Mexican Federal Judicial Police, the state police, and customs (Branigan, 1988). The complicity of the Mexican police in the death of Enrique Camarena has been detailed in Elaine Shannon's *Desperados*. Notwithstanding these events, Mexican president Carlos Salinas de Gortari appointed as his Attorney General the governor of the state of Jalisco, who American officials complain dragged his feet on the Camarena investigation (Rohter, 1988b).

When Mexican authorities recently arrested Miguel Angel Felix Gallardo—a reputed drug lord called by the Attorney General of Mexico "the number one drug trafficker in Mexico"—they also arrested the top federal antidrug official of the state of Sinaloa, six police officials, and every policeman on the force of Felix Gallardo's hometown of Culiacan (Anchorage Daily News, 1989a). The head of intelligence for the Mexico City Police recently resigned after he was indicted in the United States on charges of operating a car-theft and smuggling ring. His name has also surfaced in testimony given to American grand juries considering drug trafficking across the Mexican border (Rohter, 1989).

A former chairman of the Joint Chiefs of Staff told the Washington Post (Collett, 1988) that drug traffickers had "thoroughly penetrated" the national police force in Colombia. The State Department issued a report in 1988 that noted "drug-related corruption" in the Bahamas (Sciolino, 1989b), and evidence of official connivance in trafficking has also been noted in Bolivia (Lernoux, 1989;189), Haiti (Sciolino, 1989a), Paraguay (Riding, 1989), and other countries.

This corrosion has not only affected police institutions, but leading government and military officials as well. In March 1988, for example, U.S. authorities indicted Colonel Jean-Calude Paul of Haiti on narcotics counts (Collett, 1988). In March 1989, a close associate of Prime Minister Lynden Pindling of the Bahamas was indicted on charges of taking part in smuggling more than $1 billion worth of cocaine into the United States (New York Times, 1989d). Another associate of Pindling's was indicted in Florida for receiving bribes in exchange for allowing the Bahamas to be used for drug trafficking (Efron, 1989). Witnesses at the trial of Carlos Lehder Rivas testified that Prime Minister Pindling himself was involved (New York Times, 1989d). Even Reagan administration officials admit that Honduran military officers are involved in drug trafficking (Collett, 1988).

Secondary Criminal Activity

The enforcement tactics used against illegal drug trafficking create a host of secondary criminal activity, from murder to document forging. Enrique Camarena was evidently tortured and then murdered. The three other decomposing corpses found with Camarena's body were believed to be innocent bystanders killed because they had seen too much (Shannon, 1988).

U.S. Army General Paul Gorman, former commander of the U.S. Southern Command, testified before a Senate subcommitttee: "If you want to move arms and munitions in Latin America, the established networks are owned by the Cartel" (Washington Post, 1988a). Gunrunning and drug distribution go hand-in-hand. In February 1988 raids, Mexican police authorities captured more than 360 AK47 assault rifles and 145,000 rounds of ammunition. According to Mexican and U.S. officials, the weapons had been smuggled into Mexico from the United States and were destined for Colombia. In another series of raids in Durango, Mexico, the capture of three suspected drug dealers led to the seizure of 180 AK47s. The raids came after federal indictments in San Diego of twelve Mexicans — eight members of the Federal Judicial Police, three state policemen, and one Mexican customs official — for smuggling semiautomatic assault rifles from California (Branigan, 1988).

Disrespect for the Law

The U.S. administration has clearly shown its disdain for international law, and this disdain has led to the perception in Latin America of the United States as an outlaw nation. Bodenheimer and Gould (1989:223), in their book *Rollback!,* note that it is difficult for the American people to understand the depth of resentment people in other countries feel for the United States. The 'extradition' of Juan Ramon Matta in honduras, for example, provoked anti-American riots which culminated in an attack on the U.S. embassy in which five people are believed to have died (Rohter, 1988a). These riots were not only in response to Matta's virtual kidnapping, but also the result of widespread resentment of the U.S. use of Honduras as a staging ground for the war against Nicaragua.

Health Problems

A 1988 State Department report, maintained that aerial spraying was the only way to curb cocaine production (Sciolino, 1989b), even though eradication programs have proved largely ineffective in stopping production (Lernoux, 1989:190, GAO, 1988). In the Chapare region of Bolivia, an estimated 42,000 farming families depend on coca production for their livelihoods. The State Department has taken the position that the area should be sprayed with chemicals to destroy the coca fields, a measure the Bolivians oppose (Kerr, 1988).

Eradication programs have created health problems because they destroy not only coca but other crops and because they involve toxic chemicals. Paraquat, used to destroy marijuana in Mexico and Colombia, created disturbing health problems. The long-term environmental effects of current chemical spraying in Latin America are especially serious in a region where the poorest segment of the population is totally dependent on the land.

Why the Bush Administration Continues to Pursue the War on Drugs

The war on drugs, both domestically and internationally, has been ineffective in stopping the use, manufacture, and trafficking of drugs, and has created a host of subsidiary problems. Why, then — given the ineffectiveness of the war on drugs in terms of stopping drug use, and the negative effects of criminalization and enforcement tactics—has the Bush administration chosen to follow this course? The answer is that although the war on drugs might in some ways be ineffective and destructive, in other — perhaps more important — ways, it has been highly effective.

Moralistic Rhetoric

The war on drugs has successfully diverted public attention from fundamental social problems. The Reagan/Bush administration has managed to convince a substantial number of Americans that cocaine, marijuana, and heroin use are among the greatest dangers threatening not only the health of the American people, but the very fabric of society.

The abuse of tobacco, alcohol, and prescription drugs leads to far more serious consequences in terms of public health, violent behavior, spiritual deterioration, family disruption, death and disease — consequences that are all but ignored in the quest for a so-called drug-free culture. The drug-free culture being pursued is in fact a culture which allows citizens to consume culturally integrated drugs but excludes the drugs of other cultures.

The moralistic rhetoric about drugs and drug traffickers which is a fundamental part of this 'war' has distorted the realities of the situation and complicated any attempt to find realistic solutions to the drug problem. The issues of drug use and trafficking have been converted into a holy war, an almost religious crusade. In the ensuing fervor, the factors underlying the problems of drug use and trafficking are obscured. These real factors are obscured for a very good reason: powerful segments of society do not want to confront them because if they are confronted, something might have to be done about them.

The two main factors underlying the drug problem — factors the moralistic rhetoric has been successful in masking — are, first, the effects of economic exploitation and inequality, and second, a social reality in advanced capitalist countries that is so unbearable and stressful that most people spend a great deal of their time trying to escape it.

Economic Inequality

The war on drugs ideology has served to mask society's failure to establish fundamental economic and social justice domestically. Almost every homicide, assault, and robbery is presented in the media as "drug related." The violence and alienation of the ghetto has been redefined into a contemporary version of *Reefer Madness*.

Domestically, the war on drugs targets and blames an enemy group for social problems. Internationally, it targets and blames enemy countries (Colombia, for example) to mask its failure to even approximate international social and economic justice.

It is no surprise that inner-city ghettos are filled with drug dealers. Those who face the most obstacles to attaining the rewards of the social system predictably opt for a fast and easy route to the affluence all are taught to expect. Likewise, it is no surprise that people in countries such as Peru, Bolivia, and Colombia grow, distribute, process, and traffick in drugs.

The relationship between the dominant culture and the ghetto is similar to the relationship between developed, western, capitalist countries and Latin America, (i.e., it has historically been a relationship of structural dependence and exploitation). The economic relationship between the central capitalist countries and Latin America has historically been based on an unequal exchange. Until very recently, the outline of this exchange has been that Latin America has primarily exported cheap raw materials (which were cheap only because their prices were based on the overexploitation of land, labor, and natural resources) and imported expensive manufactured goods from the center. This exchange is violent in itself and has ensured continued poverty for a majority of Latin American people, underdevelopment of Latin American economies, and a sharpening of conflict between the powerful, indigenous oligarchies who have benefited from this relationship and the less powerful masses who have not.

In the context of these sharp inequalities in the international terms of commercial interchange, the radical fall in the prices of the traditionally exported raw materials (at present Latin American countries must sell three times more of their raw materials to obtain the same income they obtained 20 years ago), and the external debt, cocaine emerged as an exportable raw material in countries such as Colombia. None of the raw materials traditionally sold in the international market by Colombia provided enough surplus value to ensure the dynamic accumulation of capital.

Throughout perhaps all of Latin American history, cocaine has been the one raw material uniquely able to generate reasonable surplus value to producers and merchants. In Bolivia, for example, it is estimated that coca production brings in $500 million a year (Kerr, 1988). According to Lernoux (1989:190), who estimates the earnings at $3 billion a year, "the economy would collapse without cocaine income." $500 million is six times the total value of Bolivia's legal exports (Lernoux, 1989:190). It is estimated that a farmer in Bolivia can make as much as $10,000 a year selling coca (Christian, 1987). Hobsbawm notes that cocaine "has no competition as a profit maker. . . . It is basically an ordinary business that had been criminalized" (Hobsbawm, 1986).

The cocaine boom occurred in Colombia at a moment of deep and pervasive societal conflict. The concentration of power and wealth by the economic and political elites had systematically closed the possibilities of advancement and social mobility to most of Colombia's people.

Unable to manage the ensuing social conflicts, the hegemonic classes began exercising a policy of state terror in a strategy of social control which effectively silenced the Colombian people. These policies of terror were intensified by the proliferation of right-wing death squads whose bloody activities were, and still are, intimately connected to army commanders and police forces.

In this moment of deep social and political conflict—characterized by abject poverty, a growing external debt, widening economic distance between social classes, unemployment, political chaos, growing systematic violation of human and civil rights, and military and paramilitary violence against citizens—the enormous amounts of 'dirty money' provided by the cocaine boom arrived in Colombia as a new and powerful element of the conflict. In such a climate, the question asked Colombia and other underdeveloped countries of Latin America was the same one asked in urban ghettos: Why be poor forever? Why not use every tool available to gain money, which means power, when money and power are the only protection against exploitation?

The people of Latin American share a long history of exploitation through the international market. It is a history that includes the spoiling and pillaging of its natural resources by the wealthy countries of the center. Latin Americans have witnessed the methods by which these countries maintain this fundamentally unequal relationship — for example, violent military intervention or the promotion (and sometimes installation) of governments which systematically deny civil and human rights to the population (in Guatemala and Chile, for example).

And the lessons of exploitation have been well learned. The process of capital accumulation is violent and always benefits the few at the expense of the many. In Colombia, coffee and other export products brought about the accumulation of domestic capital through overexploitation of the labor force, expropriation and robbing of the fertile lands of farmers and peasants, and the bloodiest political violence during a historical period known simply as *La Violencia*. The capital that landowners, coffee merchants, and bankers accumulated as a result of expropriation and domestic violence represented elevated social, political, and economic costs to the Colombian people. These costs were only a reproduction of the violence which characterized the international arena.

The only difference between cocaine accumulation and previous processes of accumulation is that social, economic, and political costs of cocaine accumulation also affect the countries of the center. First World countries prefer to define the economy of the relationships of exploitation in such a manner that they reap all the benefits and distribute all

the costs to the Third World. At least in part, the war on drugs is a rebellion against the position of the United States in this new process of
capital accumulation. The more powerful segments of the United States
population do not want to face their own complicity in setting the pattern for such violent accumulation, and do not want to change a world
economy set up on the basis of one-way exploitative exchange.

Social Reality Which Leads to Drug Use

The second major issue masked by the rhetoric of the war on drugs
is the social and cultural reality that makes the United States such an
enormous consumer of drugs. For example, the cultural context in
which the demand for cocaine developed exists not only in ghettos, but
also in the expensive flats, sophisticated cocktail parties, and streets of
the most affluent First World Cities. Cocaine is presently the drug of
choice among the upper class. The question is, why?

Life in the postindustrial centers is highly stressful, partly because it involves the overuse of time. Constant, excessive action translates into physiological and psychological demands in excess of what the
human animal can withstand. The body must attempt to assume these
demands. Success in the post-industrial world demands overactivity,
and cocaine stimulates overactivity. It keeps a person awake, functioning, striving, and competing — in short, in sync with the accelerated
rhythms of postindustrial life. These rhythms create a permanent state
of 'organic alarm.' The ideological paradigms of postindustrial society
linked to excessive competition and consumption elevate psychological
and physical demands. In response to these demands, cocaine is a pan-
acea. In the beginning of the development of capitalism, time was
money; in the postindustrial centers, time is cocaine.

Every culture provides a particular experience of time — as a dimension of life, pleasure, work, knowledge, satisfaction, or pain. Time
is a corporal, or bodily, experience, and postindustrial capitalist society
requires bodies which are economically useful, socially efficient, and
politically innocuous. Cocaine is the drug to ensure such bodies.

Those in power do not want to examine the consequences of the
economic relationships which characterize society; nor do they want to
examine the social climate in which they have condemned themselves
to live. Least of all do they want to change them. They prefer to continually tell the American population that theirs is the most just, most free,
most fulfilled society on earth — never mind the evidence. The war on
drugs allows injustice to continue while Americans retain an image of
themselves as moral, righteous, fulfilled people struggling against the
drug demon which is the cause of all their problems.

The Real Successes of the War on Drugs

In addition to masking two fundamental issues that the ruling elite wishes to evade (the violent and unequal exchange relations characterizing the world capitalist economy and the spiritual poverty of personal life in advanced industrialized countries), the war on drugs has helped to bring about an aggressive, right-wind ideological shift and to legitimate what Bodenheimer and Gould (1989) refer to as a "global rollback strategy." This rollback strategy was present in American foreign policy during the entire postwar period, but it emerged as an especially potent force during the Reagan years. Rollback is essentially an attempt to return to a pre-Communist world, with the final goal of eliminating Communism in the U.S.S.R. Because of the dangers of confronting the U.S.S.R. directly, rollback strategy has focused on the Third World. Bodenheimer and Gould (1989:25–34) cite rollbacks or rollback attempts in China (1950 – 1961), Iran (1953), Guatemala (1954), Belgian Congo (1960), Cuba (1961–1968), Brazil (1964), the Dominican Republic (1965), Indonesia (1958 – 1965), Greece (1967), Southeast Asia (1958 – 1970), Chile (1970 – 1973), and Jamaica (1974 – 1980). More recently, rollback strategy has focused on Nicaragua, Libya, Grenada, and Afghanistan. The rollback strategy involves subverting or overthrowing any country that seeks "full independence from the economic, political, or military influence of the United States (Bodenheimer & Gould, 1989:26)."

Although the far right within the global rollback network publicly proclaim their intentions (Reagan's comment about making the Sandinistas "say uncle," for example), traditional conservatives have always preferred to keep rollback efforts covert. Proclaiming peaceful coexistence and pursuing an aggressive rollback strategy necessitates legitimating mythology and secrecy. As the Iran/Contra incidents illustrate, proclaiming respect for law and the Constitution while subverting them requires covert action and a strong legitimating ideology. Global Communist expansion is a fundamental part of this legitimating mythology.

In order to justify interventionism, the rollback network needs to keep the menace of Communist expansion in the public eye. This is why nationalist revolutionary movements (in Nicaragua, for example) must be presented as (and in some instances are probably believed to be) Communist-inspired. Similarly, the drug menace is presented as an external threat that must be fought — at the cost of intervening in some Latin American countries and propping up puppet or reactionary governments in others.

War — joining together to repel the foe — is, as Bacon suggested, "profitable and restorative." In the United States, the war on drugs has been both. The administration and as other members of the political elite continually define drugs and drug trafficking as threats to "U.S. security interest" (Washington Post, 1988a). The examples are legion. Mayor Donna Owens of Toledo, Ohio, in hearings before Congress in 1988: "America has been invaded by an enemy as cruel and powerful as any foreign enemy we have faced . . . ." (Rasky, 1988). New York Mayor Ed Koch at a meeting called by the U.S. Conference of Mayors to discuss the drug issue: "Wake up America: We are being destroyed" (Washington Post, 1988c). Robert M. Morgenthau (1989), District Attorney of New York City, in the New York Times: "We cannot wait for long-run palliatives because in the long run we are all dead." There is even talk of an 'international battle plan.'

Violence (in the form of economic boycott, military intervention, international kidnapping, and the new Anti-Drug Abuse Bill's provision of a nonmandatory death penalty for certain drug-related murders) has been elevated during the Reagan/Bush administration to the status of a positive good—a sign of restored confidence in America and an indication that Americans on the international scene and 'responsible conservatives' on the domestic scene are showing drug traffickers and the world who is boss. Whipped up by the hard right, the United States need not apologize for bombing the civilian population of another country and killing a hundred people (as in Libya). Such violence instead becomes an open celebration of restored American confidence. During the recent debates about the Drug Bill, Senator D'Amato remarked that his campaign to get the death penalty included for drug-related murders was "society's way of saying we're going to fight back" (Dewar, 1988). Tough domestic policy and interventionist foreign policy, then, have become celebrations of patriotism (e.g., Bush's invasion of Panama, Christmas 1989).

Expansion of Domestic State Power

Domestically, the war metaphor has whipped up a heightened perception of great external threat; consequently, it has led to increasing tolerance for the expansion of state power and erosion of democratic freedoms. To fight the drug problem, some Americans are calling for tougher measures that include the imposition of martial law (Beck, et. al, 1989). In reaction to a rising homicide rate, the City Council of Washington, D.C. approved a curfew for those under eighteen — even though the average age of homicide victims in D.C. is thirty, and the average age of killers is over eighteen (New York Times, 1989c). As the ideological frenzy about drugs heightens, 'effective' law enforcement becomes more important than protecting civil liberties. Norval Morris has written that the courts' attempts to restrain the police from illegal enforcement of statutes against victimless crime may herald the erosion, not the protection, of constitutional freedoms. (Eitzen and Timmer, 1985:234). It is now evident that this is the case. William Bennett has characterized the proposed federal intervention in Washington, D.C. as a "test case," implying that federal intervention could be extended to other cities (Berke, 1989c). Examples of the domestic expansion of state power justified by the war on drugs include the widespread of drug testing, assaults on procedural guarantees, the broadening of eligibility for capital punishment, and the denial of opportunity for those suspected of drug involvement.

Drug Testing. The Fourth Amendment prohibition against unreasonable search and seizure is now being assaulted by continual administration efforts to implement random drug testing. In 1986, the Reagan/Bush administration began asking federal agencies to test employees in so-called sensitive positions. State and local governments and private industry have followed suit. Addressing a 1988 meeting called by the U.S. Conference of Mayors to discuss the drug issue, then-Attorney General Edwin Meese called for virtually all workers in the country to be tested by their employers for the use of illicit drugs (McAllister, 1988).

By the time, there had been a number of federal court decisions in which judges had declared random testing in violation of the Constitution's ban on unreasonable search and seizure. The Reagan/Bush Justice Department seems to have completely ignored the Constitutional issues raised by universal drug testing.

Alan Adler of the American Civil Liberties Union told a Washington Post staff writer that Meese's remarks appeared to be an effort by the administration to get "employers to do things that the government could not do itself" (McAllister, 1988), and this effort has succeeded. By 1988, 30–50% of Fortune 500 companies were testing prospective employees for drug use (McAllister, 1988; Jacoby, 1988, Gest, 1985). Because private employers are not subject to the Bill of Rights, it may not be possible for workers to challenge these tests in federal court.

The 1988 Anti-Drug Abuse Bill contains a provision that puts companies and institutions receiving federal contracts and grants at risk of losing their federal funding if they do not make "good faith efforts" at ensuring a drug-free workplace. Stephen Sandherr, director of congressional relations for the Associated General Contractors of America, noted in an interview that this measure turns the employer into "a cop at the workplace" (Berke, 1989b).

Procedural Guarantees. The assault on constitutional protections is wide-ranging. The provisions of the new Anti-Drug Abuse Bill (HR 5210, passed by Congress in October 1988) demonstrate this clearly. In one version of the bill, the Justice Department would have been permitted to send a person accused of drug use to a civil hearing conducted by an examiner who could impose a fine if the majority of the presented evidence was against the accused. The accused would not have to be proven guilty beyond a reasonable doubt. Although the provision was changed in the Senate (giving the defendant the option of insisting on a criminal trial) (Mohr, 1988c), the proposed and defeated provisions of the current drug bill may well be the provisions of drug bills yet to come.

A provision supported by the Reagan/Bush administration which did make it into the final drug bill (New York Times, 1988c) is a codification of a 1984 Supreme Court decision permitting the admission of flawed evidence obtained with a search warrant in cases where police had a "good-faith" belief that they were acting properly. A similar provision in the House version of the drug bill passed in September 1988 allowed good-faith exceptions in searches conducted without a written warrant (Mohr, 1988a)."

In numerous decisions, the Reagan-stacked Supreme Court has validated the move toward greater and greater intrusions into privacy. These intrusions include: aerial surveillance to find indications of drug possession (*Florida v. Riley,* 1989); searches without probable cause of people in airports who fit a drug-courier profile (*Florida v. Royer,* 1983); warrantless searches of automobiles and inside glove compartments (*United States v. Ross,* 1982); surveillance of suspects by placing electronic devices in their cars, briefcases, or trunks (*United States v. Knotts,* 1983); acquisition of warrants to search private homes based on anonymous tips (*Illinois v. Gates,* 1983); police inspection of bank records without customer consent (*U.S. v. Miller,* 1976); and reading and inspecting the contents of a person's trash without a warrant or probable cause (*California v. Greenwood,* 1988) (Drug Policy Letter, 1989).

Broadening of Eligibility for the Death Penalty. The Reagan/Bush administration also supported the death penalty provisions of the new Anti-Drug Abuse Bill (New York Times, 1988c). The bill expands the administration of the death penalty to anyone "engaging in a drug-related felony offense, who intentionally kills, or counsels, commands, or causes the intentional killing of an individual and such killing results" (Congressional Quarterly, 1988). Senator D'Amato went so far as to suggest that the death penalty should also apply to drug "dealers and traffickers" not guilty of murder (Mohr, 1988b). President Bush recently advocated a mandatory federal death penalty in cases where law enforcement officers are killed (Boyd, 1989). In this expansion of the use of the death penalty, we see the eradication strategy in its most palpable form. It illustrates that the administration is increasingly resorting to violence and repressive strategies to deal with social problems and has a characteristic disdain for the constitutional arguments regarding discrimination and the death penalty.

By a vote of 52 to 35, the Senate killed a proposal introduced by Senator Kennedy that would have forbidden the death penalty in states where a disproportionate number of blacks and other minority groups are executed and where whites convicted of capital crimes customarily escape the death penalty (Mohr, 1988b). By allowing the death penalty in drug-related cases, a new kind of aggravating circumstance is created. Whereas 'aggravating circumstances' previously referred to the way in which a murder was carried out (i.e., if it was especially brutal) or to the crime itself (i.e., treason), this aggravating circumstance depends not on the offense itself but on its relationship to another activity.

Denial of Opportunity. In June 1988, a policy board chaired by Edwin Meede approved proposals to deny drivers licenses, student loans, public housing assistance, and other government benefits to persons convicted of drug use (Isikoff, 1988), and Reagan publicly voiced support for denying federal benefits to anyone convicted of using or selling drugs (New York Times, 1988e). The new Anti-Drug Abuse Bill contains provisions under which public housing tenants would lose their housing not only if they personally engage in criminal activity (including drug-related activity), but also if members of their households, guests, or other persons under their control engage in criminal activity. In April 1988, law enforcement authorities seized two apartments in New York City public housing projects because the tenants were *charged* with selling drugs from these apartments. In a statement to the New York Times, the executive director of the New York Civil Liberties Union noted that this action "turns the presumption of innocence upside down" (Lubasch, 1988).

In a memorandum issued in April 1989, Secretary of Housing and Urban Development Jack Kemp asked 3,000 public housing authorities to submit reports on their efforts to "evict drug abusers and drug dealers" from their projects. A staff lawyer with the National Housing Law Project was quoted in the New York Times (Tolchin, 1989) as responding: "Does Mr. Kemp have some magic way to find out who these people are? The issue is not whether people should be dealing drugs, but how to decide if someone really is a drug dealer."

A public housing tenant accused of dealing or abusing drugs is considered to have broken the lease, and the entire family is subject to eviction. When Kemp was interviewed on "The McNeil – Lehrer NewsHour" (1989), he was asked if a child who had been evicted from one housing project could really be considered as implicated. His answer was that children often helped their parents deal drugs. The conventional procedures for eviction — which include an administrative proceeding subject to court review — are considered too cumbersome and time-consuming by the Bush administration. When an attorney with the ACLU expressed fears that the Kemp memorandum would lead to "extra-judicial procedures that jeopardize constitutional rights," Kemp responded that the ACLU was "part of the problem" (Tolchin, 1989).

The Anti-Drug Abuse Bill also provides that contracts awarded by a federal agency are subject to suspension of payments or termination if a federal agency determines that enough of a contractor's employees have been convicted of violations to indicate that a contractor's failure to make a good-faith effort providing a drug-free workplace. Within thirty days of receiving notice from an employee of the violation of the drug-free workplace requirements, a federal contractor must take appropriate personnel action — up to and including termination — or require the employee to participate in a drug-abuse assistance or rehabilitation program.

Expansion of State Power Internationally

Internationally, the war on drugs has legitimated the expansion of control and an interventionist foreign policy in Latin America.

Extradition. The violation of the national sovereignty of Latin American countries by pressuring these countries to extradite suspected drug traffickers to stand trial in the United States is but one example. Through the threat of economic boycott, the United States maintains a virtual stranglehold on the domestic policies of Latin American countries.

The extent of U.S. pressure is obvious in the treaty forced on Colombia involving a commitment to extradite suspected Colombian drug traffickers. President Virgilio Barco went so far as to revoke the appointment of a Justice Minister, Jaime Bernal, for expressing his opposition to such extraditions. The Supreme Court of Colombia evenually declared such extraditions unconstitutional — decision presented by the administration as a function of Mafia pressure. The fact that the Supreme Court justices might actually believe that Colombia has a right to national sovereignty is not considered.

In the case of Juan Ramon Matta in Honduras, what was officially called "extradition" ended up being the virtual kidnapping of a Honduran citizen. The United States arranged Matta's arrest and deportation through Honduran military officials and security forces rather than through judicial channels. Numerous Honduran judges, legislators, and intellectuals have denounced this so-called extradition as unjustifiable under Honduran law: the Honduran constitution specifically prohibits the extradition of Honduran citizens. This was evidently not the first attempt to "extradite" Matta. In February 1988, Matta charged that U.S. agents had tried unsuccessfully to kidnap him four times before the final "extradition" (Ring, 1988).

   Flaunting of International Law and Use of the Military. The rhetoric of the war on drugs has led to open and public support for the flaunting of international law. Irving Kristol (1988), co-editor of *The Public Interest,* has gone so far as to suggest that the U.S. follow the nineteenth-century British example of stopping and searching boats on the high seas, even ships in foreign ports. He recommended that the United States employ its military to stop the flow of drugs into this country. Forget education, Kristol argues; it doesn't work. Forget international law as well; only the pansies at the State Department worry about such things. According to Kristol, the United States has a moral imperative to break the law. "If we are at all serious about a war on drugs," he argues, "let's begin by taking appropriate military action." Early in 1988, William Bennet (former Secretary of Education and now Federal Drug Czar) also suggested that the United States involve the military in combatting the flow of drugs (Kristol, 1988). At an April 1988 meeting on the drug issue, the U.S. Conference of Mayors included in their resolution a call to the federal government to use the military to keep narcotics from coming into the country (Washington Post, 1988c).

   Aside from the moral implications of becoming a criminal state in terms of international law, these policies are hardly conducive to the long-term foreign policy interests of the United States. These actions and proposals certainly win the United States no friends in Latin America. As noted, after the extradition, or kidnapping of Matta in Honduras, there were widespread riots.

   Ed Koch, testifying before Congress in 1988, put it this way: "I get so fed up with people who claim to be civil libertarians complaining about totalitarian measures. What's totalitarian about using the military to stop a foreign invasion?" Koch went on to say that if the 1878 Posse Comitatus Act (which bars military involvement in civilian law enforcement) interfered with greater use of the military in drug enforcement, it should be modified or repealed. Mr. Koch told the subcommittee, "The Posse Comitatus is not a constitutional protection, it's a law. Get rid of it" (New York Times, 1988a). Koch's statement reflects the Reagan/Bush administration's attitude toward any law that interferes with its designs. For the administration, law has become an obstacle to be overcome.

War Against Only Certain Countries. The shallowness of the war on drugs rhetoric and its use to advance rollback goals in Latin America is seen clearly in the selectivity of its use. The U.S. security threat posed by drug production and trafficking evidently involves only the drug dealings of selected people and countries. As noted in the recently issued report by the Senate Foreign Relations Subcommittee on Narcotics, Terrorism, and International Relations, the administration has been entirely willing to ignore drug involvement by military and political leaders who support the Administration's political designs. This has been the case in Panama, Antigua, the Bahamas, Colombia, El Salvador, Haiti, Honduras, Jamaica, Mexico, and Paraguay (Washington Post, 1988b).

The administration has protected high-level military officials in Honduras, for example, arguing that this policy is in the interest of national security because the Honduran military provides support for the Contras. State Department reports have previously cited Honduras as an important transit point for drugs, and key lawmakers have maintained that they have evidence of drug connections among political, governmental, and/or military forces in Honduras (Sciolino, 1989a). The Congressional Research Service, however, has reported that American military aid to Honduras was $4 million in 1980. From 1983 to 1988, military aid averaged $64 million a year (Uhlig, 1989). Reagan administration officials sought a reduced sentence for at least one Honduran general with ties to drug trafficking (Berke, 1989d). The 1989 report by the State Department's Bureau of International Narcotics contains no recommendations for a censure of Honduras (Sciolino, 1989a).

The situation with Mexico is similar. Mexico has been called by the State Department "the largest single-country source of the heroin and marijuana imported into the United States" and an important transshipment point for cocaine from South America (Rohter, 1988b). The Mexican president is praised for a few symbolic drug busts and neither Mexico nor Honduras however are rollback targets.

The Reagan/Bush administration and participants in the Iran/Contra investigation have refused to confront the drug involvement of the Contras. The scope of the Congressional investigation was extremely limited. Bodenheimer and Gould (1989:7) note:

> The inquiry into the numerous allegations of contra drug-running
> was superficial, attributable to the involvement of the Senate pan-

el's chief investigator, Thomas Polgar. This was not surprising given that Polgar, a 30-year CIA veteran, had been station chief in Saigon during the Vietnam war.

Had Contra drug involvement been adequately exposed, it would have been revealed that certain U.S. officials chose to look the other way regarding Contra drug involvement; others abetted this drug trafficking because it generated funds for themselves or the Contras (Washington Post, 1988b). Bodenheimer and Gould (1989) have detailed how covert governmental involvement in drug trafficking has generated funds and political alliances which help in the rollback effort. The Kerry investigation report cited numerous examples of governmental decisions in which political concerns outweighed concern about the drug problem. Between January and August 1986, for example, the State Department paid $806,401 to four companies owned and operated by drug traffickers for distributing contra "humanitarian" aid (Berke, 1989d).

The administration has even considered drug involvement by friendly military and political leaders a useful form of political leverage. If these officials cease to be cooperative (as in the case of Noriega), threats of public exposure can be brought to bear. When cooperation is not forthcoming, the charge of narcomilitary control can always be trotted out. In the words of Peter Bourne (1988): " . . . the cooperation of tainted leaders in the hemisphere on a host of political issues ultimately transcends our concern about drugs exported to this country."

As the cold war thaws, communism is being supplemented by narco-military control as the great enemy against which U.S citizens are called upon to fight. Putting an end to drug use and drug trafficking has become the Holy Grail for which rights are given up, and the rights of selected others are trampled — a contemporary counterpart of 1950s McCarthyism. The war on drugs, then, becomes legitimation for military, economic, and political interventionism. In the 1950s, all was legitimate in defending the United States against Communism. In the 1980s, all became legitimate in the struggle to defend the United States against drugs.

Justification of Support for Reactionary Elements. The war on drugs masks the real nature of political oppression in countries whose governments the United States supports. Political violence, terror, and repression can continually be laid at the door of the drug cartels. This is particularly evident in the case of Colombia. The assassination of newspaper editors, for example, who write or publish articles against drug trafficking becomes mafia-inspired. Articles critical of the government or the military and their interest in and history of silencing political opposition are conveniently ignored.

Illustrating this point is the 1985 attack on the Supreme Court of Colombia in which eleven of the twenty-four justices were killed. This complicated event was reinterpreted by the administration and the American media as mafia-financed, left-wing terrorism. In fact, the Colombian military drove a tank through the door of the Supreme Court and was responsible for most if not all of the deaths. The Washington Post (1987), however, called it a *"guerrilla attack,* which U.S. and Colombian officials believe was financed by traffickers, killed 11 of the 24 justices."

Even though homicide is the leading cause of death for Colombian males between the ages of fifteen and forty-four (Hobsbawm 1986) and the Colombian military has been closely linked with right-wing death squads, the U.S. administration continues to fund the Colombian military. Large areas of Colombia are essentially under military control, with only formal national government sovereignty. These areas are the most violent, and in them the military can do what it likes. In January 1989, a right-wing paramilitary group ambushed and assassinated twelve members of a judicial commission that had uncovered evidence on previous right-wing massacres (New York Times, 1989a).

The administration also continually attempts to create the appearance of an alliance between the Left and the drug cartels, even though the drug cartels have nothing to gain and everything to lose by left-wing power. The drug business is the epitome of private-enterprise capitalism. As Hobsbawm notes, the real increase in violence is on the right (1986:28):

> The real growth sector is right-wing terror. This takes the form of threats against and murders of labor leaders and activists of the UP, who during September 1986 were falling at the rate of about one a day—an apparent rise in the rate of attacks on the left, which is said to have lost about three hundred during the last two years of the Betancur era. Even more sinister are "unknown" death squads which, in defense of morality and social order, have taken to making weekend forays through cities like Cali and Medellin, killing "antisocial" elements such as petty criminals, homosexuals, prostitutes, or just plain beggars and bums indiscriminately.

The administration repeatedly attempts to justify funding the military to fight drug trafficking and refuses to acknowledge the connections between the military, right-wing violence, and drugs. In a recently released report, however, the human rights group Americas Watch makes this connection apparent. The report states that Colombian cocaine dealers financed and trained the right-wing death squads who committed most of Colombia's political killings and massacres in 1987 and 1988. Colombia's drug dealers are waging a war against leftist politicians and labor leaders. The military, says the report, often looks the other way or actively collaborates. The report's authors argue that the situation in Colombia is not narcoguerrilla, but "narco repression" (Brooke, 1989).

Even the Washington Post (1988d) acknowledges "the cartel's alliances with communist guerrilla movements and paramilitary groups often appear to be more marriages of convenience than part of some grand ideological campaign." These marriages of convenience involve access to clandestine movement and the fact that many peasants in guerrilla regions make their living growing coca. It is these peasants, for example, who suffer most from American-financed eradication programs. In Bolivia, peasants have attacked drug agents and Bolivian police attempting to destroy coca laboratories. In February 1988, when peasants who were shouting and throwing explosives surrounded American agents and Bolivian police, Bolivian police fired into the crowd and killed two people (Kerr, 1988).

Political repression—state terror—is then transformed into legitimate action against the great enemy. The Colombian and Honduran militaries might not be exemplar (so the propaganda goes), but the United States must continue to fund them in order to keep up the war against the greater evil, drugs.

Cover for Illegal Activities. The war model, in addition, helps those in power justify their policies. The war on drugs is used as a cover to help legitimate the rollback strategy. At one time, the Reagan administration planned a drug shipment to El Salvador which would be seized and planted evidence which, when discovered, would implicate Nicaragua. Similarly, repeated attempts have been made to implicate Cuba (another rollback target) in drug trafficking. For example, the Washington Post (1988d) has noted "allegations" of Cuban involvement with the Colombian drug mafia, including Cuba in a list of five countries (the other four being Panama, Honduras, the Bahamas, and Haiti), where there have been "allegations" of "links between Colombian traffickers and [government] officials."

The same article noted allegations by Jose Blandon, a former political advisor to Noriega, that Fidel Castro was involved in mediating disputes between the drug cartel and Panama. The article also included allegations by Ramon Milian Rodriguez — reputedly a former cartel money launderer — that "Cuba's involvement may be a part of some master plan aimed eventually at killing off cartel leaders and taking control of an organization with tentacles reaching into many of the region's governments and with a hold over millions of drug addicts in the United States" (Washington Post, 1988a).

The response to Blandon's allegations by the Angel Pino for the Cuban Interests Section in Washington is appropriate: He called them "science fiction." Pino also noted that, "If we had been dealing in drugs we could have solved our economic problems" (Washington Post, 1988a). Whatever one believes about Fidel Castro, he is not a stupid man, and the implication that he would attempt to bring about a subversive movement in the United States by mobilizing junkies is far-fetched, to say the least. But the intent is clear: If the American people can be convinced that Cuba and Nicaragua are trafficking in drugs, anything is legitimate.

A similar tactic was used with Noriega. The Kerry investigation noted administration decisions to turn a "blind eye" to Noriega's drug connections (Berke, 1989d). The release of information linking Noriega to drug trafficking was used to legitimate a military buildup in the region and a cessation in payments for use of the Panama Canal — bringing economic ruin to countless Panamanians. Noriega's drug connections can be used to legitimate a refusal to turn the Panama Canal over to the Panamanians, and it has been used to legitimate the invasion of Panama. The revelations about Noriega were made public not because they had only recently come to light, but because of Noriega's diminished utility in furthering the administration's Central America policy.

Thus, the war on drugs has been used to expand control in Latin America and assist the rollback effort. Penny Lernoux (1989) has detailed the activities of what were supposed to be drug-interdiction forces in one region in Bolivia. The administration poured at least $50 million in aid to the region, and Bolivia's defense minister recently announced another $25 million in U.S. military aid in exchange for an agreement to allow three military missions a year to train Bolivian troops. These joint military maneuvers, Lernoux notes, would allow the U.S. to establish for the first time since World War II permanent military presence in Latin America:

> The ostensible aim of U.S. aid is to wipe out the drug traffickers. In fact, the Pentagon is barely interested in coca leaf plantations. Its only concern in the Beni is to establish an outpost for the U.S. Southern Command which is based in Panama. . . . the Pentagon intends to use the Beni as a staging area for the rapid deployment

of U.S. troops in the event of insurrections in the region. . . . The idea . . . is to prevent a repetition of the Nicaraguan and Salvadoran rebellions through "early intervention" by US. Special Operations Forces (Lernoux, 1989:188).

Summary

The war on drugs, then, is likely not only to continue, but to expand. Especially with Bush in the White House, we are likely to see an escalation in the rhetoric, as well as an escalation in American interventionism in Latin America and increasing tolerance of right-wing terror. Americas Watch notes that "the end justifies any means at all, and certainly nothing so trivial as law—U.S. or international—should be a constraint" (Brown, 1985:39).

A recently released ABA report, "Criminal Justice in Crisis," urges that action be taken "to rethink our strategies for dealing with drugs" (Criminal Justice Digest, 1989). Mayor Kurt Schmoke of Baltimore told a House Subcommittee in 1988 that, rather than a drug policy based on law enforcement, "a measured and carefully implemented program of drug decriminalization" was needed (New York Times, 1988b). But, the 1988 Anti-Drug Abuse Bill calls legalization "an unconscionable surrender in a war [where] there can be no substitute for total victory" (Drug Policy Letter, 1989).

In the end, the negative effects of the war on drugs are largely irrelevant. The battles are likely to go on and on — with ever-increasing crime and violence, ever-increasing inequality between the center and the periphery, and ever-increasing exploitation and control of the periphery by the center. Simply put, the war on drugs is too useful a legitimation of state crime to abandon.

References

American Bar Association
1988   *Criminal Justice in Crisis*, Washington, DC: American Bar Association.

Anchorage Daily News
1989a   Mexico Arrests Top Drug Dealer in Crackdown. April 11.
1989b   Undercover Sting Nets Ex-Officer. April 11.

Anderson, John W. and Nancy Lewis
1987   D.C. Police Allegedly Protected Drug Dealers. *Washington Post*. October 16.

Beck, Melinda, Ann McDaniel, Patricia King, and Lynda Wright
1989   We Need Drastic Measures. *Newsweek.* March 13.

Berke, Richard L.
1989a   2 Admirals Named to Combat Drugs. *New York Times.* February 8.
1989b   Anti-Drug Steps Imposed on U.S. Contractors. *New York Times.* March 18.
1989c   Capital's War on Drugs. *New York Times.* April 7.
1989d   Foreign Policy Said to Hinder Drug War. *New York Times.* April 14.

Blair, William G.
1988   Jury In the Bronx Acquits Larry Davis of Attempted Murder in a Police
     Raid. *New York Times.* November 21.

Bodenheimer, Thomas and Robert Gould
1989   *Rollback! Right-wing Power in U.S. Foreign Policy.* Boston: South End Press.

Bourne, Peter
1988   Tainted Leaders in Latin America, *Washington Post.* March 25.

Boyd, Gerald M.
1989   Bush Seeks Mandatory Execution in Slaying of Federal Law Officers. *New
     York Times.* March 10.

Branigan, William
1988   Mexico Cracks Major Arms, Drug Trafficking Ring. *Washington Post.* Feb-
     ruary 26.

Brooke, James
1989   Colombia Drug Cartels Tied to Terror in Rights Report. *New York Times.*
     April 6.

Brown, Cynthia (ed.)
1985   *With Friends Like These: The Americas Watch Report on Human Rights and
     U.S. Policy in Latin America.* New York: Pantheon Books.

Christian, Shirley
1987   Bolivians Say It's Their Right to Grow Coca. *New York Times.* August 2.

Collett, Merrill
1988   Colombia's Drug Cartel Said to Aim at Military. *Washington Post.* April 11.

Congressional Quarterly
1988   October 20.

Corn, David and Jefferson Morley
1989a   Winners and Losers in Drug Capitalism. *The Nation.* (April 17).
1989b   CIA for the Defense. *The Nation.* April 17.

Criminal Justice Digest
1989   Study Finds Police Efforts Hindered by Lack of Resources. January.

Criminal Justice Newsletter
1989a Bush Budget for Justice Department an Increase over Reagan's. March 1.
1989b Survey Shows Declining Rate of Drug Use by High School Senior. March 15.

Data Clearinghouse for Drugs and Crime
1989 May.

Dewar, Helen
1988 Death Penalty in Drug Killings. *Washington Post.* June 11.

Drug Policy Foundation
1989 Mr. Bush and the 1988 Anti-Drug Abuse Act. *Drug Policy Letter.* Vol. 1, No. 1.

Eddy, Paul, Hugo Sabogal and Sara Walden
1988 *The Cocaine Wars.* New York: W. W. Norton and Company.

Efron, Sonni
1989 Bahamas: Indictments Are Political. *Anchorage Daily News.* February 1.

Eitzen, D. Stanley and Doug A. Timmer
1985 *Criminology: Crime and Criminal Justice.* New York: Wiley.

Engelberg, Stephen
1989 Antidrug Effort Floundering, Former Cocaine Dealer Says. *New York Times.* March 6.

General Accounting Office
1988 GGD-88-39. Washington, DC: Government Printing Office.

Gest, Ted
1985 Using Drugs? You May Not Get Hired. *U.S. News and World Report.* December 23.

Hills, Stuard (ed.)
1987 *Corporate Violence: Injury and Death for Profit.* Totowa, New Jersey: Rowman and Little field.

Hobsbawm, Eric
1986 Murderous Columbia, *New York Review of Books.*

Isikoff, Michael
1988 Federal Aid May Be Lever in Drug War. *Washington Post.* July 8.

Jacoby, Tamar
1988 Drug Testing in the Dock. *Newsweek.* November 14.

Jordan, Mary
1988 New Antidrug Efforts Needed, Officials Say. *Washington Post.* February 26.

Kadish, S. H.
1971 Overcriminalization. In *Crime and Justice*, Vol. 1 (The Criminal and Society): 56–71, ed. by L. Radzinowicz and M. E. Wolfgang. New York: Basic Books.

Kerr, Peter
1988 Bolivia With U.S. Aid. *New York Times*. April 17.

Kirstol, Irving
1988 The Military and the War, *Washington Post*. March 28.

Lernoux, Penny
1989 Playing Golf While Drugs Flow. *The Nation*. February 13.

Lubasch, Arnold H.
1988 Housing Agency Seizes Drug Suspects' Apartments. *New York Times*. April 28.

McAllister, Bill
1988 Meese Asks Drug Testing for 'Most' Workers. *Washington Post*. April 25.

McNeil–Lehrer NewsHour
1989 Public Broadcasting. April 17.

Marriott, Michel
1989 After 3 Years, Crack Plague in New York Grows Worse. *New York Times*. February 20.

Mohr, Charles
1988a Senate is Closer to Drug Bill Vote. *New York Times*. October 13.
1988b Penalty of Death Kept in Drug Bill. *New York Times*. October 14.
1988c Experts Say Impact of Drug Bill Remains Unclear. *New York Times*. October 30.

Morgenthau, Robert M.
1989 Bush's Lip Service on Drugs. *New York Times*. March 9.

New York Times
1988a June 10.
1988b Baltimore Mayor Supports Legalizing Illicit Drugs. September 30.
1988c Reagan Backs House Drug Bill. October 10.
1988d 3 Former Drug Agents Charged in Fraud Scheme. November 25.
1988e U.S. Looking into Undercover Drug Manipulation. November 30.
1989a Rightists Blamed in Colombia In Killings of 12 on Court Team. January 22.
1989b 33 Charged With Laundering $500 million in Drug Profits. February 23.
1989c Washington Imposes Curfew to fight Drug-Related Crime. March 1.
1989d Colombian Cocaine Network Is Target of U.S. Indictments. March 23.

Pitt, David
1988a New Drug Squad Checks Officers. *New York Times*. September 30.

1988b   Ward Criticizes a Bronx Jury for Acquittal of Larry Davis. *New York Times*. November 22.

President's Commission on Law Enforcement and Administration of Justice
1967   *The Challenge of Crime in a Free Society*. Washington, DC: Government Printing Office.

Rasky, Susan F.
1988   Officials Urge a Wide Military Role in Drug Fight. *New York Times*. June 10.

Raspberry, William
1988   Free Needles for Addicts. *Washington Post*. January 11.

Reiman, J. H.
1979   Prostitution, Addiction and the Ideology of Liberalism. *Contemporary Crisis*. Vol. 3:53–68.

Reiman, Jeffrey
1984   *The Rich Get Richer and the Poor Get Prison: Ideology, Class and Criminal Justice*. New York: Wiley.

Riding, Alan
1989   Paraguay's Leader Denies Ties to Drugs. *New York Times*. February 7.

Ring, Wilson
1988   Honduran Sought in Drug Crimes. *Washington Post*. February 26.

Rohter, Larry
1988a   Seized Honduran: Drug Baron or a Robin Hood? *New York Times*. April 16.
1988b   Mexican President Pledges to Make Life Miserable for Drug Traffickers. *New York Times*. December 12.
1989   Annual Lobbying for Mexico Begins. *New York Times*. March 1.

Sciolino, Elaine
1989a   U.S. Study Praises Mexico on Drugs. *New York Times*. March 1.
1989b   Drug Production Rising Worldwide. *New York Times*. March 2.

Shannon, Elaine
1988   *Desperados: Latin Drug Lords, U.S. Lawmen, and the War America Can't Win*. New York: Viking.

Tolchin, Martin
1989   Kemp Vows to Oust Tenants Over Drugs. *New York Times*. March 8.

Uhlig, Mark A.
1989   Honduran Army Backs Dismantling of Contras. *New York Times*. February 28.

U.S. Department of Justice
1987   *Sourcebook of Criminal Justice Statistics, 1986.* Washington, DC: Government Printing Office.

Walsh, Elsa and Nancy Lewis
1987   Probers Told Police Lied Under Oath. *Washington Post.* June 27.

Washington Post
1987a   12 Ex-Policemen Indicted in Miami. July 15.
1988a   Arms and the Cartels, February 24.
1988b   Latin America and Official Corruption, March 25.
1988c   The Military and the War on Drugs, April 27.

Wines, Michael
1989a   Drug Money Ring Smashed, U.S. Says. *New York Times.* March 30.
1989b   Law Enabled U.S. to Seize Proceeds of Drug Money Scheme. *New York Times.* April 3.

4

Multi-Tiered Terrorism in Peru*†

R. S. Ratner

Introduction

Scholarly discourse on the phenomenon of terrorism is marked by such disagreement over definition and cause that it eludes consensus even regarding its undesirability.[1] To some, terrorism threatens the very survival of democracy (Wilkinson, 1977:66) and portends a collapse of the social order (Carny, 1981:91). Others regret the focus on terrorism, believing that it diverts attention from more urgent social issues such as global debt and Third World hunger (Bakhash, 1987). Much popular and academic debate is so riddled with self-serving myths about terrorism (Stohl, 1988) and inflated by such irresponsible usage of the term that, in the worlds of one commentator, the very idea of terrorism has become "a cliche in search of a meaning" (Payne, 1988:142).[2] At bottom, the varied meanings imputed to terrorism affirm its reality as a "social construction" (Greisman, 1977). Indeed, terrorism has been described as an *ideological* construction of reality that politicizes language in order to "set up a structure of 'apologetics' for those acts not thus described" (Hocking, 1984) and, similarly, as state actions intended to reproduce the dominant assumptions about social order in a "semantics of terror" (Schlesinger, 1981). Thus, official or 'state terror' is concealed by self-exculpatory labels,[3] and conventional accounts either single out the Soviet Union and its allies as involved in a range of terrorist enterprises (Sterling, 1981), or simply reject the explanation of terrorism in terms of social inequality (Wilson, 1981). Equally complacent 'dialectical' interpretations condone terrorism as a barometer of societal *vibrancy* (Horowitz, 1973) or attribute incidences of terrorism to the political unsophistication of authoritarian regimes unpracticed in the accommodations of dominance and deference found in the mature authority structures of Western democracies (Turk, 1982). But analyses of this order merely attest to a lack of dialecticism, because it is precisely the symbiotic relationship between authoritarian and 'democratic' regimes that demands explanation. Such wide analytic nets, however, are seldom thrown out by naive protagonists of moral order.[4]

The major, and perhaps the only, analysis of terrorism cast in a genuinely dialectical mode is Edward Herman's *The Real Terror Network* (1982). Herman points to the vital interdependencies between the "development model" of U.S. imperialism, third world authoritarian regimes, and "terrorist" movements. He states unequivocally that there is

> a huge tacit conspiracy between the U.S. government, its agencies and its multinational corporations, on the one hand, and local business and military cliques in the Third World, on the other, to assume complete control of these countries and to 'develop' them on a joint venture basis (p.3).

> The National Security States (of Latin America) are in place precisely because they serve U.S interests in a joint venture with local torturers at the expense of their majorities (p.14).

Polemical in tone, this is nevertheless a compelling argument to anyone who has directly experienced the political and economic realities of the imperialist fiefdoms of South and Central America, or to anyone who has managed to obtain analyses not generated by the organs of imperialist government and business propaganda.

In a useful attempt to clarify the meaning of terrorism, Ronald Crelinsten (1987:3) writes:

> The major weaknesses in current approaches to the study of terrorism are: (a) a truncated object of study, which reflects (b) a skewed focus of the researcher, which stems from (c) a narrow policy orientation on prevention and control, which yields (d) narrow conceptual frameworks which ignore the political dimension of terrorism and (e) ahistorical, linear, causal models which ignore the historical and comparative aspects of terrorism and focus selectively on individual actors, their characteristics, their tactics, and their stated ideologies.

Crelinsten re-conceives terrorism as a form of "political communication" — i.e.," a tactic involving the use and threat of violence for communicative purposes" (p.7). In rendering his dialectical interpretation, Crelinsten identifies a 'terrorism from below,' which aims to draw political authorities away from legitimized control activities and towards state terrorism (or institutionalized terrorism 'from above'), thereby transforming government supporters into terrorist sympathizers. This movement is opposed by state initiatives aimed at suppressing legitimate dissent by treating all regime opponents as terrorists — thus alienating the populace from reform movements in favor of a control strategy that emphasizes 'national security' over civil liberties. Although Crelinsten thinks his model apposite to the "domestic, intrastate context" (p.14), he believes it can be applied in the international context as well:

> ... particularly as it relates to post-revolutionary conditions and the role of other states in what has been variously called 'state-sponsored terrorism,' aid to 'freedom fighters,' and 'surrogate warfare'. .... The distinction between controller and controlled would be clearest in the colonial context and in the spheres of influence of the superpowers (p.21, n24).

Although Crelinsten's model addresses complexities of the terrorist phenomenon unexamined in narrower, nondialectical conceptualizations, it does not encompass the dynamic of protest and control at the level of superpower intervention — where the dialectic itself appears to be orchestrated by agents of transnational capital. Even where the dialectic 'from below' is not so constrained as to thwart a liberative potential, the idea of a controlled or managed dialectic operating 'from above' resonates better with the powerful forces that envelop much of the Third World, inbuing its regimes with political impotence and terror.[5]

Start of the Downfall

Peru is a country of approximately twenty million inhabitants, one-third of whom live in or around the capital of Lima (two million dwelling in 'shantytown' squalor). Approximately half of the country's people are Amerindians; one-third Mestizo (mixed Spanish, Indian, and white); 12% white; and 5% African and Mulatto. The Quechua Indians, numbering more than eight million, represent the largest indigenous ethnic group. Peru is one of the most underdeveloped countries in South America. Its gross domestic product (GDP) totalled $19.5 billion in 1983, and GDP per capita was $1,070. Approximately 60% of total income was received by the top 20% of households, and only 40% of the economically active population were fully employed.[6] Peru's major trading partner is the United States (accounting for about one-third of its exports and imports from 1978–1982), and half of its direct foreign investment comes from the United States. Its foreign debt since 1983 has ranged from $12 billion to approximately $19 billion—60–80% of its annual GNP. In 1983, its debt-service payments amounted to 44% of its total export earnings. The country is now among the top ten in the world in terms of hyperinflation, with a 1989 inflation rate of 6000%. Over the past fifteen years, almost all economic indicators have been down.

As might be surmised from these figures, Peru's economy is in shambles. Its 'debt crisis,' can be traced back to the early 19th century —the beginning of a series of so-called stabilization programs that foreshadowed the International Monetary Fund (IMF) measures applied since the mid-1950s (Scheetz, 1986). Before that time, Peruvian governments were traditionally represented by big landowners and other elites who grew rich by selling off the country's resources to foreign (increasingly U.S.) corporations. Austerity measures geared mainly to uphold the oligarchy were imposed during the eight-year reign of General Manuel Odria (1948–56), but they failed to bring economic stability or suppress scattered peasant revolts. Fernando Belaunde Terry came to power in 1963 after six years of unmiraculous, conservative civilian rule under Manuel Prado. Belaunde presided over a mildly reformist government which also foundered on political indecisiveness and inefficiency. Although he ran on a platform of agrarian reform and resource nationalization, he was unable to reconcile the old with the more progressive bourgeoisie; with no military support, his resolve faltered. In 1968, General Juan Velasco Alvarado led a bloodless coup which ousted Belaunde and ushered in a series of sweeping agrarian reforms along with the nationalization of key industries. But a failure to assist new landowners in crop production, combined with harassment by global transnationals and the resistance of Peru's own elites to populist reforms, undermined Velasco's program. When Velasco reverted to militaristic bossism and entrusted the management of peasant cooperatives to government-appointed functionaries not controlled by the community, he was overthrown by his own troops, who installed General Francisco Morales Bermudez. Orthodox IMF economic stabilization policies were reintroduced, ostensibly to combat Peru's worst recession since the 1930s. Although Morales consolidated the regime's shift to the right, he was forced by a growing radicalization of the masses to return to the barracks in 1980. He left behind a $9.4 billion foreign debt, raging inflation, less than 50% full employment, and a drastic drop in real wages. Belaunde, who claimed he had been couped by Velasco and not allowed to govern, was restored to power in the 1980 elections on the heels of an antistatist, liberal upsurge. Free-market economic policies (dictated by the IMF) included a sweeping import liberalization drive, harsh deflationary policies, unfettered transnational investment in major export sectors such as oil and mining,[7] dismantling of the coastal collective agro-enterprises established during the Velasco regime, elimination of subsidies on foods and industrial exports, and long-term financing from foreign banks for massive infrastructure development. But debt renegotiation, an important playing card in Belaunde's neoliberal program. was arranged in the interests of international capital rather than in the interests of internal economic reactivation (Petras et al., 1983). Sharply rising prices, the decline of real wage levels, increased capital flight, and a significant drop in GNP, revealed the political and economic bankruptcy of Accion Popular (Belaunde's right-wing party). Oviedo (1987:172) states:

> The ship was leaking everywhere, and people were thinking in terms of mere survival, while the threat of repayment of the foreign debt ($14 billion dollars) and the demands of the IMF loomed on the horizon. In the grip of circumstances it could not control, and of economic forces far greater than those of its government, the country seemed to be heading toward its apocalypse.

Thus, between 1968 and 1983, the Velasco and Belaunde regimes each failed—in very different ways—to create a national capitalist class fraction capable of generating economic growth and social and political harmony. Velasco's state-corporatist program was resisted on almost all fronts, and Belaunde's efforts were hampered by inadequate financial resources and a deepening world capitalist crisis that made a development strategy based on expanding exports and increasing flows of capital difficult to sustain. So, despite reduced oligarchic domination in the Velasco years, there was still no visible strategy for nationwide economic development. Belaunde's government lacked the fortitude to apply hard measures which might generate internal sources of development finance. As Reid (1985:124) summarizes:

> The resulting foreign debt and deficits in government finances deprived Peru of all room for manoeuvre when the world entered a profound economic depression, the Latin American credit squeeze broke, and the country became the prisoner of its international creditors.[8]

In return for debt restructuring and new infustions of credit, foreign creditors insisted upon fiscal and monetary policies that led to high unemployment. Representing the interests of multinational, private, commercial banks, the IMF imposed a development strategy which strengthened exporters, stimulated the massive influx of foreign capital, and transferred power and resources to the private sector (Petras et al., 1983:52). Austerity measures further marginalized Peruvian peasants and slum dwellers to the point that, beginning in 1977, numerous strikes and riots erupted, and dozens of people were killed by the police and army (Korner et al., 1984:139).[9]

Facing presidential elections in 1985, government supporters grew alarmed at the political price of austerity. A debt moratorium was proposed as the sole alternative to orthodox IMF policies. But Belaunde retreated from a confrontative stance and instead accepted simple rescheduling of the debt interest payments — an adjustment which did little to alter the prospect of years of economic prostration.

Aggravating all these difficulties was the government's failure to limit military expenditures, which accounted for more than one-third of Peru's total external debt (Reid, 1985:124). Belaunde was reluctant to compromise the military because an insurrectionist mentality was developing among the people who had borne a disproportionate share of the cost of the failed neoliberal policies — the Sierra peasants and the urban poor in the coastal shantytowns. Agricultural cooperatives in the Andean areas were decimated by the low prices paid by the controlling agribusinesses and by their lack of access to credits and government aid. Massive impoverishment in the countryside had already sent swarms of central highland villagers to coastal cities in search of employment.[10] The deteriorating economic situation and the growing legitimacy crisis brought the repressive side of the Belaunde regime to the forefront. Under the cover of new antiterrorist laws directed at a group of Andean revolutionaries — Sendero Luminoso (Shining Path) — Belaunde militarized political life in an attempt to immobilize all forms of opposition. Increasingly frustrated by attempts to tame Sendero without terrorizing the entire rural population, Belaunde began to apply antiterrorist laws indiscriminately. The tactic backfired, pushing an increasingly organized mass movement to the left, sparking parliamentary opposition, inducing military genocide of the peasantry, and catalyzing the largest rural insurgency in Peru since Tupac Amaru's rebellion against the Spanish conquerors two centuries earlier.

The Shining Path Solution

Sendero Luminoso emerged out of the confusion of Peruvian Maoist politics in 1970.[11] Prompted by the Sino-Soviet split in 1964, Sendero's original nucleus — the Ayacucho Regional Committee of the Communist Party — joined the Bandera Roja, Peru's first Maoist party. The group then broke with Bandera Roja in 1970, denouncing the latter's betrayal of Maoist principles of armed peasant revolt in favor of urban and purely political methods of struggle. The Sendero splinter group[12] inherited Bandera Roja's considerable political influence in neighborhood trade union and student organizations in the southern highlands of the Ayacucho region, strategically located between Lima and Cuzco (one of Peru's most destitute departments). By 1979, Sendero declared itself the true revolutionary Communist Party of Peru, and it now refers to itself only by that name.

After establishing a base in Ayacucho's Huamanga University, Sendero began armed struggle in 1980. Using a Maoist strategy of rural insurgency combined with urban terrorism, Sendero formed a People's Revolutionary Army with an estimated strength of 2,500–3,000 in 1983. In 1984, Sendero proceeded to launch a full-scale guerrilla war. Terror was employed to mobilize the oppressed peasantry and to paralyze the state. Thus, the long negligence of government policy and consequent social disintegration found dramatic expression in Sendero's violent insurgency.[13]

The Sendero Luminoso movement is rooted in a combination of Andean mysticism, Maoism, and the world view of its leader and organizer, Abimael Guzman. Guzman, a former philosophy professor at the University of Huamanga, is heralded by his followers as the ''fourth sword of Marxism'' (After Marx, Lenin, and Mao).[14] Sendero's goal is to create a peasant-worker republic—a new democracy based on a primitive agrarian communism of barter exchange, reminiscent of the pre-Colombian 14th century Inca model (which was actually a transition between primitive communism and class society). Strongly anticapitalist, Sendero rejects modern technology as an imperialist tool for the domination of peasants and calls for the abolition of industrial enterprise, the national market economy, the banking system, and all foreign trade. Even the use of currency is to be replaced by a communal, village-oriented economy based on a system of barter exchange.[15] Ultimately, the war is expected to bring about the establishment of a pan-Indian socialist state embracing the Quechua-speaking peoples of Peru, Bolivia, Colombia, Ecuador, Argentina, and Chile.

Sendero regards armed struggle as the only realistic means of achieving its goal. The route of parliamentary reform is denounced as "bureaucratic cretinism." Sendero strategy is the classic one of prolonged popular war, with the peasantry the main revolutionary force and the countryside the site of principle contradiction. The initial stage of the revolution calls for the mobilization of a base of support in the countryside, the training of revolutionary cadres for guerrilla warfare, and the destabilization of government in rural areas. These goals were accomplished, for the most part, between 1970 and 1982, culminating in hundreds of dynamite attacks in the Ayacucho area and elsewhere in the Sierra against corporate state targets and imperialist technology in all their manifestations. These actions included 'people's trials' and the execution of government officials, mayors, landowners, loansharks, traders, and informants, as well as the redistribution of land to campesinos. The second stage involved the seizure (if only temporary) of 'liberated zones' to serve as strongholds and symbols of achievement, the widening of rural control, and the expansion of the war into the cities.[16] Approximately 30,000 terrorist incursions have been initiated since 1980, with the death toll exceeding 15,000 and more than $5 billion in property damage. The third and final stage anticipates a general uprising in the countryside and an encirclement of the cities which will lead to the collapse of urban society and the destruction of the Lima regime.

Guzman, who had not appeared for some time and was believed dead, resurfaced in 1988 and declared that the time had come for the siege of the cities to begin. Attacks, murders, and bombings have been carred out with increasing fervor and audacity since then. Belaunde's efforts to discredit sendero as part of an exotic foreign conspiracy have failed to stem the growth of popular support, and attempts to repress popular movements in the Sierra have merely demonstrated the government's incapacity to rule under a bourgeois-democratic form.[17] Despite serious damage inflicted by Sendero violence, popular support is said to number in the tens of thousands. The actual number of sympathizers is unknown, but estimates range as high as 30–40% of the general population, a figure government officials now dispute with less confidence.[18]

The degree of coordination among Sendero units is hard to ascertain because the organization is one of the most secretive in modern history. Earlier tactical coordination with the Tupac Amaru revolutionary group, signed agreements with Spanish Maoists in 1987 to promote the "proletarian world revolution," and unconfirmed reports of Sendero guerrillas being trained in Ecuador—all of these signs suggest that the grand design of a resurrected Quechua Nation has not been relinquished. On the other hand, Sendero does not have a clear political strategy for dealing with the market-oriented coastal peasants and the urban working class, and it disavows the organized political left. It may be that it is only in Peru's 'Fourth World' regions (such as Ayachucho,[19] where deprivation and despair is so profound), that Sendero can recruit combatants and maintain belligerence indefinitely. Indeed, Sendero's ultraleft ideology is received as alien rhetoric by many Peruvian peasants. But it is also clear that many campesinos support sendero not simply out of desperation, but because the movement advances their own historical aspirations (ownership and control of land, notwithstanding the banner of Mao). So, although appealing mainly to the young and poor, Sendero continues to expand its control in the countryside, even in the teeth of the government's augmented military presence. It has forged a cogent discourse of terror which goes beyond the ordinary understanding of terror and

> changes the discourse of meaning. It 'deconstructs' economic capital as rationality, that is, as the developmental basis of authority. It 'brackets' ordinary terms of politics to create a 'common sense' of radical intentions. . . . If innovation leads to marginalization and the latter predisposes to violence, it is violence that forms an anti-discourse. As a disordering and re-ordering *mytho-logics*, it 'develops' into symbolic capital and the struggle between good and evil (Apter, 1987:42).

Garcia's Impasse

The presidential election of 1985 brought renewed hope to counter the despair sown by Belaunde's misguided policies.[20] Alan Garcia, the young and charismatic candidate of the previously outlawed centre-left American Popular Revolutionary Alliance (APRA) party won with an impressive 47% of the vote, reinforced by a loyalty pledge from the army.[21] Garcia was an intellectual populist who — from the moment of his election as General Secretary of the APRA party in 1982 — had tried to steer Peru in the direction of a broad-based socialist democracy. The task of reviving Peru's economy was a daunting one: Garcia inherited the most serious economic crisis in Peru this century. But early encouragement was provided by a 70% approval rating in public opinion polls, followed by APRA's mayoralty victories in twenty of Peru's twenty-four department capitals in November 1986.[22] Garcia's image grew to heroic proportions among the dispossessed and troubled people whose expectations he stimulated.[23]

In addition to the high costs of the guerrilla war and the consequent difficulty in suppressing military terrorism, Garcia's major obstacle to achieving the 'profound social revolution' he had promised was the paralyzing effect of the fiscal and monetary policies decreed by the IMF in return for new credits and debt restructuring. The 1982 austerity package had imposed the familiar stabilization' program of deep budget cuts, continuous currency devaluations, and sharp reductions in real wages — policies intended to curb domestic demand and conserve foreign exchange for service on the external debt. Garcia's first move was to declare that Peru would pay only ten percent of the annual value of its exports towards amortization of the $14 billion foreign debt. This, he argued, would free resources to promote a burst of economic activity through stepped-up government spending, price controls, and across-the-board wage increases. In order to reduce the military budget, Garcia unified the armed forces and began talks with Chile and Ecuador aimed at ending their regional skirmishes. In the hope of stemming the peasant migration to Lima and wooing peasants away from Sendero, he decentralized political power by reorganizing Peru's twenty-four departments into twelve regions that were promised a degree of autonomy in policy-making and administration, and he set up a peace commission which offered to negotiate with Sendero. Garcia's program — an odd mixture of supply-side and demand-side economics aimed at both growth and redistribution — resulted in a temporary economic boom during the first two years of his administration. Business profits were up due to newly created demands, protective import duties, and low interest rates. Peru's gross domestic product grew by an impressive 8.5% in 1986 and 7% in 1987. In the first year of economic recovery, the rate of inflation fell from 185% to 65%. But Garcia's constant vilification of the IMF and his refusal to heed the Fund's threats led to a renewed crisis. The inflationary upsurge and the cost of increased imports seriously depleted foreign reserves, producing an enormous trade deficit. Coupled with heavy government deficit spending, Peru plunged into a deep recession that was unrelieved by international creditors still angry over Peru's noncompliance with IMF dictates. Garcia had expected increased investment and industrial activity to follow increased demand and government stimulation of the economy, thus, keeping the economic boom alive.[24] Instead, the business community put most of its profits into foreign real estate and banks — a betrayal which prompted Garcia to nationalize the banks in order to prevent capital flight, democratize credit, and break up the power concentrated in a few economic families and groups.[25] The proposed nationalization of banks sparked the consolidation of a new political coalition among the weak right-wing political parties, who denounced the nationalization plan as political demagoguery. Garcia's subsequent introduction of a 'war economy' budget—which implemented policies exactly opposite to those he had originally championed—led to mass protests by workers, students, and civil servants. With the government unable to pay its bills and inflation running at over 2,000%,[26] Garcia sought to repair relations with international bankers and entreated the IMF back to the negotiating table.[27]

Needless to say, the rapid decline in purchasing power since 1987, the alienation of international creditors, and the discord registered within the APRA party on the merits of Garcia's economic plan have jeopardized the survival of Garcia's presidency. He has already resigned the leadership of his party and, to carry favor with the right, appointed the conservative Alberto Sanchez as Prime Minister. Garcia's public opinion ratings have nose-dived, and leaders of both left- and right-wing parties have proposed advancing the 1990 presidential elections by means of a constitutional amendment. General strikes and unabated terrorist violence are viewed by Garcia's critics as evidence that Peru is being driven into a preevolutionary state by the government's mistakes. Fears of civil war and a military coup are now rife.

This deterioration is compounded by developments in the guerrilla war, where escalating terrorist activity has forced Garcia to repudiate his own reformist pacification policies. The military—eager to utilize the sophisticated weaponry purchased over the last decade, and buttressed by U.S training and support[28]— knows it is in position to gain political leverage as the chaos spreads. At first, Garcia attempted a conciliatory stance towards Sendero, seeking to distance himself from Belaunde's one-dimensional, military approach.[29] But Sendero's obdurate response—a flurry of bombings and assassinations—prompted Garcia to announce new antiterrorist measures. He decreed states of emergency in Lima and other provinces, authorized police occupations of San Marcos University (a known hotbed of Sendero indoctrination and recruitment),[30] and decreased monitoring of the military's handling of the insurgency — even when flagrant human rights abuses had obviously been committed. Predictably, military tactics became more ruthless. Counterspecialists of the civil guard (the Sinchis) have committed undeniable excesses while searching villages for guerrillas. In retaliation for Sendero ambushes, soldiers have massacred entire hamlets where peasants were thought to be Sendero sympathizers or refused to cooperate and submit to recruitment by the army. In June 1986, the coordinated uprising of Sendero prisoners at three Lima-area penitentiaries was crushed by the military, who executed more than 200 prisoners *after* they had surrendered to guardsmen.[31] More indigenous communities are being resettled under military control, and the army has propagated terrorism with the countryside by paying or forcing villagers to form paramilitary peasant patrols. These ragtag militias are armed with knives, stakes, and slingshots to hunt Senderistas. Often confused with the Rondas (self-defense units of the Peasants Federation) these paramilitary units are no match for Sendero's automatic weapons, but some Indians have used the government's invitation to violence and done battle with traditional rivals on the pretense of rounding up Sendero suspects.

The peasants are trapped between the abuses of the military and the atrocities of Sendero. For many, the only alternative to theft, torture, murder, and disappearances is to leave their homes and migrate to Ayacucho or Lima, where conditions are no less harsh. As this scenario unfolds, the inclination of APRA party leaders to reject calls for a rapid military solution is giving way to a hardening of the antisubversive strategy—a change in attitude not unaffected by the 300-plus murders of APRA leaders since Garcia's inauguration. Indeed, a new level of terrorist violence has been introduced by extremists within Garcia's own APRA party, as members of the vigilante Rodrigo Franco Command carry out reprisals, not only for terrorist actions committed by the Shining Path, but also against conservative critics of Garcia and APRA.[32]

So Garcia has had to rely increasingly on the military but not allow his response to become solely coercive. At times, momentum in the struggle seems to shift to the government, as when Garcia lifted the curfew in Lima and restored civilian government in the Ayacucho region in July 1987. But neither gloved hand nor iron fist has stopped Sendero from expanding its control in the country side and, in May 1988, Garcia considered declaring a state of siege.[33] Meanwhile, the military has steadily gained ground. Securely installed in the Andean provinces, it is now threatening to crush worker-peasant mass organizations and the Left (Sanchez, 1987), and it is poised to stage what many observers believe will be the inevitable coup.[34]

Military supremacy is given further impetus by the complex drug *traficante* problem in Peru. Peru leads Bolivia as the world's largest grower of coca. Its prime cocaine region is the Upper Huallaga Valley, about 250 miles northwest of Lima, where thousands of peasants grow coca plants. Drug traffickers operate landing strips and jungle laboratories in the valley, attacking police posts, convoys, and military helicopters in defense of their lucrative enterprise. Although the exact relationship between Sendero and the drug traffickers is unclear, Sendero has increased its activities in the eastern jungles, and the Huallaga Valley has been declared a liberated zone by the Shining Path. The Garcia government directs a U.S.-backed drug eradication program, but Sendero —which regards the chewing of coca leaves as an ancient and beneficial practice[35]— supports the coca leaf farmers (Werlich, 1987:16). Sendero guerrillas thus provide protection for coca farmers, allowing Colombian planes unlimited access to the area as long as farmers and coca paste producers get a fair price for their product. They assist drug traffickers in order to ensure that the farmers prosper and the peasants earn a livelihood cultivating and picking the crop.[36] In return, local traficantes support Sendero and pay for its protection because Shining Path guerrillas both divert police resources and make it difficult for the military and police to enter the coca-growing areas (McCormick, 1987). Sendero itself vehemently opposes cocaine drug use, but its depiction of the eradication campaign as an example of the national governments alignment with an imperialist power attempting to deprive the native of his livelihood provides fertile grounds for recruitment (Craig, 1985:109).[37]

Even without Sendero's involvement, the government's war on drugs is fraught with contradiction. Coca paste is actually Peru's major export commodity, and cocaine export revenues have been used to prop up Peru's international reserves and provided financing for urban property development (Reid, 1985:104). In 1987, a convicted traficante offered to liquidate the Peruvian national deficit in exchange for his release. The penultimate contradiction, however, lies in the pretext afforded by the alleged war on drugs to justify foreign control over anti-guerrilla operations (i.e., the coca regions as staging grounds for the proliferation of U.S. military personnel), and for the recirculation of cocaine profits to finance the destabilization of other Third World regimes.[38] These developments do little to enhance the probability of democratic reforms.

At the start of his presidency, Garcia was bolstered by wide public support that afforded some protection against a military coup while he confronted Peru's creditors. But the task of reaching a national accord has proved insuperable given the difficulty of reconciling competing objectives such as defeating Sendero while restraining the military's own contra-terror. Garcia's limited concessions to the poor will not mollify workers and peasants who seek liberation from the cumulating toll of debt bondage. Furthermore, right-wing forces distrust even circumscribed reforms, and the capitalist financial world eyes Garcia with open hostility because of his contemptuous attitude toward the IMF. Should external financing continue to decrease and economic benefits cease, Garcia can expect opportunistic allies to desert his government. Thus, the APRA project is full of contradictions and already appears to have run its course. Popular mobilization without structural change cannot create the industrial base needed to develop new export products and expanded domestic markets (Branford and Kucinski, 1988). Ever since the debt strategy ran out of steam in 1987, the president who was adored in 1986 has been struggling fitfully to complete his term.

Dialectic of Terrorism

Garcia's antiimperialist APRA party has been unable to cut new paths in a global economic order dominated by capitalist imperatives, international banks, and multinational corporations — all of which are structurally disposed to equate the growth of democracy in underdeveloped countries with diminishing supplies of cheap labor and raw materials. Like other semicapitalist colonies, Peru falls victim to the tendency for dominant capitalist countries to mitigate their own internal economic problems at the expense of other socio-economic formations. It is not surprising, therefore, that imperialist penetration of underdeveloped countries contributed mainly to the growth and stabilization of the advanced capitalist economies.[39] The initial stimulus provided by direct foreign investment usually leads to the repatriation of profits produced by capital to the mother country, starving the underdeveloped regions of new investment, Moreover, the increased product efficiency of the dependent nation's export sector results in lower export prices and a consequent deterioration of the commodity terms of trade of the underdeveloped country. This leads to a deterioration in the balance of payments associated both with falling export prices and the repatriation of profits — offsetting the initially positive effect of direct investment on the balance of payments of the underdeveloped country. Amid these larger determinations, Scheetz (1986:8) observes, " ... the room for manoeuvering or self-determination of development objectives is extremely limited, especially for a small country like Peru. ... " Even in sectors of the economy with a high degree of public ownership (e.g., Peru's petroleum industry), the state seems unable to transform the structures of dependent capitalism within which it operates (Hamilton, 1981),[40] and it continues to function largely in the interests of private (usually foreign) capital. The failure of both dominat class fractions and the state to implement projects of national dominion exposes the reality of what Bamat refers to as the "chronic hegemonic barrier in dependent social formations" (1977:83), a problem that has certainly plagued Peru's governments since its absorption into the imperialist economic order.

Since 1976, when Peruvian authorities accused the international banks of "Wall Street Imperialism," the IMF has been orchestrating lending arrangements and the course of the ensuing debt crises. Garcia's proposal to limit Peru's debt payment to 10% of export earnings could be viewed as a sensible attempt to alleviate his nation's enormous debt burden and enable his government to modernize the economy and carry out mandatory social welfare programs. At $14 billion, Peru's foreign debt would not inflict crippling losses on the international banks, and only 18% of Peru's debt was owed to U.S. banks. But Washington (and thus the IMF) feared that other larger debtor nations might be tempted to adopt Garcia's "ten percent solution" and cause a major financial crisi.[41] When Garcia rejected an ultimatum to make up his arrears, the IMF declared Peru ineligible for future loans. Since August 1986, it has continued a hard line on debts and credits, demanding further austerity-based adjustments. Precisely because such 'stabilization' policies endanger the survival of governments subjected to them, the IMF tends to favor conservative and authoritarian regimes, sometimes bringing them to power when governments are reluctant to apply IMF remedies (Korner, et al., 1984:139). When human rights, democratic expression, social equity, and internal development are all sacrificed in order to protect the stability of the system of payments for foreign bankers," . . . it is no wonder that the IMF must work in tandem with the armed forces of a country to guarantee compliance with the rules of the game" (Scheetz, (1986:152).

The specificity of terrorism in Peru, therefore, must be understood against the backdrop of Peru's status as an exploited, semicapitalist, Third World nation trapped in ever-growing spirals of indebtedness and poverty. Workers and peasants bear the brunt of policies—resulting in suffering, resignation, and ultimately, rebellion. Terrorism from above, therefore, elicits terrorism from below, although growing insurgent movements are rapidly depoliticized in order to justify accelerated *state* terrorism—from Sinchis, to 'self-defense' forces, to vigilantism, to foreign 'advisors,' and back to international creditors. The multitiered terrorism that soon envelops the entire society becomes grounds for importuning the National Security State, the only 'commonsensical' means to quash violence that threatens to escalate out of control. Revolution is much less likely (though not inconceivable should the guerrilla movement itself deploy terror successfully).[42] Of course, the principal role of agencies such as the IMF is to ensure that such revolutionary outcomes do not occur. This is why, finally, the relationship between guerrilla and state terrorism must be understood as a *managed dialectic*, precipitated and controlled by multinational capital through its international brokers — immiserating Third World majorities, fixated on the terror of the left, and ignoring or justifying official state terror. At the very least, Peru's struggle lends credence to Edward Herman's condemnation of the development model as "a huge tacit conspiracy," even if it does not exactly demonstrate that the collusion between foreign, local, and military interests has become glaringly overt.

Conclusions

Peru today is in an extremely turbulent state, although it is not clear which group will eventually take power. The centrist alternative has clearly collapsed as the APRA government barely clings to power— unable to repel mounting Sendero attacks[43] and immobilized by soaring inflation,[44] spreading fear,[45] and daily privation.[46] A right-wing 'Chilean strongman' solution seems imminent, despite widespread oppostion to a military coup. A presentiment of this already exists in the figure of Mario Vargas Llosa, the famed author and right-centrist (Fredemo) presidential candidate. His plans to introduce a 'Thatcherite' set of economic solutions hinge on the possibilities of attracting foreign capital and blocking capital flight — even though neither objective can be accomplished without guarantees of domestic security, and this is improbable amidst the warring factions in Peru. The United Left party (Izquierda Unida) is far from united.[47] Should the constitutional framework survive long enough for elections to be held in 1990, a left triumph is unlikely given the lack of ideological and pragmatic cohesion. Indeed, the United Left's failure to win a significant number of mayoralties in the November 1989 municipal elections (when all signs pointed to a sweeping victory) is indicative of the parliamentary Left's chronic inopportunism. If Vargas Llosa does not win a strong mandate and achieve political stability, the current crisis will likely result in another military takeover, with the armed forces forming a junta to avoid the fragmentation experience of the left. The military may then install a civilian (and his political party) or swing over to Sendero — although this latter course is unlikely given the history of bloody recriminations between the two groups. Therefore, the recrudescence of a National Security State—a familiar IMF-engineered, Third World solution—is the most likely future for the beleaguered and moribund democratic state of Peru.

Another possible future for Peru lies in economic reorganization by international lending institutions and the IMF to relieve the debt crisis unilaterally. Throughout the 1980s, efforts have been made to negotiate new deals with debtors, but even middle-income developing countries such as Brazil, Venezuela, and Argentina continue to be caught in investment – export growth – debt-repayment crunches that cause severe political and social strains. Cash outflows from debtor nations have actually risen in recent years, curtailing domestic income investment and growth.[48] Conventional measures to ease debt with new loans, partial write-offs, and economic reform fail to address the magnitude of the problem. Other recently bruited proposals involve more radical reform of tax laws to spur banks to write off debts, buying up of shaky loans by

First World economies, and further extension of credit to stimulate growth export industries. But channeling more resources to the Third World and unilateral debt moratoriums are unwanted remedies in the international financial ecommunity, which fears that unmet loans will destabilize its home economies.[49] Nevertheless, some South American countries are insisting on temporary debt moratoriums and other changes in the rules of the IMF game, but this approach has no chance of working unless such governments are resolute, prepared for confrontation should negotiations fail, and able to demonstrate substantial popular support—all political resources difficult to muster at the very time such changes are urgently required.[50] When Peru, for example, ran out of reserves to honor some letters of credit needed to import food staples, its government announced in January 1989 that it was welcoming a mission by the IMF—the very institution it had denounced since 1985 as an oppressor of the Third World and to which it had, for a time, stopped paying its debt.

In the latest chapter of Peru's national degradation events are now moving rapidly toward a climax. Paradoxically, terrorism may represent Peru's only hope by galvanizing the mass movements, the Peasants Federation, and the shantytown associations into concerted radical action. But it may also ensure Peru's continued exploitation should liberation struggles merely rationalize increased authoritarianism. Oviedo (1985:178) observeds plaintively:

> The collective wisdom of a people that has maintained its sense of resignation and tenacity in so many harsh situations keeps alive a saying that is ironic but consoling. 'God is a Peruvian.' Maybe with this in mind, the great poet Cesar Vallejo wrote in 1919: "I was born on a day when God was very, very sick.'

Perhaps the solemn lesson of Peru's fate is that it is not to God but to international monopoly capitalism that we need raise hapless prayers or pitiable swords.

Notes

*Revision of paper presented at the 40th Annual Meeting of the American Society of Criminology, Chicago, Illinois, November 9–12, 1988.

†I wish to thank Alar Olljum and Claudio Vidal for their research assistance; and Alicia Barrasalo, Maureen Cain, and Blanca Muratorio for their careful reading of earlier drafts of this paper. I am also grateful to my many informants and interviewees in Lima, Peru and Vancouver, B.C.

1. See the extensive compilation of meanings, typologies, and etiological theories of terrorism in Schmid and Jongman (1988).

2. In this paper, the term *terrorism* is given the widest possible referent, encompassing political violence committed at the levels of insurgent, state, or international action. According to Stohl and Lopez, "terrorism is the purposeful act or threat of violence to create fear and/or compliant behavior in a victim and/or audience of the act or threat" (1984:7). This definition is taken to include economic policies that knowingly inflict serious harm on selected groups and rely on intimidation to ensure compliance.

3. Chomsky and Herman (1979) draw the distinction between the *retail* terror employed by isolated individuals or small groups and the *wholesale* terror employed by states. Military and political establishments focus almost exclusively on the former. *Terrorist Group Profiles*, a volume recently published by the U.S. Department of Defense, categorizes almost all terrorist groups as "Marxist-Leninist" or "Socialist," and ignores the multitude of right-wing terrorist groups in Asia, Western Europe, and even the United States—not to mention the CIA's ongoing links to terrorism throughout most of Central America. Charles Whitehouse, the assistant defense secretary responsible for antiterrorism, has admitted that what makes an individual a terrorist depends in large part on the individual's attitude toward the United States: "One has to distinguish between what the objectives are, and the degree to which what has taken place is contrary to U.S. interests and hostile to the people of the United States" (*Globe and Mail*, 16 January, 1989).

4. See, for example, the scant and conceptually amorphous items referring to "regional and global etiological factors" in Schmid and Jongman's updated encyclopedic survey of political terrorism (1988:112–188). In his critique of "development" and its relationship to terrorism, Apter (1987) noted the same deficiency: "Even less examined is what one can speak of as a 'dialectic' of terrorism, especially of the Left-Right variety. For example, in Argentina, Brazil, and elsewhere in Latin America, and in Italy as well, left-wing and right-wing terrorism have literally fed off each other, and in the first two instances, terrorists have been divided between anti-state versus pro-state forces, the right wing being in part sponsored by the police."

5. Cuba and Nicaragua, for example, have so far managed to escape the transnational trap, although broken filaments in the web of superpower domination can be respun. *Perestroika*, it should be noted, has ominous implications for Latin American countries that rely on Soviet economic support.

6. The firgures reported here are drawn from Reid (1985:1–16). After a short-lived consumerist surge in 1985–86, all economic indicators have worsened over the past three years.

7. Those overtures included the opening of the Amazon jungle to multinational capital.

8. As Werlich notes, this economic decline "translated into widespread malnutrition, disease, and a sharp rise in the rate of infant mortality" (1984:78).

9. Reid states that, by 1984, "real income per head had fallen back to the level of 20 years before, but the aggregate figures concealed a widening inequality in the distribution of income" (1985:97).

10. In 1963, Lima had a population of 1.5 million. By 1983, its population had grown to 6.5 million—or nearly 40 percent of the country's then 18 million people. By 1985, unemployment and underemployment had skyrocketed to about 65 percent, and the real minimum wage was barely a dollar a day—less than half the 1973 wage (McClintock, 1987:240).

11. The discussion of Sendero Luminoso is based on Berg (1987), Bonner (1988), McClintock (1983–1984), McCormick (1987), and Werlich (1984).

12. Sendero's full name is *Partido Communista del Peru—Por El Sendero Luminoso de Jose Carlos Mariategui*. The term *Sendero Luminoso* refers to a statement by Mariategui, Peru's first prominent Marxist, that "Marxism-Leninism will open the *shinging path* to the revolution."

13. Although the Shining Path is the largest and most successful of Peru's so-called terrorist organizations, there are at least five other terrorist groups operating on Peruvian soil. One of these is the Tupac Amaru Revolutionary Movement (MRTA), a Castroite guerrilla group successful in recruiting urban supporters. Tupac Amaru was a freedom fighter put to death in the late eighteenth century for leading a popular uprising against the Spanish conquerors. Drawing on this inspiration, the white Sendero leadership learned the native Quechua language and nurtured the messianic tradition of Incan rebellion against the conquistadors.

14. Guzman's *nom de guerre* is "Comrade Gonzalo."

15. The Sendero program has been compared with the rural economic schemes of the Khmer Rouge under the genocidal rule of Pol Pot in Cambodia.

16. Sendero forays have expanded since 1982 to include military, economic, imperialist, and international political targets—among them army barracks and installations, embassies, Kentucky Fried Chicken franchises, and beauty contests. Direct killings of public officials and other political targets are now carried out in provincial capitals and in Lima.

17. Starting in January 1983, Belaunde deployed more than 1,500 U.S.-trained troops in the Ayacucho region. These troops — Sinchis (the Quechua word for 'warrior') — have proved more wanton than the Senderistas in their killing and plundering, and, consequently, have done little to win back the countryside for the government.

18. In September 1982, more than 10,000 people crowded the streets of Ayacucho to mourn Edith Lagos, a young Sendero leader killed by the policy. In May 1988, hundreds of Sendero militants marched through downtown streets tossing dynamite, waving flags, and chanting revolutionary slogans. Just before the police arrived, the guerrillas dispersed into the large crowd, making it impossible for the police to identify them.

19. McClintock notes that, "Rural smallholders who are not particularly active in the market economy or non-agricultural networks have been Sendero's primary peasant base. In addition, the Ayacucho area is expecially advantageous to revolutionaries because it is relatively inaccessible and because it has a university (many of whose students are currently destined for unemployment)" (1984:82 – 3). Despite martial law, Ayacucho has been under de facto Sendero control.

20. In addition to the increasing toll taken by the guerrilla war, the failure of Belaunde's conservative free-market policies and a 40 percent plunge in the average price for Peru's exports almost destroyed the economy, thus necessitating new loans to service the foreign debt and cover huge deficits. By the time of the 1985 elections, the foreign debt had climbed to $13 billion—73 percent of the gross domestic product, or $713 per person (Branford and Kucinski, 1988:9). The annual inflation rate approached 250 percent, over half of Peru's industrial capacity was idle, almost two-thirds of the labor force was inadequately employed, real wages had plummeted at least 40 percent since 1980, and per capita income had fallen to the level of the mid-1960s (Werlich, 1971:29). By the time Garcia assumed office in 1985, inflation had spiraled—from 50 *soles* to the dollar to 14,500 *soles* to the dollar. The Treasury replaced the *sol* with the *inti* (which means *sol*, or sun, in Quechua) as the new monetary unit.

21. Not surprisingly, Belaunde's Popular Action party won only 6 percent of the ballot in the 1985 presidential election.

22. For the first time in its 55-year history, the APRA party won in Lima, and Jorge de Castillo ousted Mayor Alfonso Barrantes Lingan, a Marxist leader of the United Left.

23. Garcia is a spellbinding orator. According to Bonner (1988:49), "Six times in his first month in office, he spontaneously addressed crowds from the balcony of the Presidential Palace, earning the nickname of the 'Balcony President.' "

24. Garcia also expected economic reactivation as a result of improved credit for farmers, but by the time of the 1987 inflationary spiral, higher food prices could not be passed on to already hard-pressed urban consumers, and the government could not afford additional food subsides. In the industrial export area, the Aprista government has been unable to curtail and control the reinvestment of profits extracted by the mining companies. Most of these are foreign monopolies (e.g., the Southern Corporation and the American Smelting Corporation), and they account for nearly half of Peru's exports.

25. Gunmen tried to assassinate Garcia's key aide responsible for the plan to nationalize Peru's financial industry (*Globe and Mail*, 7 August 1987). Actually, the attempt to nationalize the banks failed in response to right-wing opposition. Only two banks were nationalized, and the decree ordering investment in government securities was eventually nullified by the government.

26. In the last few months of 1988, workers in Peru lost 70 percent of their real wage value. The current average wage is $120 per month, and purchases other than food are out of reach for almost all workers.

27. Third World debtor nations usually require the IMF seal of approval to obtain debt renegotiation from their creditors.

28. The U.S. military mission opened in Peru in 1932 and is still functioning. Between 1949 and 1979, 33,000 Latin American army officers (including Peruvian military) were trained at a U.S. 'school of coups' in Panama. U.S. Green Berets led counterinsurgency operations against guerrillas in the eastern jungles of Peru in the early 1960s. President Reagan's fiscal budget in 1984 requested a five-fold increase in military aid to support the purchase of high-tech counterinsurgency equipment by the Peruvian armed forces(*NACLA Report*, Jan./Feb. 1984). The current Bush initiative is widely regarded as an attempt to gain a U.S. military presence in the Andes in order to crush political guerrillas, rather than as a serious effort to wipe out the cocaine trade at its source.

29. Garcia's blue-ribbon police commission recommended partial amnesty for guerrillas, repeal of Belaunde's sweeping and vague antiterrorist law, restoration of civilian control over the Ayacucho emergency zone, and steps toward the prosecution of security personnel who had violated human rights (Werlich, 1987:32). In fact, however, Garcia did not punish military officers who were responsible for the Accomarca massacre in August 1985 (in which 69 persons were killed), nor did he take effective punitive action after the prison massacres in June 1986.

30. The police raids on universities in Peru were unusual in that they violated the centuries-old Latin American tradition of university autonomy.

31. U.N. and Amnesty International reports have documented and condemned these atrocities and the subsequent government cover-ups. In a 1983 television interview, President Belaunde called Amnesty International "a Communist organization" and said that AI letters were "thrown directly into the wastepaper basket" (*Amnesty International Bulletin*, April 1985:1). When Garcia attempted to punish those responsible for the prison massacres, the military responded by kidnapping members of the middle and upper classes. In general, few suspected terrorists are brought to trial because judicial authorities fear reprisals.

32. The command takes its name from an APRA leader slain by guerrillas in 1987. Ironically, Franco had been utterly opposed to the violent activities of groups such as the Rodrigo Franco Command. The command is active primarily

in Lima and in the Andean region of Ayacucho, and it appears to have links with the police (*Globe and Mail*, 5 December 1988). It has been associated with a series of bombings and thefts, and on 28 July 1988, it claimed credit for the murder of the defense lawyer of a captured Shining Path commander.

33. See *The Christian Science Monitor* 27 June–3 July 1988:5).

34. A top general and close ally of Garcia was forced to resign his command because he had warned Garcia of a possible military coup (*Globe and Mail*, 13 October 1988).

35. For at least five thousand years, the coca bush has grown on the lower slopes of the eastern Andes, and its leaves have been chewed by the Sierra Indians to help them work in extreme cold on an inadequate diet (Reid, 1985:104).

36. See *Lima Times* 19 June 1987:2).

37. Sendero's attempts to persuade the peasants to grow other crops (e.g., food) are incompatible with the objectives of narco-traffickers—who are interested only becoming rich, not in changing the social system (*Si Magazine*, 8 June 1987).

38. This is believed to be the case in Bolivia, where drug production finances the attempted destabilization of Nicaragua and the presence of North American elements in the campaign against drug trafficking has turned into collusion with it'' (Garcia, 1988:24). Bonner reports that "the United States has provided money, equipment, and training for a special unit with the Civil Guard which was ostensibly set up as a part of the war on drugs. This unit, which Peruvian police officials refer to unofficially as their SWAT team or Delta Force, will actually be used in the war against Sendero as well. In fact, one police official told me that this would be its principal mission" (1988:56).

39. Peru is a clear example of imperialist penetration changing traditional habits and opening new markets for colonial powers' export surpluses. The staple grain of indigenous peoples in Peru used to be the *quinoa*, a nutritious foodstuff well-adapted to the ecological and climactic conditions of the high sierras. But President Truman's aid programs, which brought wheat to Peru, popularized consumption of wheat bread and other wheat products. Aid was soon followed by trade, and Peru now imports large quantities of this cereal, devoting to this purpose a sizable proportion of its overall export earnings (Schatan, 1987:52–53).

40. Indeed, the limits of the state capitalist area in dependent class formations are revealed by the growth of the national debt.

41. Not irrelevant to the IMF attitude was the Reagan administration's anger over Garcia's persistent condemnation of U.S. policies toward Nicaragua. This grievance has hardly been assuaged by Garcia's condemnation of the recent U.S. invasion of Panama and by Peru's tentative withdrawal from a U.S.-organized cocaine interdiction conclave in the Andean region.

42. In his survey of Latin American guerrilla movements Hobsbawn noted: "If the past ten years suggests that, in purely technical terms, the forces of government should be able to eliminate, control, or side-track practically any irregular armed force, they also suggest that these governments have rarely even looked like being able to create the conditions of long-term economic, social, political, and institutional stability. Revolutions are not, as Debray and Guevera thought, around the corner. But neither are they beyond the range of realistic politics" (1974:88–89). It may be that, especially in Peru, so-called revolution ultimately depends less on guerrilla movements than on the mass movements of peasants and workers. The United Left certainly maintains this view in critiquing Sendero violence and dogmatism.

43. Sendero has blown up hydroelectric pylons at the rate of a dozen a day. For three consecutive months in 1989, Lima did not have even one 24-hour period of continuous electricity.

44. The 1988 annual inflation rate was officially listed at 1700%, but the actual rate was well over 2000%. For 1989, it was close to 6000%.

45. More people are being shot and kidnapped, more are withdrawing children from school and colleges, and more are leaving Peru.

46. The price of a tin of milk has gone up numerous times in the past two years. In the autumn of 1988, a tin cost 250 *intis,* and the average daily wage was 800 *intis.*

47. Izquierda Unida (IU) was formed after divisions on the left resulted in disaster in the 1980 presidential elections. IU's president, Alfonso Barrantes, a labor lawyer and nonaligned Marxist, was elected mayor of Lima in 1983. IU is composed of approximately 10,000 militants and represents a coalition of center-left and left parties. No unions are affiliated as such, but workers tend to support the party. On the plausibility of an IU electoral triumph, Reid commented that "there were powerful reasons to suppose that neither the armed forces nor the U.S. would permit the left-wing forces grouped in IU to win a poll and exercise national power through the electoral system. The fate of the Allende government in Chile and statements from Peruvian military officers, who made little distinction between IU and Sendero, tended to reinforce this supposition" (1985:123).

48. *Vancouver Sun* (19 December 1988).

49. *Globe and Mail* (27 December 1988). Indeed, the most exemplary statesmen of our time, Mikhail Gorbachev of the Soviet Union, suggested a 100-year moratorium on Third World debt repayment.

50. A Latin American Reserve Fund was recently created as a self-help alternative to the IMF. Its aim is to grant loans to ease balance of payments deficits in the region without attaching the usual economic policy adjustment conditions demanded by the IMF. The fund has assets of only $4 billion—but a fraction of the total debt owed by its member countries (*Globe and Mail,* 18 January 1988).

References

Apter, Daivd E.
1987   *Rethinking Development.* Beverly Hills, Sage Publications Inc.

Bakhash, Shaul
1987   "The Riddle of Terrorism." *The New York Review of Books,* Vol. XXXIV, No. 14, 24 September 1987:12–15.

Bamet, Thomas
1977   "Relative State Autonomy and Capitalism in Brazil and Peru." *The Insurgent Sociologist,* Vol. VII, No. II, (Spring) 1977: pp. 74–83.

Berg, Ronald H.
1986   "Sendero Luminoso and the Peasantry of Andahuaylas." *Journal of Interamerican Studies and World Affairs,* Vol. 28, No. 4, (Winter 1986/1987):165–196.

Bonner, Raymond
1988   "Peru's War." *The New Yorker,* Vol. 63, 4 January 1988:31–58.

Branford, Sue and Bernardo Kucinski
1988   *The Debt Squards: The U.S., The Banks, and Latin America.* London: Zed Books Ltd.

Bulletin (Canadian Section)
"Peru respondes to A.I. Report," April 1985, vol., XII, no. 3, pp. 1–2.

Carny, Phillips
1981   "France: Non-Terrorism and the Politics of Repressive Tolerance." In *Terrorism: A Challenge to the State.* Ed. by Juliet Lodge. Oxford: Martin Robertson.

Chomsky, Noam and Edward S. Herman, *The Washington Connection and Third World Fascism* 1979 Boston: South End Press.

Craig, Richard B.
1985   "Illicit Drug Traffic and U.S. Latin American Relations." *The Washington Quarterly,* Fall 1985:105–115.

Crelinsten, R. D.
1987   "Terrorism as Political Communication: The Relationship Between the Controller and the Controlled." In *Contemporary Research on Terrorism.* Ed. by Paul Wilkinson and Alasdair M. Stewart. Aberdeen: Aberdeen University Press.

Garcia, Fernando
1988   "Coca Leaves, Contra Wars, and Contraventions." *Socialist Studies Bulletin* 13 (July/September) 1989:21–26.

Gatt-Fly
1985   *Debt Bondage or Self-Reliance: A popular Perspective on the Global Debt Crisis.* Toronto: Gatt-Fly.

Greisman, H. C.
1977   "Social Meanings of Terrorism: Reification, Violence, and Social Control." *Contemporary Crises* 1:303–318.

Hamilton, Nora
1981   "State Autonomy and Dependent Capitalism in Latin America." *British Journal of Sociology* 32 No. 3 (September 1981):305–329.

Herman, Edward S.
1982   *The Real Terror Network.* Montreal: Black Rose Books.

Hobsbawn, E. J.
1974   "Latin American Guerrillas: A Survey." In *Latin American Review of Books.* I. Ed. by Colin Harding and Christopher Roper. Palo Alto: Rampart's Press.

Hocking, Jenny
1984   "Orthodox Theories of 'Terrorism': The Power of Politicized Terminology." *Journal of the Australian Political Studies Association* 19, No. 2 (November) 103–110.

Horowitz, Irving Louis
1973   *Journal of Political and Military Sociology* 1, No. 1:147–157.

Korner, Peter, et al.
1986   *The IMF and the Debt Crisis: A Guide to the Third World's Dilemmas.* London: Zed Books Ltd.

Lima Times
1987   24 July "Lima Blackout, Upper Huallaga Emergency." No. 633:1–2.

Mariategui, Jose Carlos
1971   *Seven Interpretive Essays on Peruvian Reality.* Austin: University of Texas Press.

McClintock, Cynthia
1983   "Sendero Luminoso: Peru's Maoist Guerrillas." *Problems of Communism* (September/October):19–34.

McCynthia
1984   "Why Peasants Rebel: The Case of Peru's Sendero Luminoso." *World Politics* 37, No. 1 (October):48–84.

McClintock, Cynthia
1987   "Capitalist Expansion and the Andean Peasantry." *Latin American Research Review* 22, No. 2:235–244.

McCormick, Gordon H.
1987 "The Shining Path and Peruvian Terrorism." *The Journal of Strategic Studies* 10, No. 4 (December):109–126.

Oviedo, Jose Miguel
1987 "Peru: Can This Nation Save Itself?" *Dissent* 34, No. 2 (Spring):171–178.

Payne, Johnny
1987 "Talking Around Terrorism: A Conference Report." *Telos* 75 (Winter): 141–146.

Petras, James
1985 "Authoritarianism, Democracy, and the Transition to Socialism." *Socialist Register*. London: The Merlin Press.

Petras, James, Morris Morley, and Eugene Havens
1983 "Peru: Capitalist Democracy in Transition." *New Left Review* 142 (November/December:30–53.

Quijano, Anibal
1982 "Imperialism and the Peasantry: The Current Situation in Peru." *Latin American Perspectives* IX, No. (Summer) No. 3:46–61.

Reid, Michael
1985 *Peru: Paths of Poverty*. Nottingham: Latin American Bureau (Research and Action) Limited, Russell Press Ltd.

Sanchez, A.
1987 "Populism with Military Supremacy." *Peru Link* 5 (Spring):2–12 (Published by the Committee for the Defense of Human Rights in Peru, Vancouver, B.C., Canada.)

Schatan, Jacob
1987 *World Debt: Who is to Pay?* Zed Books Ltd.: London 1987.

Scheetz, Thomas
1986 *Peru and the International Monetary Fund*, Pittsburgh: U. of Pittsburgh Press.

Schlesinger, Philip
1981 "Terrorism, the Media, and the Liberal-Democratic State: A Critique of the Orthodoxy." *Social REsearch* 48, No. 1:74–99.

Schmid, Alex P. and Albert J. Jongman
1988 *Political Terrorism* (Rev. ed.) Amsterdam; North-Holland Publishing Company.

Si Magazine
1987 "Shining Path Takes Tocache: Alliance between Drug-Traffickers and Terrorists." *Si Magazine* 1, No. 15 (8 June):76–85.

Stallings, Barbara
1985   "International Lending and Relative Autonomy of the State: A Case Study of Twentieth Century Peru." *Politics and Society* 14, No. 3:257–288.

Sterling, Claire
1981   *The Terror Network*. New York: Holt, Rinehart & Winston.

Stohl, Michael
1988   "Demystifying Terrorism: They Myths and Realities of Contemporary Political Terrorism." In *The Politics of Terrorism*. Ed. by Michael Stohl. New York: Marcel Dekkar, Inc.

Stohl, Michael and George A. Lopez (Eds.)
1984   *The State as Terrorist: The Dynamics of Governmental Violence and Repression*. Westport, Connecticut: Greenwood Press.

Turk, Austin S.
1982   "Social Dynamics of Terrorism." *Annals AAPSS,* No. 463 (September): 119–128.

Ugarte, Susana
1988   "Peru: Time for Alliances." *Gramma* 23, No. 5 (31 January):11. (Havana.)

Werlick, David P.
1984   "Peru: The Shadow of the Shining Path." *Current History* (February 1984):78–82, 90.

Werlick, David P.
1987   "Debt, Democracy, and Terrorism in Peru." *Current History* (January 1987):29–32, 36.

Werlick, David P.
1988   "Peru: Garcia Loses his Charm." *Current History* (January):13–16, 36–37.

Wilkinson, Paul
1977   *Terrorism and the Liberal State*. London; MacMillan.

Wilson, James Q.
1981   "Thinking About Terrorism." *Commentary* 72, No. 1 (July):34–39.

5

Piracy, Air Piracy, and Recurrent U.S. and Israeli Civilian Aircraft Interceptions

Daniel E. Georges-Abeyie

Introduction: The Reality of Redirections

When one thinks of piracy and air piracy, the image of gunmen with no allegiance to any current *jure gentium* nation-state usually emerges. One does not usually associate the terms *piracy, air piracy,* and *hostage taking* with uniformed agents or representatives of a *jure gentium* recognized nation-state. However, the mid- to late-twentieth century has borne witness to the unusual spector of the uniformed armed services of Israel, the United States, and South Africa intercepting and redirecting civilian aircraft under the threat of being shot from the skies, and the U.S.S.R., the United States, the Sudan, Iraq, South Korea, and Israel have literally demanded the so-called redirection of civilian aircraft—and then shot them from the skies when they failed to redirect. In February 1973, for example, Israel downed a Libyan airliner (Chomsky, 1986). And on October 19, 1986, South Africa may have downed (i.e., 'redirected') a Mozambican nonmilitary, presidential aircraft into a mountainside (New York Times, 1988:811; Mozambique Embassy, 1988). Table 1 lists well-documented incidents of civilian aircraft that have been intercepted and redirected by the uniformed armed forces of Israel and the United States.

I have used the term *redirect* guardedly. These so-called redirections may have been grievous acts of official or state terrorism and violations of international law. This chapter will explore the concepts of terrorism and international law in general—as well as the specifics of piracy, hijacking, air piracy, and hostage taking—in an attempt to determine whether these so-called redirections can or should be labeled any of the crimes noted above.

TABLE 1

Israeli and U.S. Interceptions and Redirections* of
Civilian Aircraft and Civilian Sea Transit

Date	Nation	Vessel	Vessel's Flag
December 12, 1954	Israel	Civilian Airliner	Syria
February 1973	Israel	Civilian Airliner	Libya
June 1984	Israel	Ferry Boat	Lebanon
April 25, 1985	Israel	Fishing Boats	Lebanon**
October 10, 1985	U.S.	Egypt Air Boeing 737	Egypt
February 4, 1986	Israel	Civilian Aircraft	Libya
January 7, 1987	Israel	Commercial Ferry	Cyprus
July 3, 1988	U.S.	Iran Air Flight 655	Iran

*Includes attempted redirections.
**Palestinians on board were seized and sent to Israel for interrogation.

Source: Chomsky, N. *Pirates and Emperors: International Terrorism in the Real World*. New York: Claremont Research of Publications, 1986; *New York Times*.

Defining *Terrorism, Terror, State or Official Terrorism, Piracy, Air Piracy, Skyjacking,* and *Air Hijacking*

The central issue is whether the so-called interception and redirection of civilian aircraft by the uniformed armed services of a *jure genitum* recognized nation-state constitutes an act of terror (i.e., state or official terrorism) and can be litimately labeled piracy, air piracy, skyjacking, or air hijacking.

Before one can discuss the terms *terror* and *state or official terrorism,* one must first comprehend the concept of terrorism, for which there is no single, universally accepted definition. Brian Jenkins notes that the term has "become a fad word used promiscuously and often applied to a variety of acts of violence which are not strictly terrorism by definition. It is generally pejorative. . . . What is called terrorism thus seems to depend on one's point of view" (Jenkins, 1980:1). The report of the Vice President's Task Force on Combating Terrorism contends that

Terrorism is a phenomenon that is easier to describe than define. It is the unlawful use or threat of violence against persons or property to further political or social objectives. It is generally intended to intimidate or coerce a government, individuals or groups to modify their behavior or policies. (Vice President's Task Force on Combating Terrorism, February 1986:1).

This report also notes that "... neither the United States nor the United Nations has adopted official definitions of terrorism. ... " (Vice President's Task Force on Combating Terrorism, 1986:1). Ten years earlier, however, the National Advisory Committee on Criminal Justice Standards and Goals, in its *Report of the Task Force on Disorders and Terrorism* (1976), noted that

> Political terrorism is characterized by: (1) its violent, criminal nature; (2) its impersonal frame of reference; and (3) the primacy of its ulterior objective, which is the dissemination of fear throughout the community for political ends or purposes. "Political terrorism may be defined, therefore, as violent, criminal behavior designed primarily to generate fear in the community, or a substantial segment of it, for political purposes." (Task Force on Disorders and Terrorism, 1976:3).

For the sake of closure on the definitional complexities of the general term *terrorism*, one can note that the U.S. Congress has not passed a federal law which succinctly defines terrorism. One can, however, state that terrorism is characterized by its illegal challenge to the power of the state — i.e., the illegal challenge to the state's *ability* to carry out its political policies. It is not an illegal challenge to the state's *authority* — i.e., to the state's right to legislate and to exist as a *jure gentium* recognized political entity. (Such an illegal challenge would be the essence of guerrilla warfare.) This illegal challenge to the power of the state is carried out by means of violence or threats of violence. It is directed not only against official uniformed or nonuniformed representatives of a state but against animate and inanimate civilian targets as well.

If one accepts this definition of terrorism, one can define *terror* or *official or state terrorism* as the use of legal violence or threat of such violence by state agents and representatives (both uniformed and nonuniformed) as well as by vigilante representatives of state interests. Examples of such vigilante representatives include the Orden in El Salvador and the numerous right-wing, private armies organized by the Philippine uniformed and nonuniformed social control forces to help combat the communist threat of the New Peoples Army. The essence of terror (i.e., of state or official terrorism) is psychological (i.e., fear), although violence or the threat of violence is the instrumentality of this fear. The purpose of terror is the enforcement of state policies, laws, and executive orders. It is not a challenge to the state's own authority. Unlike *terrorism* from below, *terror* from above is legal. The state has the power to legislate or simply declare by executive order restrictive and all encompassing political dictates (e.g., in South Africa, the Group Areas Act and the state of emergency declared on July 21, 1985). The essence of terror goes beyond the simple physical implementation of an oppressive act upon a specific individual. Its essence lies in its psychological impact upon society as a whole or upon a specific, targeted sector of society. Terror attempts to paralyze the will of dissidents to act against the state's power and/or authority.

The case of so-called redirection and destruction of civilian aircraft by the uniformed armed forces of *jure gentium* recognized nation-states introduces an interesting possible application of the concept of terror or state or official terrorism. Does the downing and redirection of civilian aircraft constitute acts of terror—i.e., state or official terrorism, piracy, air piracy, skyjacking or air hijacking?

The terms *skyjacking* and *air hijacking* are mass media terms, not *jure gentium* defined legal entities. In fact, the aforementioned terms are not *de jure* realities in most nation-states. When one speaks of law, one is usually referring to case law (court-ordered and enacted or created by court interpretation), administrative law (law created by executive order or fiat), statutory law (legislative-initiated and enacted), or *jure gentium* law (law by international convention or treaty). The terms *skyjacking* and *air hijacking* are pseudolegal terms, media inventions that describe other criminal interventions, such as piracy, kidnapping, and hijacking. The term *piracy* does exist as a *jure gentium* legal entity, and the term *hijacking* exists as a statutory offense in most, if not all, nation-states.

> Article 101 of the Informal Composite Negotiating Text of the Law of the Sea Conference defines the crime [of piracy] as consisting of any illegal acts of violence, detention or . . . deprivation committed for private ends by the crew or the passengers of a private ship or private aircraft . . . against a ship or aircraft (Hikadish, 1983:905).

Hikadish, a legal expert on piracy and aircraft interventions notes:

> Although aircraft hijacking is a form of piracy, the unusually strong worldwide reaction to unlawful seizures of aircraft caused the offense to become a separate international crime. As defined, the crime consists of the seizure or destruction of aircraft, the placing of a destructive device in an aircraft, the damaging of air navigation facilities, or interference with the operation of or communication to an aircraft. These prohibitions are found in three conventions on [according to Hikadish] air piracy [i.e., sky-jacking] that were signed in 1963, 1970 and 1971. The United States is a signatory to these conventions and had incorporated their provisions into law" (Hikadish, 1983:905).

Although different *jure gentium* and *de jure* definitions of piracy exist and will be discussed in detail later in this chapter, most *jure gentium* definitions of piracy involve the seizure of a private vessel by another private vessel or by on-board offenders over or in international waters or air space for private gain (i.e., a profit motive), with the offender vessel not being a military or police vehicle or a vessel of a recognized nation-state. Thus, the basic motivation for piracy appears to be profit, not politics. Piracy shares this apparent profit motive with the legal definitions of *hijacking*, which note that hijacking includes "to take by force goods or merchandise being transported. . . . Many passenger-carrying airplanes have been hijacked and forced to fly to a foreign country that was not the original destination" (Martin and Astone, 1980:127).

Jure Gentium Definitions of *Air Piracy* and the Issues of Jurisdiction and Enforcement

Professor D. H. N. Johnson notes that "International law . . . is mainly concerned with the questions when a State should exercise jurisdiction and when it should not. It cannot compel States to exercise jurisdiction when they lack power to do so under their own laws. . . . " (1965: 77). Johnson notes that the purpose of international law "is to say when a State may exercise jurisdiction and when it may not, not to deal with possible conflicts of jurisdiction" (Johnson, 1965:76) — in other words, concurrent jurisdiction. The issue of sovereign nation-states engaging in air piracy, a possible form of terror, centers upon this issue of *jure gentium* jurisdiction. There are five *jure gentium* principles of jurisdiction:

1. The *Active Nationality Principle*, the concept that "each State may . . . punish crimes committed anywhere by its own nationals; this principle is in [no] way controversial" (Johnson, 1965:75).
2. The *Territorial Principle*, "the concept that each State may punish crimes committed on its own territory, whether by its own nationals or by foreigners" (Johnson, 1965:75). This principle is in no way controversial.
3. The *Passive Nationality Principle*, which notes that the claiming nation-states "arrogate to themselves the right to punish crimes, wherever committed, of which their own nationals are victims . . . " (Johnson, 1965:75). Claimed by some nation-states, this principle is highly controversial.

4. The *Universal Principle,* which "authorizes all States to punish crimes of a heinous nature which threaten the international community as a whole (Johnson, 1965:76).
5. The *Protective Principle,* which declares that "States may punish crimes, wherever commited, which directly threaten their own security" (Johnson, 1965:76).

Nation-states such as the United States, South Africa, and Israel claim the Universal Jurisdiction Principle when interdicting air pirates (whom they label terrorists or air hijackers) because traditional piracy is viewed as a heinous act that threatens the international community as a whole. Nation-states have frequently used the Active Nationality Principle to punish their own nationals apprehended for various criminal offenses commited upon the territory of allied or client-states; the Territorial Principle to punish the apprehended nationals of other nation-states who have committed felony offenses on vessels bearing the claimant nation-state's flag; and the Universal and Protective Principles to punish the nationals of enemy nation-states. In addition, Israel and South Africa have frequently relied upon the highly disputed Passive Nationality Principle in order to strike at alleged Palestinian and African National Congress guerrillas, respectively, or the base camps for such guerrilla organizations located in neighboring nation-states. The jurisdiction principle used is largely determined by where the felony offense occurred, and whether the site of the occurrence—or the current site of the residence, training camp, or base camp of the offender—is in a friendly or hostile nation-state. The key problem with all *jure gentium* enforcement is that only signatory nation-states are obligated to obey an agreement or jurisdictional mandate. Nonsignatories must be controlled by international behavior designed to limit their mobility, access or rights.

Civil Aviation Security and the International Scene: The Treaties

The term *air piracy* is similar to the terms *terrorism* and *ghetto* in that all three are media darlings used promiscuously to describe a myriad of behavior. However, according to the renowned international law scholar Joyner, traditional piracy as a *jure gentium* reality must be: "(1) . . . adequate in degree . . . (2) committed on the high seas as opposed to similar acts committed within some state's territorial jurisdiction. . . . (3) The offenders, at the time of the commission of the act, should be, in fact, free from lawful authority . . . [and thus be] in the predicament of outlaws." Joyner also notes (1974:236) that traditional "piracy *jure gen-*

tium is predicated upon indiscriminate plunder by a private (i.e., pirate) vessel against commercial vessels on the high seas," and it involves an attack by a private vessel, not a public warship (1974:240). Joyner's definition of piracy is based upon Article 15 (and, to a lesser extent, Article 16) of the Convention on the High Seas (Geneva, 1958). Articles 15 and 16 of this convention specifically declare:

Article 15

Piracy consists of any of the following acts:

1. Any illegal acts of violence, detention or any act of depredation, committed for private ends by the crew or the passengers of a private ship or a private aircraft, and directed:

   (1) On the high seas, against another ship or aircraft, or against persons or property on board such ship or aircraft;

   (2) Against a ship, aircraft, persons or property in a place outside the jurisdiction of any State;

2. Any act of voluntary participation in the operation of a ship or of an aircraft with knowledge of facts making it a pirate ship or aircraft;

3. Any act of inciting or of intentionally facilitating an act described in sub-paragraph 1 or sub-paragraph 2 of this article.

Article 16

The acts of piracy, as defined in article 15, committed by a warship, government ship or government aircraft whose crew has mutinied and taken control of the ship or aircraft are assimilated to acts committed by a private ship.

It is important to note that the Geneva Convention was not a true aviation convention concerned with civil aviation security. Even so, its definition of piracy does introduce the *jure gentium* concept of air piracy, thus removing it from the arena of media hyperbole.

The three true aviation conventions focusing on civil aviation security and criminal acts have been:

1. *The Tokyo Convention on Offenses and Certain Other Acts Committed on Board Aircraft* (Tokyo, 1963). Signed in Tokyo on September

14, 1963, this convention came into force on December 4, 1969. The United States ratified the Tokyo Convention on June 30, 1969, thus being the twelfth state to do so. According to a U.S. Federal Aviation Administration (FAA) fact sheet, the basic purpose of this convention was to "promote safety through the establishment of continuity of jurisdiction among the contracting States over acts occurring on board aircraft. Article 11 deals with hijacking and provides: (a) positive obligation on each contracting State to take every appropriate measure to restore control to, or preserve control in, the lawful commander of an aircraft; and (b) an obligation on contracting States to permit the passengers and crew of a hijacked aircraft to continue their journey as soon as practicable, and to return the aircraft and its cargo to the persons lawfully entitled to possession" (Federal Aviation Administration).

2. *The Hague Convention for the Suppression of the Unlawful Seizure of Aircraft* (Hague, 1970). This convention was signed at the Hague on December 16, 1970 and came into force on October 14, 1971. The United States ratified the Hague Convention on 14th September 1971, thus being the tenth state to do so. According to the FAA, "This treaty obliges the contracting parties to: (a) establish jurisdiction over hijackers; (b) make the offense punishable by severe penalties; and (c) submit any offenders found in their territories to the competent authorities for prosecution, or extradite them. . . . The U.S. implemented this convention by enactment of Public Law 93-366 (Antihijacking Act of 1974) on August 5, 1974" (Federal Aviation Administration).

3. *The Montreal Convention for the Suppression of Unlawful Acts Against the Safety of Civil Aviation* (Montreal, 1971). This convention was signed in Montreal on September 23, 1971 and came into force on January 26, 1973. "The U.S. ratified the Montreal Convention on November 1, 1972 . . . [and] implemented [it] on October 12, 1984 by Part B of Chapter 20 of Title II of Public Law 98-473 Aircraft Sabotage Act. This treaty deals with sabotage and armed attacks against international civil aviation facilities and creates the same obligations with respect to these offenses as the Hague Convention creates with respect to hijacking" (Federal Aviation Administration).

It is important to note that none of the three conventions concerned with civil aviation security used the terms *pirate* or *air piracy,* and all three skillfully avoided any terminology that would associate or identify the offending agent or vessel as a legal representative of a *jure gentium* recognized nation-state. They thus limit the applicability of these conventions to outlaw agents acting without the flag of a *jure gentium* recognized nation-state. The inapplicability of these conventions to an agent acting in the name of a *jure gentium* recognized nation-state is similar to the legal parameters established under the Convention on the High Seas (Geneva, 1958), which entered into force on September 30, 1962.

Aircraft Hijacking: Categories and Motivations

An examination of typical aircraft hijacking categories results in the following list (Aggarwala, 1971:585; Clyne, 1973:183):

1. Criminals or suspects fleeing (i.e., escaping) from the law
2. Mentally disturbed persons
3. Persons who see hijacking as their only means of escape from a particular political or social system
4. Political militants who hijack aircraft for the purpose of political blackmail
5. Those who hijack for money
6. A nonpolitical criminal attempting to get to a specific location (a transit rather than escape situation)
7. An expressively suicidal individual dedicated to killing and being killed
8. A political extremist seeking media coverage and publicity for a specific cause or organization

Thus, the typical motivations for air-hijacking appear to be (Wilkinson, 1977:208; Crelinsten and Szabo, 1979:14 – 15; Joyner, 1974:204 – 208):

1. Advertisement of a cause
2. Demand for international attention
3. Securing important tactical gains for the terrorist
4. An attack on a symbol of the affluent and powerful capitalist ruling class
5. Proof that anyone and anything is vulnerable to attack
6. Kidnapping for ransom, extortion, and escape
7. Kidnapping of political personalities for political ends
8. Kidnapping for facilitating escape
9. Securing of a vehicle for escape

10. Illegal restraint upon the active victim to facilitate commission of an infraction
11. Establishing a bond between active and passive victims
12. Expression of "expressive suicidal" tendencies by the emotionally unbalanced or mentally disturbed
13. Expression of a desire for personal attention
14. Avenge of a defeat
15. Demand for the release of a fellow terrorist from the custody of another individual, organization, or nation-state
16. Discontent with the policies of the nation-state from which the aircraft originated or in which the hijacker boarded
17. Political asylum
18. Dropping of political leaflets
19. Supplying comrades, refugees or others the hijackers identify with
20. Using the aircraft as a bargaining counter

The typical motivation and categorization of air hijackers and air hijacking does not appear to explain the sociopolitical behavior of nation-state interceptions and redirections. However, if one assumes that terror is simply (1) an extension of the implementation of state power and (2) a form of low-intensity, unconventional warfare, the motivation behind state terrorism via interceptions and redirections is comprehensible. Any threat against an unarmed aircraft must be viewed by the pilot of the threatened aircraft as a mortal threat. Even the least sophisticated airborne armament system (and to great extent land based armament system) must be viewed as mortally serious. Thus, minor military powers become regional powers for the duration of an incident. The unarmed aircraft can neither outdistance nor outgun the threatening agent.

In the case of the U.S. interception of the Egyptian Boeing 737, the U.S. interception and redirection was an obvious, self-proclaimed act by the United States to secure custody of the Palestinian hijackers of the Italian cruiseship Achilles Lauro and the alleged murderers of U.S. citizen Leon Klinghoffer. The United States cited its alleged right and obligation to bring the Palestinian gunmen of the Abu Abbas faction of the Palestine Liberation Front (PLF) to justice under the stipulations of the Hague Convention and the *jure gentium* jurisdictional rights of the highly controversial Passive Nationality Principle and the noncontroversial Universal Principle. The United States claimed that the Egyptian pledge to deliver the Abu Abbas PLF gunmen to the custody of the Arafat-dominated Palestine Liberation Organization (PLO) headquarters in Tunis violated the Hague Convention (which demands severe penalties for the unlawful seizure of aircraft) and that this Hague principle was applicable to unlawful seizures of vessels on the High Seas (The Geneva Convention, Article 15). Although, the U.S. *jure gentium* position is interesting, it may not be legal. Egypt is not a signatory of the Hague Convention. Egypt vociferously accused the United States of air piracy and noted that it had acted in the spirit of the Hague convention by its intention to release the Abbu Abbas PLF gunmen to the custody of the PLO. The PLO had vociferously condemned the hijacking and the alleged murder of Leon Klinghoffer, noting that in November 1985 the PLO had announced it would limit its military operations to within the borders of the nation-state of Israel and Israeli-occupied territories. Furthermore, the PLO had conducted executions of PLO gunmen who had conducted military operations without the authority of the PLO.

The U.S. downing of Iranian Airbus Flight 655 presents another intriguing dilemma for the United States. The United States claims that its downing of the Iranian Airbus was an unfortunate case of mistaken identity and mistaken intent — of a civilian aircraft which refused to identify itself or to deviate (i.e., redirect) from a path that appeared to threaten the U.S. Aegis cruiser U.S.S. Vincennes. U.S. presence in the Arabian Sea at the time of this incident was predicated primarily upon its interpretation of the Universal Jurisdiction Principle applied to the U.N. Convention on the Law of the Sea (adopted on April 30, 1982, opened for signature on December 10, 1982, and signed by the United States on December 10, 1982. The U.S. claim, based on this treaty, was that civilian merchant transit had the right of unimpeded transit through, or within, the Arabian Sea.

If one examines the Israeli, Soviet, Iraqi, or Sudanese interceptions and redirections or downings of civilian aircraft (or South African redirections and interceptions and alleged involvement in the redirection and involvement in the crash of the Mozambican government plane on October 19, 1986, which resulted in the death of Mozambican President Samora Moises Machel), one notes that all of these republics have relied upon the *jure gentium* Universal Jurisdictional Principle. On the other hand, Israel and the United States have relied upon the Passive Nationality Principle as justification for the interdiction of nonmilitary aircraft while allegedly in "hot pursuit" of terrorists. The centrality of the political motivation behind these flagged-vessel interceptions of civilian aircraft highlights one of the numerous problems associated with the current *jure gentium* definitions of air hijacking and air piracy.

The Need to Revise the *Jure Gentium* Definitions of Piracy, Air Piracy, Hijacking, and Air Hijacking

The *de jure* definitions of piracy, hijacking, air piracy and air hijack-ing have traditionally included a profit motive and excluded the actions of legal, flagged representatives of *jure gentium* nation-states acting within the official purview of their military statutory function. These aforementioned criminal offenses have traditionally involved at least two vessels and—in the case of piracy—the unlawful actions of the of-fender vessel or the legal actions of the victimized vessel. Moreover, these violations originate within international waters or air space, or from one or both vessels being within international waters or airspace at the time of the criminal event. However, the reality of contemporary military technology and electronic surveillance and guidance systems negate the necessity of a confrontation involving two or more vessels. Contemporary ground-to-air defense systems and electronic guidance and surveillance systems now make it possible for land-based military forces to intercept and redirect noncombatant aircraft under threat of destruction. It is not necessary for a vessel to confront another vessel directly, nor is it necessary to board another vessel in order to seize and redirect it. The extension of state power via armed threat or direct com-bat now extends into the arena of unconventional, low-intensity war-fare. Contemporary nation-states have used their official militaries to intercept, redirect, and occasionally destroy civilian aircraft or un-armed government aircraft of nonbelligerent nation-states. The current definitions of piracy, air piracy, hijacking and air hijacking—which note the profit motive and the violent or threatening posture of gunmen aligned to no *jure gentium* nation-state—is only partially applicable to the current reality of civil aviation security. Contemporary nation-states have intentionally interfered with the lawful transit of noncombatant civil and government aircraft, allegedly in the pursuit of terrorists or in the name of the *jure gentium* jurisdictional principles of Universality and Passive Nationality.

Quite simply, the Convention on the High Seas (Geneva, 1958), the Convention on Offenses and Certain Other Acts Committed on Board Aircraft (Tokyo, 1963), the Convention for the Suppression of the Unlawful Seizure of Aircraft (Hague, 1970), and the Convention for the Suppression of Unlawful Acts Against the Safety of Civil Aviation (Montreal, 1971) are antiquated. The 'two vessel concept,' the profit mo-tive, and armed intervention are as antiquated as the previously cited conventions. The 1980s have ushered in an era of official, state terrorism —i.e., terror via direct violence or the threat of violence for a political purpose — as well as the reality of nation-states possibly interfering with the navigation systems of noncombatant aircraft (as in the possible South African involvement in the death of Mozambican President

Samora Machel. A new civil aviation security convention is needed in order to deter terror (i.e., official, or state terrorism) via sea-, air-, or land-based military forces as well as via electronic interference (i.e., intervention) with the navigation system of noncombatant aircraft.

An essential element of any true act of terrorism or terror is the bond between the primary (active) victim and the secondary (passive) victim. The motivation behind true political terrorism or true terror is political advantage — i.e., the extension or restraint of state power by instilling an environment permeated by fear. Thus, the motivation is political gain, not monetary or private financial reward. Were the recent Israeli and U.S. interceptions, redirections, and downings *terror?* From this author's perspective, the only logical answer is Yes. The apparent intent of the Israeli interventions was not the mere capture of wanted criminals (labeled terrorists by Israel and its allies), but the delivery of a message to the Palestinian resistance and the Palestinian people in general. The message was that Israel will allow no safe quarter for terrorists, regardless of their mode of attempted escape. Israeli security forces will strike out whenever and wherever they deem necessary to protect Israeli citizens (the Passive Nationality Principle) and Israeli national integrity and national security (the Protective Principle), even if allegedly innocent individuals are harmed or killed. Innocent people must not allow themselves to be used as shields for terrorists, because Israel will not honor such shields. Israel's message is clear: You need fear Israeli military might more than the spasmatic Palestinian or Islamic fundamentalist-inspired violence. Israel can be neutral, friend, or foe, but fear or ethnically induced neutrality that victimizes or endangers Israeli citizens or national security will not be tolerated, no matter what the price in blood and suffering.

The U.S. downing of the Air Iran Flight 655 appears to have been an unfortunate American overreaction, not legitimately labeled an act of terror or terrorism. There obviously was no intervictim bond. However, a geopolitically cynical application of the *jure gentium* Universal Jurisdiction Principle to include free, unimpeded transit within a war zone certainly increased the likelihood of the occurrence of such a disaster. The interception and redirection of the Egypt Air Boeing 737, in this author's opinion, serves as an ideal case study for the need to redefine the terms *official or state terrorism* and *air piracy* or *air hijacking* to include the acts of flagged vessels acting within the purview of their statutory function. The U.S. message was essentially the same as that delivered repeatedly by Israel and South Africa to their enemies as well as to those who might willingly, or unwillingly, shield such enemies: The enemy may run, but it cannot hide. The enemy cannot shield itself behind the innocent, nor can it hide behind the niceties of a civilian or non-combatant label. The intervictim bond was distinct: The passive victims in the U.S.-Iranian tragedy were the alleged PLF terrorists and the Egyptian aircraft and its crew; the active victims were the Egyptian government, the PLO, and the amorphous Palestinian resistance in general. Does the U.S. action constitute an act of air piracy, air-hijacking, or terror via rational, objective, and revised contemporary definitions of air piracy and terror which include political motivation and the use of flagged vessels acting within the purview of their statutory military or police function in pursuance of state power? Yes.

References

Aggarwala, N.
1971   Political Aspects of Hijacking. *Air Hijacking: An International Perspective.* New York: Carnegie Endowment for International Peace. November (No. 585).

Chomsky, N.
1986   *Pirates and Emperors: International Terrorism in the Real World.* New York: Claremont Research & Publications.

Clyne, P.
1973   *An Anatomy of Skyjacking.* London: Intertext Publishing Limited.

Crelinsten, R. D. and Szabo, D.
1979   *Hostage-Taking.* Lexington, MA: Heath.

Federal Aviation Administration
No date   Memorandum on Civil Aviation Security. Washington, DC: FAA

Geneva
1958   Convention on the High Seas.

Hague
1970   Convention for the Suppression of the Unlawful Seizure of Aircraft.

Hikadish, S. (ed.)
1983   *The Encyclopedia of Crime and Justice.* New York: Collier Macmillan.

Jenkins, B. M.
1980   The Study of Terrorism: Definitional Issues. *Rand Corporation Monographs.* December: P-6363.

Johnson, D. H. N.
1965   *Rights in Airspace.* Dobbs Ferry, New York: Oceana Publications.

Joyner, N. D.
1974 *Aerial Hijacking as an International Crime.* Dobbs Ferry, New York: Oceana Publications.

Martin, J. A. and Astone, N. A.
1980 *Criminal Justice Vocabulary.* Springfield, Illinois: Charles C. Thomas.

Montreal
1971 Convention for the Suppression of Unlawful Acts Against the Safety of Civil Aviation.

Mozambique Embassy
1988 Oral Conversation with U.S. Information Officer. October 20.

National Advisory Committee on Criminal Justice Standards and Goals
1976 *Report of the Task Force on Disorders and Terrorism.* Washington, DC: Government Printing Office.

New York Times
1988 *The New York Times Index,* vol. 75.

Tokyo
1963 Convention on Offenses and Certain Other Acts Committed on Board Aircraft.

New York
1982 U.N. Convention on the Law of the Sea.

New York
1985 U.N. Convention on the Law of the Sea: Final Act.

Vice President's Task Force on Combating Terrorism
1986 *Public Report of the Vice President's Task Force on Combating Terrorism.* Washington, DC: Government Printing Office.

Wilkinson, Paul
1977 *Terrorism and the Liberal State.* New York: Wiley.

6

The Abandoned Ones: A History of the Oakdale and Atlanta Prison Riots*

Mark S. Hamm

Introduction

On Friday, November 20, 1987, Tom Brokaw reported on the NBC *Nightly News* that a treaty had been signed in Mexico City between the United States and Cuba concerning the repatriation of Cuban inmates under custody of the Federal Bureau of Prisons (BOP). For most viewers, Brokaw's report meant very little. After all, what did it mean to "repatriate" a convicted criminal from a communist country? Even if we knew, who really cared?

Yet, within minutes of this televised announcement, a drunken Cuban detainee at the federal detention center in Oakdale, Louisiana staggered into the prison dining room, threw his food on the floor, and then hurled his empty food tray into the forehead of a food service supervisor. This act of violence, declared the detainee, was a protest against the repatriation treaty. Exhilarated by this spontaneous demonstration of outrage, nearly one hundred Cuban detainees in the dining room — equally frustrated by the new accord — began throwing their food, trays, silverware, and salt and pepper shakers against the walls of the cafeteria. This situation was quickly stifled by BOP staff, and the Cubans were returned to their housing units without further incident.

Twenty-four hours later (at 6:50 P.M., November 21), approximately 250 Cuban detainees gathered in the center of the Oakdale compound. From beneath their prison-issue coats and jackets, they suddenly pulled rocks, clubs, and baseball bats. In unison, this group began chanting, *somos los abandonados''* ("We are the abandoned ones"), as they charged toward the front gate of the Oakdale facility. In the meantime, another group of detainees broke into the prison's mechanical services building and armed themselves with fire axes and picks. Still another group ran onto the prison yard with homemade machetes and began chasing and capturing staff as hostages. At 7:15, hundreds of detainees went on a rampage — breaking windows, hurling rocks, and setting fires. By 8:30, they had captured twenty-eight hostages and destroyed ten of the fourteen prison buildings. By 9:00, the Cubans had control of Oakdale.

On Sunday, November 22, negotiations began in earnest between the Cubans and BOP officials. At about 9:30 P.M., detainee representatives were called to the front gate by Oakdale administrators and offered a plan to end the takeover. The detainees were handed a photocopy of a letter from Attorney General Edwin Meese proposing an ''indefinite moratorium'' on repatriations to Cuba in exchange for the hostages. The detainees said, in effect, that they would sleep on it.

These events were reported by the print and broadcast media over the weekend of the November 21 – 22. Among the media's audience were 1,394 Cuban detainees at the federal penitentiary in Atlanta, Georgia. When these inmates were turned out for their work assignments on Monday morning (November 23), they began gathering in small groups to discuss the Oakdale disturbance and the implications of the repatriation treaty. At about 10:30 A.M., a group of detainees started a fire in the institution's Federal Prison Industries shop (UNICOR). Concomitantly, a second group of detainees raced out of the dining room and began overpowering staff in the prison yard. A third group started to take staff as hostages in the UNICOR building and the dining room. Hundreds of Cubans then exited the UNICOR building brandishing boards, homemade machetes, clubs, chains, blowtorches, and bolt cutters. They joined the detainees who had captured staff on the prison yard, taking radios and keys from staff and handcuffing staff members with their own handcuffs.

At this point, tower guards opened fire on the Cubans. One detainee was shot in the head and killed. Twelve others were struck by gunfire, leaving them painfully wounded on the ground. After this, guards withheld their fire because detainees threatened to slit the throat of a hostage if the shooting did not stop. Within a matter of minutes, the detainees had successfully captured 102 hostages and destroyed the huge UNICOR factory. By noon, almost all of the penitentiary had been seized by the Cubans with what one hostage later described as ''military precision.''

At 1:00 P.M., a BOP lieutenant made contact with several detainees by radio and began negotiations. A lone Cuban leader was permitted to enter the main corridor of the prison for a discussion with Atlanta administrators. The detainee was given a photocopy of Attorney General Meese's letter promising a moratorium on deportations to Cuba in exchange for the hostages. Like the detainees at Oakdale, however, the inmate leader said that the Cuban population in Atlanta did not believe in Meese's assurances, and they were unwilling to release the hostages at that time.[1]

So began the longest siege in the history of American penology. The Oakdale takeover lasted nine days (until November 29); and the Atlanta rebellion lasted eleven days (until December 4). During this time, hostages were subjected to intense psychological torture as the demands issued by the Cubans shifted and wavered through the negotiation process. Two things, however, remained perfectly clear throughout the crisis. First, the detainees were ready to die in American prisons rather than be deported to Cuba. Second, they had no faith in the U.S. government's plan to end the long and difficult seige.

The purpose of this chapter is to examine this unique political consciousness. Who were these "Abandoned Ones?" Why had they come to the United States in the first place? What crimes had they committed to end up in federal penitentiaries? And, most importantly, what caused them to so violently oppose deportation to their homeland and to so adamantly reject the offers of Attorney General Meese?

Background: The Freedom Flotilla of 1980

The 2,400 inmates involved in the rebellions at Oakdale and Atlanta came to the United States primarily on shrimp and lobster fishing boats as part of the Freedom Flotilla which brought more than 120,000 refugees to the United States from the tiny port city of Mariel, Cuba between April and June 1980. These people (soon to be called "Mariel Cubans" or "Marielitos") came to the United States as a result of an intricate set of factors related to economic, social, and political developments occuring in Cuba during the late 1970s and the early months of 1980.

Essentially, a complex set of forces interacted to 'push' Cubans out of their country. These forces included increased unemployment, demographic shifts, natural disaster, spectacular increases in educational opportunities for Cuban women, increased incentives for work on behalf of Cuban women (e.g., more durable consumer goods), food and housing shortages, declining prices on the world sugar market, and a growing unwillingness on the part of international banks to extend credit to Fidel Castro because of his government's military activities in Angola and Ethiopia. In addition, certain social and political forces operated as 'pull factors' in the mass exodus. These included the normalization of visitation permits granted Cuban-Americans and the passage of the U.S. Refugee Act of 1980 (Betancourt and Dizard, 1984; Brundenius, 1984; Mesa-Lago 1978; Sklar, 1984, Winn, 1980; Womack, 1980).

U.S. reaction to the Freedom Flotilla was mixed. On the one hand, President Jimmy Carter said during the early days of the sealift:

We'll continue to provide an open heart and open arms to refugees seeking freedom from Communist domination, brought about primarily by Fidel Castro and his government (*The New York Times*, 1980).

On the other hand, many refugees soon found themselves in what has been described as "an Orwellian purgatory with little chance of escape in which the United States government took the position that as a matter of law, the Mariel Cubans were not really here" (Leshaw, 1988:2). This "matter of law" was primarily shaped by the political ramifications of the Freedom Flotilla itself.

Politics and the Freedom Flotilla: The Making of a Myth

During the second week of the boatlift, U.S. Immigration and Naturalization Service (INS) officials at Key West, Florida began to notice Cuban men who were "more hardened and rougher in appearance" than men who had come on earlier arrivals (Sklar, 1984:70). Because of their appearance, the INS concluded that the Cuban government was taking advantage of the immigration accord and emptying Cuba's prisons of hard-core criminals. The Carter White House endorsed this line of reasoning, and on May 14th President Carter accused the Cuban government of "taking hardened criminals out of prison and mental patients out of hospitals and forcing boat captains to take them to the United States" (U.S. Department of State, 1980a:70-1).

The Cuban government denied such a deliberate policy. On May 19, President Castro characterized the refugees as simply "anti-social lumpen" (socially displaced individuals) and "anti-government reactionaries" who were making the decision to leave Cuba of their own accord. Castro further explained that mentally ill persons on the boatlift were there because family members in the United States had requested their passage through Mariel (Sklar, 1984). Fidel Castro made no additional comment about the Mariel people during 1980.

Analysts in the United States, however, overlooked Castro's simple description of the Mariel refugees in favor of the more derogatory picture offered by the Carter administration. Essays began to appear in the U.S. press accusing Castro of saying that the Mariel people were "murderers, vagrants, and homosexuals." Moreover, Castro had branded them all *"escoria"* ("scum") (*Newsweek*, 1980a; *U.S. News & World Report*, 1980a and 1980b; Hunt 1980; Mayer, 1980; Winn, 1980). Although official INS relocation figures would later refute this pejorative description of the Mariel Cubans, the damage had already been done. That is, the collective imagination of the Carter administration and the U.S. press brought into being the belief that a number of Mariel Cubans were dangerous people who could not be trusted in the United States or any other land.

This popular myth served an important purpose for the Carter White House. By making Castro appear as if he were using the Freedom Flotilla as a giant 'drudge drain' for his society's ills, then the 'real cause' of the mass exodus could be exposed—the moral failure of Cuban socialism. Under such a strategy, communism became an easy target for criticism, and it was sure to be an issue in the forthcoming presidential race between Carter and the conservative California statesman Ronald Reagan.

Resettlement in America

Despite Jimmy Carter's humanitarian interests in the Mariel people, the U.S. State Department (under the direction of Cyrus Vance) held that the Mariel sealift was unlawful and that refugees were technically illegal aliens. Under the terms of the Refugee Act of 1980, illegal aliens could, however, be admitted to the United States as "excludable entrants." As applied to the Freedom Flotilla, this meant that the Mariels were technically not really in the United States because they lacked valid passports or visas. Because they lacked this necessary documentation, the Refugee Act stipulated that all excludable entrants be processed and screened by government officials before they be allowed to actually relocate in America (U.S. Department of State, 1980b; Minneapolis Lawyer's Human Rights Committee, 1986). Such precautions were necessary, said Representative Elizabeth Holtzman (head of the House Subcommittee on INS activities), because "as many as 700 ex-convicts had been rounded up by the Cuban government and given a choice of going to the United States or back to jail" (*Newsweek*, 1980b).

In accordance with the law, the INS established relocation camps in Miami, Key West, Elgin Air Force Base, and Fort Walton Beach, Florida; Fort McCoy, Wisconsin; Fort Indiantown Gap, Pennsylvania; and Fort Chafee, Arkansas to process the Cuban aliens. In strict adherence to the 1980 Refugee Act, each Cuban underwent a medical examination (complete with x-rays and lab tests) and interviews with members of the INS, the Federal Bureau of Investigation (FBI), the Pentagon, and the Central Intelligence Agency (CIA). If an alien was determined to pose no threat to the safety of the U.S. public, then he or she was placed on parole by the INS, with the stipulation that if aliens remained free of law violations for seven years, they would become eligible for permanent U.S. citizenship. If they were convicted of a crime during those seven years, however, they would be deported back to Cuba (U.S. Department of State, 1980c; *U.S. News & World Report*, 1980c; Minnesota Lawyers Human Rights Committee, 1986).

The tremendous daily flow of Cubans into the relocation camps, however, made the policy of case-by-case review nearly impossible. By June 1, 1980, more than seventy thousand Mariels were backed up in these camps waiting to be relocated. Many — who had arrived in the United States tired, seasick, and with no personal belongings beyond the clothes on their backs—began to complain about weeks of boredom and their "burning impatience" to be reunited with loved ones (*Ibid.;* see also *U.S. News & World Report*, 1980d; *Newsweek*, 1980c).

The Fort Chafee Incident

On June 6, 1980, nearly one thousand anxious and weary Mariel Cubans went on a rampage at the Fort Chafee relocation camp, burning five wooden Army buildings and storming through the front gates toward a confrontation with the Arkansas State Police. This riot lasted two hours and resulted in one refugee dead, forty refugees seriously injured, and fifteen state troopers who filed for disability benefits (U.S. Department of State, 1980a; Hoeffel, 1980; *Newsweek*, 1980d). Consistent with the Carter campaign strategy, presidential press secretary Jody Powell said on June 7 that "evidence exists to show that Fidel Castro exported to the United States some hardened criminals" (Sklar, 1984:32).

Two days later, Jimmy Carter ordered expulsion proceedings against the riot's ringleaders and then sent one thousand troopers of the Eighty-second Airborne Division to stand guard over Mariels at the Indiantown Gap facility. Meanwhile, INS officials began to streamline their review process, often reviewing as many as five hundred restless refugees in a single day (*Time*, 1980; *Newsweek* 1980d). By October, nearly all of the Mariels had been processed and the camps were closed down.

Armed with 20/20 hindsight, two important lessons were learned. First, there were serious problems with implementing the Refugee Act of 1980. The INS had simply not been equipped to effectively deal with a mass migration like the Mariel boatlift. Contributing to this problem,

the times were not right for an 'open hearts and open arms' policy. In
1980, America was drifting into an economic recession. Many Americans were troubled by an oil crisis, and some had begun to hear about
plant closings. Moreover, Americans did not especially want to invite
one percent of the entire population of Cuba to come live in their country during the summer of 1980 (*Newsweek*, 1980e).

Second, it was clear that the Mariel Cubans did not hold up well
under indefinite terms of confinement in relocations camps. In less than
two weeks, the Cubans had incurred the wrath of the President and his
Eighty-second Division. The internment of Mariel Cubans had became
a serious concern among high-ranking U.S. military base commanders
and federal prison wardens.[2]

The Relocation Figures

Of the 120,737 illegal Cuban aliens processed in 1980 by INS,
119,081 were immediately placed on parole and passed along to private
relief groups in Miami; Los Angeles; Phoenix; Chicago; New York City
and Rochester, New York; and West New York and Union City, New Jersey. These community groups worked to reunite exiles with relatives
and otherwise facilitated the resettlement of the Mariel people in America (Sklar, 1984; *Time*, 1980c).

The INS also identified 1,306 aliens who had questionable backgrounds,, and they were sent to various federal correctional institutions
for further questioning and observation. Evenually, nearly all of them
were paroled (*Ibid.*). The remaining 350 Cubans—*less than one-half of one
percent of the entire Freedom Flotilla*—were found to have serious criminal
backgrounds. These Cubans were transferred to the federal penitentiary at Talladega, Alabama to serve indefinite prison terms (Chandler,
1987; Dolman, 1986; *The New Republic*, 1980; *Time*, 1981; U.S. Department of State, 1980b).[3] Upon processing into the Talladega facility, aliens
were told their release "would be determined by their behavior in
prison over the course of the next several months" (Shepard, 1987:6B).
This policy would later cause great anguish among thousands of Mariels who failed to follow the conditions of their parole in America.

Rates of Incarceration for Mariels: 1980 – 1987

The overwhelming majority of Mariel Cubans handled resettlement in America quite well. In a news conference held on December 11,
1987, U.S. Deputy Attorney General Arnold I. Burns declared that "approximately 117,400 refugees [or 97 percent of the original Mariel pop-
ulation] had become productive, law-abiding members of their communities." "However," continued Burns, "7,600 Cubans had violated

the conditions of parole" over the seven year period, and they had been "placed in prisons or detention facilities supervised by federal or state authorities" (Burns, 1987:1).

Because of their status as excludable entrants, these 7,600 parole violators were excluded from constitutional rights to due process. Under the terms of the Refugee Act of 1980, excludable entrants had no more rights than persons stopped at a U.S. border. Excludable entrants on parole were therefore entitled to no hearing rights and their paroles would be revoked at any time. In other words, paroles could be revoked at the pleasure of the government, and parolees were not entitled to hearings of the charges being brought against them (Eig, 1986; Pirie, 1986).

Numerous accounts indicate that paroles were revoked and Mariels were imprisoned because they lacked no visible means of support, a fixed address, or an American sponsor. Other Mariels wound up in prison for violating curfew or travel restrictions, or for failing to participate in various government relocation programs. The case of Pedro Prior Rodriguez exemplifies this type of violation.

In 1983, while living in a halfway house in Rochester, New York, Prior was mugged on a city street and taken to a local hospital for treatment of an eye injury. INS officials revoked Prior's parole on the grounds that he could not afford specialized medical care, and then sent him not to an eye specialist but to a mental hospital. The mental hospital did not employ an eye specialist, so Prior was transferred to the federal penitentiary in Atlanta, where he was treated and given a glass eye in November 1983. Having committed no crime in the United States, Prior remained locked up in Atlanta until the riot of 1987 (Golden, 1987; *ABC Nightline*, 1987).

Other Mariel parolees were sent to prison for minor infractions such as driving without a license, shoplifting, or possession of small amounts of marijuana or cocaine. One such parolee, Rafael Ferrer, arrived at the Atlanta penitentiary on March 19, 1984 after pleading guilty to possession of three grams of cocaine. Like other Mariels, Ferrer was indefinitely detained until his prison behavior warranted release. Like Prior, Ferrer took part in the Atlanta Rebellion which occurred three years later (Dwyer, 1987).

Some parole violators wound up in federal prisons after they had already completed sentences in city lockups. In 1984, for example, Guzman Gonzalez was convicted of strong armed robbery by a Miami court. He received and served a one-year jail sentence for this crime. Upon release, Gonzalez was rearrested by INS officials and sent to the Atlanta penitentiary. In 1986, he was transferred to the Oakdale detention center to await placement in a BOP halfway house. Gonzalez was patiently awaiting his halfway house placement when the Oakdale riot broke out in November 1987 (Chandler, 1987; Leshaw, 1988).

To be sure, over the seven-year period (1980–1987), a number of Cuban parolees were said to have committed serious crimes in the United States. The Reagan administration estimated that "about one-fourth of the Cuban detainees in Oakdale and Atlanta at the time of the riots [approximately 600] had been convicted of crimes of violence including murder, kidnapping, sexual assault, robbery, and arson" (Burns, 1987:1).

In summary, five tentative conclusions can be drawn about the Mariel Cubans who populated U.S. prisons during the 1980s. First, these inmates were a heterogeneous group of refugees who had been allowed to live in the United States under the policies of the INS—and they had failed. Most of these failures took place as the result of either misdemeanor infractions or the inability of refugees to develop an adequate community-support apparatus. Second, statistics from the Reagan White House indicate that the remainder of the Mariel detainees had committed serious crimes while on parole in America. Third, these statistics are troublesome.

For example, of the six hundred violent offenders identified by the U.S. Justice Department, Congressman Pat Swindall (the ranking Republican on the House Immigration Subcommittee) indicated during the Oakdale-Atlanta rebellions that "Cubans at the Atlanta prison are a hard-core lot and 500 of them are convicted murderers") Woolner, 1987a:8). Conversely, Congressman Robert Kastenmeier (Chairman of the House Subcommittee on the Administration of Justice) found that *absolutely none* of the Cubans incarcerated in Atlanta were serving criminal sentences as of February, 1986 (Subcommittee on Courts, Civil Liberties, and the Administration of Justice, 1986, hereafter referred to as the *House of Representatives Report;* see also Dolman, 1986; Donzinger, 1987; *The New York Times*, 1988).

History has confirmed Kastenmeier's description of reality. The U.S. Department of Justice opened the medium-security Oakdale prison in March 1986 for the express purpose of housing the overflow of nonviolent Cuban prisoners from the Atlanta penitentiary (Treadway, 1987). In his recent "Anatomy of the Oakdale Riot," criminologist Burk Foster (1989) further documented that none of the Oakdale detainees were serving criminal sentences at the time of the riot. Additionally, Foster's research shows that the tremendous overflow of nonviolent detainees from Atlanta, in fact, caused the newly established Oakdale facility to become overcrowded in less than six months.

Fourth, criminality notwithstanding, the very fact that these refugees were found in violation of their parole made them all subject to deportation to Cuba in accordance with the Refugee Act of 1980. Although the vast majority of detainees had no criminal sentences to serve, the terms of their release from prison were contingent upon their behavior while under custody.

Several questions emerge which (if correctly answered) may shed some light on the causes of the Oakdale-Atlanta riots. These questions lead to a fifth conclusion — namely, that U.S.-Cuban political relations superseded the factualities of Mariel criminality.

1. Why weren't these refugees deported to Cuba once they had violated the conditions of their parole?
2. Why did the INS continue to lock up so many Cubans in federal prisons either for misdemeanor charges or no criminal charges at all?
3. Why were official estimates of Mariel criminality so diverse?
4. Exactly how were these Cuban detainees supposed to act in order to demonstrate the so-called good prison behavior necessary to live in the community?

Deportation

In practice, the U.S. deportation of Mariel parole violators to Cuba proved to be an empty threat. Between 1981 and 1984, the Cuban government refused to acknowledge U.S. law relating to the deportation of any Cuban residing in America (Boswell and Rivero, 1985; Hampton, 1987; McAfee, 1986). The basis for this emigration discord took shape largely as a result of the foreign policy initiatives of the Reagan administration.

Cuba's revolutionary imperative in the 1980s (as it has been since 1959) states that Cuba has the moral right and duty to support Marxist-Leninist governments throughout the world. It has been Cuba's striving, with support from the Soviet Union, to support revolutionary and national liberation movements in Africa and Central America—support which was at the heart of U.S.-Cuban discord during the 1980s (Kissinger, 1984). Wayne Smith, former Chief of the U.S. Interests Section in Cuba, aptly summarized these effects on the Reagan White House:

The problem [was] rooted in an "ideological mindset." The Reagan administration [saw] the world in Manichean terms, and Castro [represented] the darkest of the forces of darkness (Smith, 1987:286).

U.S.-Cuban relations reached an all-time low with Ronald Reagan's intervention into Cuban-supported Grenada in October 1983. For Castro's Cuba, Grenada represented the first direct (noncovert) military conflict between the U.S. and Cuba in history. Although rarely mentioned in the United States literature, more than two hundred Cuban soldiers and civilians lost their lives in this short-lived war. Another eight hundred Cubans were taken captive by the U.S. Marines in Grenada, and many haven't been heard from since. In total, the conflict cost Cuba the lives of nearly one thousand well-trained revolutionaries (Castro, 1987). Additionally, the U.S. Marines destroyed an elaborate (and enormously expensive) ground-based communication network linked with the Soviet Sputnik satellite system. After this, the Marines blew up the newly built Granadan National Airport because Cuban engineers had been responsible for its construction. Finally, the Marines destroyed an air defense system designed to protect Grenada against foreign invaders such as Ronald Reagan (LeoGrande, 1986; Skoug, 1984; The International Security Council, 1985).

As a result of this war, Fidel Castro came to hate Ronald Reagan. Castro called the U.S. invasion of Grenada "a cheap, political, opportunistic operation" which amounted to "a cowardly and ridiculous act." "Ronald Reagan," said Castro, "has proven that he cares little for reason and law. . . . He's a total liar" (*Newsweek*, 1984).

As such, Grenada seriously effected emigration policy between the United States and Cuba. Indeed, neither side spoke to one another for a year after this conflict (Coleman and Herring, 1985). Then, in late 1984, an event occurred which would ultimately lead to the establishment of limited diplomatic arrangements between the two nations.

The Atlanta Riot of 1984 and U.S.-Cuban Emigration Policy

On October 14, 1984, a group of fifty Cuban detainees gathered together on the recreation yard of the Atlanta penitentiary and quietly held up two bedsheets inscribed with the word *freedom* on them. They were protesting their indefinite confinement in this deeply troubled, old prison. The Cubans were immediately handcuffed by guards and taken to Cellhouse E, the prison's segregation unit.

On October 16, several detainees began small fires in their cells in protest of the segregation decision. The next day, prison officials removed every item of personal property from each Cuban detainee and —against BOP policy—used American prisoners to tear up and destroy all personal mementos belonging to Cuban detainees. For the most part, these mementos consisted of bibles, pictures, and religious charms.

On November 1, detainee Jose Hernandez Mesa got into an argument with a guard over his transfer to Cellhouse E. At this point, other detainees began to mill around Hernandez's cell to see what was going on. Within minutes, the Atlanta riot squad appeared on the scene and sprayed Cellhouse B with tear gas. In turn, the Cubans began to set fires and break windows. As tear gas saturated the air of Cellhouse B, detainees left the building and gathered on the recreation field, where they were captured and put on the ground by guards. Detainees were handcuffed 'hog-style', and forced to lie on the cold ground for approximately six hours, during which they were beaten by baton-wielding guards.

On November 2, the Atlanta penitentiary went on emergency lockdown, which meant that all detainees were confined to their cells for twenty-three hours a day. Such measures were necessary, said prison officials, "because of unrest among the Marielitos."[4]

Less than two weeks later, on November 14, representatives of the U.S. State Department and the INS sought out officials of the Cuban government and restored limited diplomatic relations. The U.S. position was clear: The dangerous Marielitos had to go. As a result of these diplomatic discussions, Cuba agreed to take back (or repatriate) 2,746 excludable entrants, starting with approximately 1,500 troublemaking Mariels confined to the Atlanta penitentiary. In exchange, the United States would open its borders to the legal migration of some 20,000 Cubans (including 3,000 political prisoners) who had recently applied for exit visas to the United States (U.S. Department of State, 1985).

Between January and April 1985, 201 Mariel prisoners from the Atlanta penitentiary were deported to Cuba by the U.S. Marshal's Service. According to an official Cuban news release, at least seventy-three of these Mariels were immediately incarcerated in Cuban prisons (*Diario de Las Americas*, 1986). These events set in motion a series of legal battles over which detainees the United States could deport. Attorneys for the Cubans in Atlanta made a desperate bid to keep the Mariel detainees in America — even if that meant staying in prison.

These legal cases were initially heard in Atlanta by U.S. District Court Judge Charles A. Moye, Jr. between January and May 1985. Moye became outraged at the INS for what he called "its unseemly haste" in trying to deport Cubans who had pending court challenges to their deportations, and he began ordering that Cubans be held off deportation planes from Atlanta until they could receive fair hearings. One by one, however, Moye's decisions were reversed by the Eleventh Circuit Court of the United States during 1985. The appellate court held, on balance, that the INS had the right to deport virtually any illegal alien it wanted, regardless of pending legal challenges (Eig, 1986; Woolner, 1987b).

Just as the INS was winning its right to deport Mariels from Atlanta, however, Fidel Castro unexpectedly suspended the immigration accord between the United States and Cuba on May 10, 1985. Most sources indicate that Castro had become outraged by the CIA-operated *Voice of America* radio program which started beaming aggressively anticommunist propaganda to Cuba, including incitive statements about human rights abuses in Cuban prisons made by President Ronald Reagan and Vice President George Bush (*House of Representatives Report*, 1986; Dolman, 1986).[5] As a result, some 2,500 Mariel Cubans who had already been selected for repatriation entered a diplomatic twilight zone — unwanted by officials in either Washington or Havana. To compound their problems, they were incarcerated in federal prison without constitutional rights to due process.

The Struggle for Justice

The indefinite imprisonment of Mariel Cubans at the Atlanta Penitentiary was being challenged in the courts. Since 1981, attorneys for the Cubans had been trying to win due process rights for their clients, and they were partially successful in the U.S. District Court in Atlanta. Indeed, between 1981 and 1985, some three hundred Cubans were released from the prison in cases where the INS conceded that it could find no evidence of a criminal record for detainees. Another twenty-five hundred Cubans had also won release from Atlanta because of a recent probation system established by the INS under threat of a court order from U.S. District Court Judge Marvin Shoob (*Ibid.*).

In the series of orders issued during six years of litigation in the Atlanta District Court (1980 – 1985), Judge Shoob ruled time and again that Mariel Cubans in Atlanta did indeed have certain constitutional rights — such as the right to know why they were being confined to a maximum-security prison for an indefinite period of time. Shoob granted Mariel inmates a limited right to counsel, a presumption of releasability, and a right to prior written notice of factual allegations supporting continued detention. In short, Judge Shoob held that the INS had to either prove its cases against the Mariels or set them free (Eig, 1986).

Like its reaction to the Moye rulings of 1985, however, the Eleventh Circuit Court often reversed the Shoob decisions. By January 1985, Eleventh Circuit Judge Robert S. Vance began to complain that Shoob was exceeding his "very, very narrow" authority and had "poached on the prerogatives of the executive branch." Vance told to an attorney for the Mariels, "The government can keep them in the Atlanta pen until they die" (*Ibid.*:16). In October 1985, an Eleventh Circuit Court ruling reversing Shoob on the question of rights for the Cubans reached the U.S. Supreme Court. By an overwhelming margin, the high court denied *certiorari*. That is, Vance's word had become law: Mariel detainees were exempt from due process protections afforded by the constitution.[6]

Accordingly, some five thousand Mariel detainees — abandoned by both the U.S. and Cuban governments — were stuck in federal prisons without legal rights to due process. Hence the application of U.S. law in the case of Mariel detainees demanded indefinite imprisonment until diplomatic accords could be achieved between the United States and Cuba. And so the waiting began. Meanwhile, the INS continued to assert its legal authority as investigator, prosecutor, and paroling agent of the Mariel people. By the end of 1985, the Atlanta prison was filled far beyond capacity with nearly two thousand Mariel Cubans (*House of Representatives Report* 1986). Why was the INS continuing to incarcerate so many low-risk offenders?

The Dangerous Marielito

During the Reagan era, law enforcement officials throughout the United States were strongly influenced by the Carter-induced myth that many Mariel Cubans were murderers, vagrants, homosexuals, or 'scum'. The Fort Chafee incident and the 1984 Atlanta riot were startling reminders of this. Yet, except for those cases heard in the Shoob court before October 1985, there was no adversarial system of justice in the United States to determine in individual cases whether Mariel Cubans were dangerous or not. Hence, Mariels could be incarcerated in a federal penitentiary merely because they were *thought* to be dangerous.

These developments made the Mariels an easy target for racism. The seeds of this racism flourished, especially in the Cuban-American community of Miami, where Mayor Maurice Ferre welcomed the first wave of Mariels to his city with this statement:

> While many refugees are good and decent people, we're also getting the dregs of society. Castro is sending his worst element here. My God, I've never seen people like some of these. Hard-core thugs (*U.S. News & World Report*, 1980a).

Unquestionably, the resettlement of the Mariel people took an extraordinary toll on the city of Miami. Nearly seventy thousand Mariel Cubans (thiry-five percent of the Freedom Flotilla) started their lives anew in this city during 1980. Within the first three months of the sealift, the city's crime rate increased thirty percent. In 1981 as the Mariels began to compete for jobs with blacks, Haitians, and union workers in Miami's construction, restaurant, and hotel industries, the city's unemployment rate skyrocketed—from 6.5 to 12 percent. These events finally erupted into four days of bloody rioting in Miami that brought to the fore a racist hatred of the Mariel Cubans (Burkholz, 1980; *Business Weekly*, 1980). The term *Marielito* emerged in Miami as a synonym for thief, drug dealer, rapist, and murderer (Boswell and Rivero, 1985; Lewis, 1987).

Among criminal justice administrators, the term *Marielito* then came to represent one of the most despised immigrations in the history of the United States. By 1984—as Mariels began to organize and revolt at the Atlanta penitentiary—police officials in Miami, New York City, Las Vegas, and Los Angeles estimated that "as many as 40,000 of the Mariel exiles in America are veterans of Castro's prison system." According to police authorities in Los Angeles, the "Marielitos [are] absolutely the meanest, most vicious criminals we have ever encountered." So dangerous, in fact, "that even hardened American criminals are terrified of them" (*U.S. News & World Report*, 1984).

In addition to the diplomatic problems surrounding this scenario, INS officials were growing very sensitive to the political heat they were receiving because of the Marielitos. In short, any problem experienced by a Mariel Cuban became a serious problem for the INS. The official INS approach during the 1980s was to exaggerate the criminal propensity of Mariels already in custody, thereby justifying increased imprisonment of Mariels while simultaneously responding to the hue and cry of urban police departments. Examples of this strategy abound.

On ABC's *Nightline* on July 3, 1987, Mike Inman, general counsel to the INS, reported that:

Some 2,700 Marielitos have been found to have been guilty of serious crimes. We are trying to protect the citizens of this country by preventing [these] people from being released into society. We have a decision to make whether to detain someone who we think is violent or to let that person on the streets and subject the citizens of this country to violence. And between the two alternatives, I think it's appropriate to take the conservative approach (*Nightline*, 1987).

This "conservative approach" to the indefinite detention of Mariel Cubans became downright vicious during the summer of 1987. On July 13, the INS district director in Atlanta charged that, "We've got everything from skyjackers, arsonists, rapists, murderers, aggravated assaults, crimes of virtually every type you can think of. A couple hundred . . . are hardcore deviates that do strange things. They are psycho cases. *I would be for keeping all these people in jail for the rest of their lives* before I would take a chance of letting one harm your child" (emphasis added) Dwyer, 1987:4A).

This strange hybrid of caution and racism also came to dominate the thinking of prison officials responsible for keeping the Mariels detained under this peculiar system of justice. But there would ultimately be a price to pay for this mentality. Shortly after the Supreme Court decision of October 1985, guards at the federal penitentiary in Atlanta began to hear a brave new cry echo through the cellblocks of their decrepit old prison. "*Somos los abandanados*" ("We are the abandoned ones").

The Pains of Imprisonment: Atlanta 1984–1986

In January 1986, Jose Hernandez Mesa and another detainee were brought to trial in the U.S. District Court in Atlanta to answer for the riot of November 1, 1984. According to the *Atlanta Constitution,* the jurors believed that there were no real leaders of the disturbance, and that the living situation of the detainees was shameful.

This shameful situation became the focus of a class-action lawsuit filed on behalf of the Mariels by Atlanta attorney Gary Leshaw in July 1984. In *Owens v. Hanberry,* Leshaw argued that Mariel Cubans in the Atlanta penitentiary were being denied adequate lighting, recreational facilities, access to personal property, and privacy. Furthermore, Leshaw charged that detainees were frequently given poor and unsanitary food, limited medical care, only weekly access to showers, and no air ventilation during the brutally hot Atlanta summers. A compassionate and courageous attorney, Gary Leshaw, also worked tenaciously to bring the Mariel story to the attention of the U.S. Congress. In February 1986, he succeeded.

The House of Representatives Report

On February 3, 1986, Congressman Robert W. Kastenmeier conducted an oversight inspection of the Atlanta penitentiary. The purpose of his visit was to assess the conditions of confinement for the Mariel detainees and to determine the appropriate congressional response. Based upon his inspection and supporting documents, Kastenmeier drew the following conclusions:

1. Absolutely none of the 1,869 Mariels incarcerated in the Atlanta penitentiary were serving criminal sentences. That is, one hundred

percent of the Atlanta Mariel population had either committed no crime at all, or had already served terms of confinement for the crimes they may have committed. (They were *not*, as the INS claimed, a group of "Psycho cases" who "do strange things." Instead, they were a group of incarcerated Cubans who had absolutely no debt to pay society.)

2. The Atlanta facility was about forty-five percent overcrowded, representing the worst condition anywhere in the federal prison system. Detainees in Cellhouses A and B were being held eight to a cell, with an average space of about seven feet by four feet per inmate. Each cell included an open toilet without partitions, a sink, and four bunk beds. Detainees in Cellhouses B, C, and E were confined to their cells for twenty-three hours a day. Atlanta Warden Jack Hanberry admitted to Congressman Kastenmeier that these conditions did not meet the basic standards of the American Correctional Association.

3. Violence within the prison was deemed a "significant problem." From 1982 to 1986, there had been seven successful suicides among the detainees, 158 serious suicide attempts, two thousand serious incidents of self-mutilation, and nine homicides. The inmate-on-inmate assault rate among detainees averaged about fifteen per month, representing over one-half of the total for the entire BOP. Inmate-on-staff assaults averaged between eleven and forty-one per month, accounting for about one-third of the total for the Bureau. From 1984 to 1985, the number of inmate-on-staff assaults referred by the Atlanta penitentiary to the U.S. Attorney increased tenfold (from five to fifty).

4. Approximately two hundred detainees were classified as mentally retarded, mentally disordered, or psychotic. Another 587 had some sort of medical problem. Most of these detainees were housed in Cellhouse C, where they were routinely administered psychotropic medication (e.g., lithium or Haldon).

5. Fewer than twenty percent of the Atlanta prison staff spoke Spanish.

6. The staff turnover rate in Atlanta was one of the highest in the BOP. Atlanta staff also demonstrated the highest disciplinary rate in the Bureau.

7. The cost of housing Mariel detainees in the Atlanta Penitentiary was approximately about $40 million a year.

In conclusion, the *House of Representatives Report* states that:

The current living situation for Cubans at the Atlanta Federal Penitentiary is intolerable considering even the most minimal correctional standards. These detainees—who are virtually without legal rights—are worse off than virtually all other Federal *sentenced inmates.* They are required to live in conditions which are brutal and inhumane. They are confined without any practical hope of ever being released. These conditions . . . present a strong possibility of future violent confrontations. For these reasons alone, Congress and the Administration should be motivated to seek out a constructive solution (emphasis added) *House of Representatives Report*, 1986:7).[7]

The Constructive Solution of 1987

The *House of Representatives Report* called for two solutions to the "Brutal and inhumane" treatment of Mariel Cubans at the Atlanta Penitentiary. First, the report recommended implementing a structured review plan which would give "careful consideration to releasing those detainees who can be sent into the community without endangering community safety" (*Ibid.*). Under the plan, each detainee would be interviewed by a panel of two INS officials to determine the possibility of parole based upon (a) the nature and number of prison disciplinary infractions, (b) past criminal behavior, (c) psychiatric and psychological reports, (d) prison program participation, and (e) any other information that would assist the panel in making a prediction of parole success (Immigration and Naturalization Service, n.d.).

Second, the report recommended spending $42 million for immediate renovation of the Atlanta prison. Congress subsequently approved both of these solutions to the Atlanta crisis.[8] Before these reforms could be enacted, however, something happened in Atlanta which had a profound effect on Cuban detainees throughout the federal prison system.

The Birth of a Martyr

Throughout the years of confinement, a detainee named Santiago Peralta Ocana became a source of inspiration for many Mariel Cubans struggling with the pains of imprisonment. Perhaps Peralta can be best described as one who would not knuckle under to the pressures of confinement at the Atlanta penitentiary during its darkest hour. He was, if you will, the Cuban equivalent of George Jackson, the legendary "Soledad Brother." For this, Peralta was both highly respected by inmates and utterly feared by guards.[9]

Peralta was an extremely muscular, black Mariel Cuban who stood only five feet seven, yet weighed over 250 pounds. Although he was only in his twenties, Peralta's thick arms and massive torso were already covered with old knife wounds—the marks of a seasoned prison fighter. Santiago Peralta had allegedly killed another inmate in a Cuban prison, and he had been responsible for a number of staff and inmate assaults at Atlanta. Accordingly, he was assigned to Cellhouse E where he could be caged—not behind the bars of a regular cell—but behind a three-inch-thick steel door with only one small food slot in it. Peralta was strong enough to kick down this massive door and had done so on two occasions. Both times, Peralta created great excitement among the other detainees of Cellhouse E. He became a personification of Latin *machismo*—the only intrapsychic strategy known to the Cubans in their efforts to cope with life in the belly of the Atlanta beast.

On February 8, 1987, Peralta began an argument with a guard while the Mariels in Cellhouse E were being served lunch in their cells. Claiming that he was being served cold food, Peralta began kicking down the door of his cell as the other detainees in Cellhouse E cheered him on. At this point, the assistant warden of the prison and approximately twenty guards came to Peralta's cell. Seeing this show of force, Peralta grew docile. Accordingly, the assistant warden left the area because he thought the situation was under control.

Following standard prison procedure, an officer told Peralta to back up to his food slot, put his arms behind his back, and stick his hands through to be cuffed. Once handcuffed, guards opened the cell door and brought Peralta outside his cell.

Peralta was then asked to explain the trouble. He responded that "the guard had been messing with my food." The accused guard called Peralta a liar, and Peralta reacted by spitting in the guard's face. The guard then kicked Peralta in the groin hard enough to make him double over and fall to the floor. Peralta then cried in Spanish, "Help me! Help me, please!"

In this condition (with his hands cuffed behind his back), Santiago Peralto was choked to death by three prison guards—in full view of the other Cellhouse E detainees and as many as seventeen guards of the Atlanta penitentiary.[10]

Stories about Peralta's murder began to circulate throughout the federal prison system. In late February 1987, newly appointed Atlanta Warden Joseph F. Petrovsky received a letter from a Mariel spokesman stating:

> We all know it was a brutal crime and we all are witness of that crime. And you know that any crime is neither legal nor justifiable. And although Santiago Peralta Ocana has been [a bad] Cuban detainee, his death will not be justified (The Commission Pro-Justice Mariel Prisoners, 1987:63).

Petrovsky told the Mariel spokesman that the FBI was investigating the Peralta case and that the BOP would reach a decision as soon as possible. After more than a month of waiting, the Cubans grew restless. On April 4, 1987, an officer was stabbed in the back by a Mariel detainee in Cellhouse A. Guards subsequently shook down all detainee cells and found more than thirty homemade machetes, as well as ropes, clubs, and sawblades (*Ibid.*).

It was within this troubled context that the U.S. government implemented its "Constructive Solution of 1987." As might be expected, these governmental reforms offered very little hope, delivered much too late, for the average detainee.

The Cuban Review Plan: A Case of "Pocket Freedom"

On June 22, 1987 (five months before the riots), the INS implemented its congressionally mandated Cuban Review Plan at the Atlanta penitentiary. By November 1, approximately thirteen hundred federal Cuban detainees had been interviewed under this plan.[11] Of this number, only eighty were released (Leshaw, 1988).

Another eight hundred detainees, however, were considered approved for release pending placements in BOP halfway houses or with community sponsors. These eight hundred detainees had received what came to be known in prison argot as "pocket freedom." Mariels at Oakdale and Atlanta used this term to refer to the fact that, while they had earned their liberty on paper, they were destined to wait a year or more in a harsh federal prison for a community placement opportunity to open up for them. In the minds of detainees, their long-awaited freedom was practically worthless (*Ibid.; The New Orleans Times-Picayune*, 1987).

Those denied release altogether were told that "if they maintained good behavior, kept a clean record, took educational courses, performed their prison jobs, and maintained contact with their family and community," then there was a ray of hope that someday they would be released from prison to live in the United States (*Ibid.*).

The Repatriation Treaty of 1987

As the U.S. Justice Department was just beginning to implement its feeble set of reforms, the U.S. State Department reactivated a series of low-key discussions with Cuba concerning the deportation of the remaining 2,563 Mariels who had been selected three years earlier (in November 1984) for expulsion to Cuba. These quiet discussions blossomed into full diplomatic accord when two U.S. State Department officials met secretly in Mexico City with several Cuban officials on November

19, 1987. Suddenly, a new deal was cut: Cuba would accept the 2,563 Mariels and, in return, the United States would accept a number of political prisoners from Cuba and speed the handling of immigration requests from Cubans who wanted to join families in the United States (*Newsweek*, 1987a).

Twenty-four hours later, in New York City, Tom Brokaw began preparing his notes for the NBC *Nightly News* of November 20, 1987. At the same time, a frightened Cuban detainee in Oakdale, Louisiana began drinking heavily from a jug of homemade wine.

Conclusions: Explaining the Oakdale and Atlanta Riots

In his essay on, "Why Prisoners Riot," Vernon Fox (1971:9) points out that "finding valid, consistent, and reliable information as to why prisoners riot defies most standard methods of gathering data on human behavior." The present research is no exception to this axiom. Indeed, the empirical evidence of the factors leading up to the Oakdale-Atlanta riots was often sketchy and frequently contradictory. As a result, the analysis was forced to rely primarily on *post hoc* reconstructions of events and circumstances surrounding the insurrections. Consequently, this information produced more descriptive than expanatory evidence.

These events and circumstances are, however, an important part of the explanation for the riots. Had any one of them been different, the crises at Oakdale and Atlanta could possibly have been deterred. Albert Cohen (1976:8) has expressed this idea another way.

The history of a [violent] incident is the history of an interaction process. The intention and the capacity for violence do not pop out, like a candy bar out of a vending machine. They take shape over time. One event calls forth, inhibits, or deflects another; it invites, provokes, abets, tempts, counsels, soothes, or turns away wrath. Every violent episode, whether it is an altercation between friends, a mugging, or a riot is the product of such an interaction history.

Following Cohen's insight, it becomes possible to identify several key events and circumstances which explain the problems witnessed at Oakdale and Atlanta.

The Precipitating Factors

To begin with, the televised announcement of the deportation treaty seems to have played a part in precipitating the disturbance at

Oakdale. But it may actually have played only a small part. Information concerning the U.S. intention to reactivate the 1984 emigration accord had been presented by the broadcast media prior to Brokaw's announcement of November 20, yet nothing happened inside the walls of Oakdale and Atlanta following this broadcast (*Nightline*, 1987). Likewise, staff working in the cellhouses in Atlanta reported that detainees learned of the Oakdale disturbance over the radio around 9:00 P.M., Saturday, November 21. Again, nothing happened. In fact, the Atlanta staff noticed that only a few of the detainees showed an interest in watching the eleven o'clock television news that night. Those who did watch it showed little reaction to the story about Oakdale and the newly signed deportation treaty (U.S. Department of Justice, 1988).

Therefore, the Oakdale dining room incident of November 20 seems to have been more a function of timing and individual deviance, rather than a function of the televised announcement *per se*. In essence, one intoxicated and uninhibited detainee saw the Brokaw report, walked to the dining room, and proceeded to demonstrate his fear concerning the repatriation treaty in the most dramatic way he could think of. His spontaneous action, in turn, sparked the fear of other detainees gathered together for the evening meal.

The detainees of Oakdale actually heard the news of the repatriation treaty six hours before the dining room incident. Shortly after noon on November 20, Oakdale Warden J. R. Johnson and all bilingual staff of the prison circulated to each of the detainee work details to inform the population of the following:

> The United States and Cuban governments have announced that some Marielitos will be returned to Cuba under a previous agreement. Parole reviews, halfway house and family release at Oakdale will continue as before. Cubans at Oakdale can help their chances to gain community release through continued positive behavior and respect towards staff and other detainees. *We have no details on how many, if any, Cubans at Oakdale will be deported.* We will keep you advised as we receive more information (emphasis added) (*Ibid*, 13).

Immediate detainee reaction to this announcement was mixed. A few became vocally critical, many asked who would be going back to Cuba, and others became sullen and quiet. Many walked off their jobs and mingled in small groups. The next several hours represented a gestation period for the detainees. Despite the well-intentioned efforts of Warden Johnson and his staff to calm the Cuban population, detainees grew extremely negative and anxious about the treaty. Even those already scheduled for release under the Cuban Review Plan began to doubt their futures (*Ibid.*).

In the first few hours after Johnson's statement, the Cubans (as a group) didn't quite know how to deal with their powerful emotions and wondered what they should do. At 6:30 P.M., a drunken detainee in the dining room gave them an answer. The violence that ensued could have been avoided if the BOP had offered a full explanation of the treaty. But they did not, despite the fact that such information was available.

The 2,563 Cubans affected by the repatriation treaty had been identified by the INS back in November 1984. By 1987, these Cubans were scattered throughout the various BOP institutions, and some were living in the community on parole. According to initial INS reports, *only 95 of the 1,394 Cubans in Atlanta were even subject to this treaty (Ibid.)*. It is still not known how many, if any, Oakdale detainees were affected (Nacci, 1989).

If the BOP could have isolated the small number of Cubans who were subject to the treaty (identified by the INS more than three years earlier), then staff could have explained to the remaining detainees, the vast majority, that the treaty did not even apply to them and there was nothing to worry about.

Behind these important management information problems, however, lies a more fundamental set of circumstances that precipitated the Oakdale-Atlanta riots. Essentially, the activities of staff and administrators in these two prisons between November 20 and November 23 demonstrate that they did not recognize the full magnitude of what had transpired in the minds of the detainees as a result of the reactivated treaty. Three important examples highlight this sense of unawareness.

First, as the dining room incident at Oakdale was occurring, most of the prison's administrators were either on their way to, or already at, a retirement party for two prison employees. Warden Johnson learned of the incident on his car radio en route to this party (U.S. Department of Justice, 1988). Prison administrators had obviously failed to detect any significant sign of discord among the detainees throughout the afternoon of November 20, despite the fact that many Cubans had walked off their jobs at midday to gather in groups.

Second, although the dining room incident was a significant event in the minds of the detainees, the Oakdale administration failed to report it to the BOP's regional and central offices (*Ibid.*). In the minds of Oakdale administrators, the dining room incident was nothing more than an episode instigated by a single intoxicated, Cuban. (In reality, it was really much more than this.) In other words, the dining room incident was not viewed by Oakdale administrators as being related to the repatriation treaty.

Third, staff members at Oakdale and Atlanta overlooked several critical events that were signals of rebellion among the Cubans. In so doing, these staff members also contributed to the precipitation of rebellion. Most importantly, guards in Atlanta witnessed an unusually high volume of mail being sent by detainees the day the riot began. Normally, one bag of mail left the Atlanta penitentiary on Monday mornings. However, on Monday, November 23, three bulging sacks of mail showed up on the mailroom floor. Most of this mail was packaged and consisted of small mementos, including personal photographs, bibles, and religious charms (*Ibid.*). Given the sentimental value that Cuban detainees placed on these mementos, and the BOP's history of destroying these items in times of conflict, this event should have caused staff to become concerned enough to report their discovery to the Atlanta administration. But they did not.

Another signal of disorder ignored by prison staff was the fact that Atlanta detainees left their cells that Monday morning wearing layered clothing and tennis shoes and carrying newspapers — three practices explicitly prohibited by BOP security policy (*Ibid.*). Nevertheless these behaviors were allowed to occur by BOP staff, almost as if they were expected.

The most extraordinary blunder, however, took place when (on the mornings of November 21 and 23) BOP staff failed to act on repeated warnings from detainee informants that riots were imminent at both Oakdale and Atlanta. Prior to both disturbances, all female staff and staff with medical problems were asked by the detainees to leave the prison grounds (*Ibid.*).

If the Oakdale and Atlanta staffs had reacted to these events in a collective (organizational) fashion, they might have thought to offer detainees an alternative to their normal prison routine. If, for example, on the morning of November 23, Atlanta inmates—already dressed in riot gear—had been allowed to loosen up by returning to their cells, going to the chapel or recreation building, making phone calls to family and friends, or simply visiting with one another and staff on the prison yard, then another (but certainly not the only) precipitating cause of the Atlanta riot may have been avoided.

Once Oakdale and Atlanta were seized by the Cubans, BOP Director Michael Quinlan told *Newsweek* reporters, "We instructed the staff to be on the lookout for signs that there might be problems. They reported none . . . We thought we were on top of it" (*Newsweek*, 1987a).

Unfortunately for the dead and wounded detainees and the hostages, the U.S. government was far from "on top of it." In sum, the inability of the INS to provide timely information to the BOP concerning the implications of the repatriation treaty and the BOP's miscalculation of the effects of this treaty in the minds of detainees combined to form the most influential precipitating cause of the Oakdale-Atlanta riots. Yet Fox postulates that the precipitating causes of prison riots are seldom the real causes.

The Predisposing Factors

In addition to the important precipitating factors, several key events and circumstances created conditions conducive to rebellion at Oakdale and Atlanta. Most obviously, the relative deprivation experienced by Mariel detainees served as a predisposing factor in the disturbances. Years of poor food, overcrowding, heat, open toilets, brutality (especially the violent murder of Santiago Peralta), official indifference to harsh sentencing, idleness, and monotony no doubt provided emotional and psychological impetus for the uprisings. In effect, these conditions created a time bomb waiting to be detonated by the repatriation treaty of November 20.

Perhaps these conditions could have been avoided by better prison management and a little more compassion on behalf of the INS. Then again, perhaps the ruthless treatment of the Mariel detainees could have been avoided altogether had the Carter administration and the U.S. press not created such an hysteria about the so-called undesirable elements of the Freedom Flotilla back in 1980.

In this vein, a second predisposing factor can be traced to the failure of governmental reform. As a group, the detainees had great expectations for the Cuban Review Plan of 1987. Because almost none of the Cubans were serving criminal sentences, they saw the new plan as their ticket out of hell. Instead, they were given only "pocket freedom." In essence, rising expectations and the perceived discrepancy between what Mariels had been led to expect and what they were actually given became the major causes of the extended rebellion. In other words, the failure of the Cuban Review Plan seriously affected the government's credibility when it came time for negotiating an end to the Oakdale-Atlanta crisis. In the minds of detainees, Attorney General Meese's photocopied letter promising a moratorium on deportations to Cuba represented only another form of "pocket freedom."

Had Attorney General Meese gone to Oakdale and Atlanta and met face-to-face with the detainees during the early stages of the takeovers — fully explaining to them what was actually meant by his letter — the detainees might have put more faith in the integrity of his proposal. If the detainees could have been convinced that Meese's plan was more than just "pocket freedom," the rebellions might have ended much sooner than they did. But the Attorney General was concerned with more urgent issues, and his credibility was highly suspect.

Two days before the Oakdale dining room incident, the 690-page Iran-Contra Committee Report was released, indicating that Attorney General Meese had demonstrated an overall "disdain for the law in America" (U.S. President's Special Review Board, 1987; Stewart, 1988). This portrayal of Meese was widely covered by the print and broadcast media on November 17 and 18, 1987. Combined with his personal involvement in the Wedtech scandal, an extremely corrupt characterization of Meese emanating from the media served to tarnish the reputation of the Attorney General in the eyes of the detainees. Soon they would receive a photocopy of a letter from Meese promising a moratorium on deportations back to the "horrors" of Castro's Cuba (see U.S. Senate, 1987; *Newsweek*, 1987b; *U.S. News & World Report*, 1987).

If the U.S Supreme Court had given Mariel Cubans access to due process protections of the Constitution in the first place, perhaps there would have been no need for a "Cuban Review Plan." And perhaps the embattled Attorney General would have faced less of a credibility crisis in his attempts to resolve the Oakdale-Atlanta riots. Similarly, had the U.S. Supreme Court allowed due process protections, the INS would not have been afforded such wide discretion in exercising its cautious and racist arrest, prosecution, and paroling policies.

In the final analysis, the Oakdale-Atlanta riots were political events: Detainees preferred to die in American prisons rather than live again under Fidel Castro's form of government. This unique political consciousness, as we shall see, was formed by individuals at the highest level of the American legal order.

Cuban Prisons and the U.S. Human Rights Offensive

At the same time that information was misused by the U.S. government to vilify the Mariel Cubans throughout the 1980s, the government was also waging an aggressive diplomatic offensive against human rights abuses in Cuban prisons. The U.S. government did so despite the fact that scholars and human rights specialists from around the world have pointed out many humane and constructive aspects of the Cuban system of penology. In fact, research shows that the conditions of confinement in Cuban prisons were far superior to those at the Atlanta penitentiary in the months and years preceding the November 1987 riot.[12]

Nevertheless, following the invasion of Grenada, the U.S. government issued an unprecedented verdict on Castro's prison system. On January 2, 1984, Assistant Secretary of State Elliott Abrams asserted that Fidel Castro had become "one of the most vicious tyrants of our time" (Platt, 1988a:40). Four days later — on the twenty-fifth anniversary of the Cuban Revolution — the U.S. House of Representatives issued a report claiming that "The Castro government engages in acts of torture and harassment, as well as other drastic steps to suppress all forms of political dissent" (U.S. House of Representatives, 1984:1). On the same day, President Reagan addressed a group of Cuban-Americans in Miami and said, "Castro's revolution has not won freedom for your people. Prisoners of conscience can expect to be in prison well into the 21st century if the present system in Cuba lasts that long" (Platt, 1988a:39–40).

The U.S. offensive against human rights abuses in Cuba reached a fever pitch during 1986. In its annual report, the State Department claimed that "repression of basic human rights is so pervasive that Cuba holds the dubious distinction of being the Western hemisphere's most serious violator of human rights . . . " (U.S. Department of State, 1986:459). On May 21, Vice President George Bush told an audience of Cuban-Americans that "it's a sad truth, but under Castro today Cuba has only two big exports — sugar and death of its young" (Platt, 1988b:7). As the year came to a close (December 11), Ronald Reagan hosted a nationally televised ceremony at the White House commemorating Human Rights Day. At his side was the guest of honor, Cuban dissident Armando Valladares, who had been recently released from a Cuban prison after serving a twenty-two-year sentence for the crime of terrorism. Together, Reagan and Valladares expressed "outrage" at "the horrors and sadism" of the Cuban prison system. "Throughout the communist world," said Ronald Reagan, "the cupboards are empty and the jails are full" (Ibid.:8) Two weeks later (December 26), the Reagan administration took its wrongheaded diplomatic offensive to the United Nations where U.S. Ambassador Vernon Walters said:

> Since Castro took control on January 1, 1959, this regime has become a brutal dictatorship. [This] system . . . has driven some fifteen percent of its population into exile [and] operates a vast network of prisons, labor camps, and firing squads to keep itself in power. Cuba still holds some fifteen thousand political prisoners (Platt, 1988a:41).[13]

These phony facts and figures about the Cuban prison system were reported *carte blanche* by the U.S. media, without any effort to substantiate and verify them with independent third parties (a major journalistic ethic). On June 8, 1986, for example, the *New York Times* launched its simpleminded attack on Fidel Castro with a review stating that "Mr. Castro has . . . institutionalized torture as a mechanism of social control." On July 26, the *Washington Post* arrantly asserted that "Fidel Castro takes his place as yet another of this century's mass murderers." And on May 19, the *Wall Street Journal* falsely reported that the Cuban prison system offered "more variations on human cruelty than anyone should ever know." Moreover, the U.S. press had created an untrue media image of a "Cuban Gulag" (Quoted in Platt, 1988a:41).

This bogus image was taken very seriously by Oakdale and Atlanta Cubans who called themselves "The Abandoned Ones." After all, they were the ones who would actually suffer Castro's alleged brutality. Quite naturally, The Abandoned Ones experienced a profound sense of panic at the thought of returning to Cuba. According to the U.S. government and press, the treaty of November 1987 promised to send them all to an early grave. Ironically, then, the most immediate impact of the U.S. political offensive against human rights abuses in Cuban prisons was to politicize Cubans locked up in U.S. prisons.

So it was with great joy that The Abandoned Ones won "a moratorium on the return of the Cuban nationals to Cuba with reference to the Cubans who came to the U.S. in 1980 via the Port of Mariel" (Meese, 1987). They had escaped the early grave! In other words, the Oakdale-Atlanta riots had been a *magnificent success.*

To the extent that my conclusions reflect an underlying dimension of reality in the case of Oakdale and Atlanta, the major finding of this essay is not hard to explain. Essentially, this analysis revealed that when the political and social aspects of a prison system operate to deprive inmates of accurate information, good management, fundamental human rights, and an adversarial system of justice, prisoners are forced into an absurd existence.

Borrowing from the Nobel Prize–winning work of Albert Camus, I use the term *absurd* to mean a condition of existence which is out of harmony with reason. To live an absurd existence, according to Camus, means that no matter how hard you try, you will never improve the condition of your insane live. This is a tragic existence. It is *absurd.* It cuts off the fundamental motivation for human existence (hope through reason). Alas, you have been *abandoned.*

Camus also maintained that once people are divested of hope for improving their lives (once they have entered the realm of the *absurd*), then violence becomes more than a viable alternative. In fact, with violence, says Camus (1942:75):

> The body, compassion, the created world, action, and human nobility will then resume their place in this insane world!

Epilogue

In February 1988, two guards from the Atlanta Penitentiary were brought before the Eleventh District Court to respond to charges concerning the homicide of Santiago Peralta Ocana. Both were acquitted of any criminal wrongdoing and the Peralta murder was ruled accidental.

Notes

*Dedicated to the memory of Santiago Peralta Ocana.

1. This chronology of events is based in the following reports: U.S. Department of Justice, Federal Bureau of Prisons, 1988 (thereafter referred to as the *After-Action Report; Newsweek,* 1987; *Time,* 1987; Nacci, 1989; The Commission Pro-Justice Mariel Prisoners, 1987; as well as interviews with over one-hundred Cuban detainees who participated in the riots. These interviews were conducted at the U.S. Federal Penitentiary at Terre Haute, Indiana between January 1988 and June 1989.

2. This concern was heightened by the fact that 16 Cubans, upon release from the relocation camps, participated in a spree of airline hijackings during the summer of 1980. In the month of August alone, seven American airliners were hijacked from Miami to Havana by members of the Freedom Flotilla (*Newsweek,* 1980f; *Time,* 1980b).

3. During 1980, approximately 6,000 out of every 100,000 persons residing in the United States committed an index crime as reported in the Uniform Crime Reports (Bureau of Justice Statistics, 1988). In other words, criminality within the general population of the U.S. was roughly *seventeen times greater* than that among members of the Freedom Flotilla from Cuba.

4. This chronology of events is drawn from the *House of Representatives Report,* Appendixes 7 and 8.

5. Another interpretation of this event comes from Castro biographers, Szulc (1986) and Betto (1987) who argue that Fidel Castro did not really care about the substance of the remarks made by Reagan and Bush in May 1985. Instead, what Castro resented was the station's call name—*Radio Marti.* By using this call name, the U.S. government belittled the hallowed image of Jose Marti, the ideological 'father' of the Cuban Revolution and Fidel's personal role model. (A statue of Jose Marti sits in the middle of downtown Havana, and is looked upon as a national shrine by the Cuban people. In a way, the Marti shrine is equivalent to the Lincoln Memorial or the Washington Monument in the capital of the United States.)

6. The U.S. Supreme Court based its decision on the case of *Leng May Ma v. Parker* 357 U.S. 189, (1958).

7. There is evident that conditions were even worse than this. Denny McLain (a former pitcher for the Detroit Tigers and two-time winner of baseball's Cy Young Award) was confined to the Atlanta Penitentiary in 1986 for a drug violation. McLain writes that, "Representative Kastenmeier didn't even see the worst of it." According to McLain, "One time there was as mainy as 300 Cubans refusing to eat for days on end, hoping to bring attention to their plight" (McLain with Nehrstadt, 1988:239). The Atlanta administration, says McLain, responded to the hunger strike by mass forced feeding: "The cops (guards) cuffed a guy to a hospital bed, hands to the top and feet to the bottom, and held his arm while somebody shoved a needle in it to feed him intravenously. Less fortunate guys got fed through tubes in their noses. Milk was poured through the tubes which were oversized and gave the Cubans bloody noses. Their blood mixed with the milk and drained into their stomachs. Some guys almost drowned in their own blood" (*Ibid.*).

8. Letter transmitted from Congressman Pat Swindall to Assistant Attorney General John R. Bolton, 22 December 1987.

9. Personal interviews with Mariel detainees and members of the BOP.

10. This chronology was reconstructed through interviews with two former Cellhouse E detainees who witnessed Peralta's murder, and information in Thompson (1987); autopsy reports from the Armed Forces Institute of Pathology, 21 April 1987; The Office of the Medical Examiner, Decatur, Georgia, 20 February 1987; the Dekalf Bounty (Georgia) Medical Examiner, 19 February 1987; and the Division of Forensic Sciences, Georgia Bureau of Investigation, 23 March 1987.

11. Letter transmitted from Swindall to Bolton.

12. For more than twenty years now, researchers have documented a number of positive aspects of the Cuban prison system. For early examples, see: John (1966) and Lockwood (1969). For more recent examples, see: the Institute for Policy Studies (1988); Platt and Platt (1987); Platt (1988a); The Human Rights Project (1987); Hamm (1989).

13. Contrary to this strong rhetoric produced by the Reagan White House, the Amnesty International (1987a) Report on Political Imprisonment in Cuba estimates that about 500 prisoners (not 15,000) are being detained for political offenses. Also, Amnesty International has been able to verify only 29 cases of legal execution in Cuba throughout the 1980s; whereas the United States, in contrast has carried out 64 executions during the same period (Amnesty International, 1987b).

References

Amnesty International
1987a   Political Imprisonment in Cuba. London: Amnesty International Publications.
1987b   United States of America: The Death Penalty. London: Amnesty International Publications.

Betancourt, Ernesto F. and Wilson P. Dizard
1984   Fidel Castro and the Bankers: The Mortgaging of a Revolution In *Cuban Communism*, ed. by Louis Irving Horowitz, New Brunswick, NJ: Transaction Books.

Betto, Frei
1987   *Fidel and Religion*. New York: Simon and Schuster.

Boswell, Thomas D. and Manuel Rivero
1985   Cubans in America. *Focus* April:2–9.

Brundenius, Claes
1984   *Revolutionary Cuba: The Challenge of Economic Growth with Equity*. London: Westview Press.

Bureau of Justice Statistics
1988   *Report to the Nation on Crime and Justice*. Washington, D.C.: U.S. department of Justice.

Burkholz, Herbert
1980   The Latinization of Miami. *The New York Times Magazine*. September 21: 45–7.

Burns, Arnold I.
1987   U.S Department of Justice Press Release. December 11.

Business Weekly
1980   The New Wave of Cubans is Swamping Miami. August 25.

Camus, Albert
1942   *Le Mythe de Sisyphe*. Paris: Gallimard.

Castro, Fidel
1987   Speech Given at the Eight Conference of the American Jurists Association. Havana. September 17.

Chandler, Kurt
1987   Despite INS Parole Plan, Uncertainty Remains for State's Mariel Cubans. *Minneapolis Star and Tribune*. August 23:7B.

Cohen, Albert K.
1976   "Prison Violence: A Sociological Perspective." In *Prison Violence*, ed. by Albert K. Cohen et al. Lexington, Mass.: D.C. Heath.

Coleman, Kenneth M. and George C. Herring
1985   *The Central American Crisis: Sources of Conflict and the Failure of U.S. Policy.*
       Wilmington, Delaware: Scholarly Resources, Inc.

Diario de las Americas
1986   "Seventy-three of the 201 Cuban refugees who were deported to Cuba
       are still in Cuban prisons. June 23.

Dolman, Joe
1986   Locking Up Liberty in the Atlanta Pen. *Southern Changes.* December 8:
       1–3.

Donzinger, Steven
1987   INS Treatment of Cubans Offends American Sense of Justice. *The Atlanta
       Journal and Constitution.* November 8:A1.

Dwyer, Timothy
1987   U.S. Prisons a Limbo for 5,000 Cubans. *The Philadelphia Inquirer.* July
       13:1A–4A.

Eig, Larry M.
1986   *Indefinite Detention of Freedom Flotilla Cubans: A History of the Judicial Re-
       sponse.* Washington, D.C.: Congressional Research Service, Library of
       Congress. February 25.

Foster, Burk
1989   "Oakdale: Anatomy of a Prison Riot." Paper presented at annual meet-
       ing of Academy of Criminal Justice Sciences. April.

Fox, Vernon
1971   Why Prisoners Riot. *Federal Probation* 35:9.

Golden, Daniel
1987   U.S. No Haven For These Cuban Refugees. *The Boston Globe.* (March
       29:A23–6.

Hamm, Mark S.
1989   Political Rehabilitation in Cuban Prisons: The Plan Progresivo. *The Jour-
       nal of Correctional Education.* 40, 2:72–79.

Hampton, Jim
1987   Caged Logic on Cuban Prisoners. *The Miami Herald.* October 19:A12.

Hoeffel, Paul Heath
1980   Fort Chafee's Unwanted Cubans. *New York Times Magazine.* December
       21:30–54.

Hunt, E. Howard
1980   Castro's Worms. *National Review.* June 13:6–8.

Immigration and Naturalization Service
n.d.   Cuban Review Plan. (unpublished report).

Institute for Policy Studies
1988   Cuban Prisons: A Preliminary Report. *Social Justice*. 15, 2:55–62.

John, Erwin Roy
1966   Seeing Oriente in a Jeep: An American in Cuba Part 1. *The Nation*. March 14:296–299.

Kissinger, Henry A.
1984   *The Report of the President's National Bipartisan Commission on Central America*. New York. Macmillan Publishing Company.

LeoGrande, William M.
1986   "Cuba." In *Confronting Revolution: Security Through Diplomacy in Central America*, ed. by Morris J. Blachman et al. New York: Pantheon Books.

Leshaw, Gary
1988   Statement of Gary Leshaw. U.S. House Judiciary Committee, Subcommittee on Courts, Civil Liberties, and the Administration of Justice. February 4:2.

Lewis, John
1987   "A Mocking Memory." U.S. Congressional Record. April 27.

Lockwood, Lee
1969   *Castro's Cuba, Cuba's Fidel*. New York: Vintage Books.

Mayer, Milton
1980   Messaging the News. *The Progressive*. August:44–5.

McAfee, Cindy
1986   Shoob Urges Fairness to Detainees. *MArietta Daily Journal*. February 26:1.

McLain, Denny with Mike Nahrstedt
1988   *Strikeout: The Story of Denny McLain*. St. Louis: The Sporting News Publishing Co.

Meese, Edwin
1987   Letter transmitted between U.S. Attorney General Edwin Meese and the Cuban Nationals of Atlanta and Oakdale. December 4.

Mesa-Lago, Carmelo
1978   *Cuba in the 1970s: Pragmatism and Institutionalization*. Albequerque, N.M.: University of New Mexico Press.

Minneapolis Lawyer's Human Rights Committee
1986   *The Freedom Flotilla Six Years Later: From Mariel to Minnesota*. Minneapolis, Minn.: Minnesota Lawyer's International Human Rights Committee.

Nacci, Peter L.
1989   The Oakdale-Atlanta Prison Disturbances. *Federal Probation* 52:3–12.

Newsweek
1980a   Cubans Vote with Their Feet. April 21:52.
1980b   Coping with Cuba's Exodus. May 12:60.
1980c   The Cuban Conundrum. September 29.
1980d   The Refugees: Rebels with a Cause. June 16.
1980e   Carter and the Cuban Influx. May 26.
1980f   Cuban Hijackers—And Those Who Stay. September 1.
1984   Castro's Challenge to Reagan. January 9:38–9.
1987a   A Cuban Explosion. December 7.
1987b   Another Blow for Ed Meese. November 30.

Nightline
1987   Marielitos: The Forgotten Refugees. ABC News. July 3.

Pirie, Sophie H.
1986   The Need for a Codified Definition of 'Persecution' in the United States Refugee Law. *Stanford Law Review* 39:187–234.

Platt, Tony
1988a   "Cuba and the Politics of Human Rights." Social Justice 15, 1:38–54.
1988b   "The United States, Cuba, and the New Cold War." Social Justice 15.

Platt, Tony and Cecilia Platt
1987   "XXXIX International Course in Criminology." Crime and Social Justice 30:125–127.

Shepard, Scott
1987   Cuban Inmate's Rights Violated, Group Says. *The Atlanta Constitution.* April 16.

Sklar, Barry
1984   Cuban Exodus 1980: The context. In *Cuban Communism,* ed. by Louis Irving Horowitz. New Brunswick N.J.: Transaction Books.

Skoug, Kenneth N., Jr.
1984   The United States and Cuba. Address before the "Face-to Face" Program of the Carnegie Endowment for International Peace. December 17.

Smith, Wayne S.
1987   *The Closest of Enemies: A Personal Account of U.S.-Cuban Relations Since 1957.* New York: W.W. Norton.

Stewart, James B.
1988   *The Prosecutors: Inside Offices of the Government's Most Powerful Lawyers.* New York: Simon and Schuster.

Subcommittee on Courts, Civil Liberties, and the Administration of Justice
1986   *Atlanta Federal Penitentiary.* Washington, D.C.: U.S. Government Printing
       Office.

Szulc, Tad
1986   *Fidel: A Critical Portrait.* New York: Avon.

The Commission Pro-Justice Mariel Prisoners
1987   *The Mariel Injustice.* Coral Gables, Fl.: The Commission Pro-Justice Mariel
       Prisoners.

The Human Rights Project
1987   *Report on Boniato Penitentiary, Santiago Cuba.* October 9. Washington, D.C.:
       The Human Rights Project.

The International Security Council
1985   *The Soviet Challenge in Central America and the Carribean.* New York:
       CAUSA.

The New Orleans Times-Picayune
1987   Feature articles. August 30.

The New Republic
1980   A Half Opened Door. May 24.

The New York Times
1980   President says U.S. offers 'open arms' to Cuban refugees, May 6:1.
1988   Fairness of case reviews for Cubans is challenged. January 3.

Thompson, Tracy
1987   Cubans, Guards Trapped in Cycle of Violence at Atlanta Pen. *The Atlanta
       Journal.* April 19.

Time
1980a   Time Wears Thin. September 1.
1980b   Havana-Bound. August 25.
1980c   The Cuban Refugees Move On. October 13.
1981   Refugee Rights. January 12.
1987   We are the Abandoned Ones. December 7.

Treadway, Joan
1987   'The Abandoned' Await Their Chance for a New Life. *The New Orleans
       Times-Picayune.* August 30:C1–2.

U.S. Department of Justice
1988   A Report to the Attorney General on the Disturbance at the Federal De-
       tention Center, Oakdale, Louisiana and the U.S. Penitentiary, Atlanta
       Georgia. Washington, D.C.: U.S. Department of Justice, Federal Bureau of
       Prisons.

U.S. Department of State
1980a   *Cuban Refugees.* Washington, D.C.: U.S. Government Printing Office (June).
1980b   *Exodus from Cuba.* Washington, D.C.: U.S. Government Printing Office (July).
1980c   *Cuban Refugees.* Washington, D.C.: U.S. Government Printing Office (August).
1985   *U.S., Cuba Resume Normal Migration.* Washington, D.C.: U.S. Government Printing Office.
1986   *Country Reports of Human Rights Practices for 1986.* Washington, D.C.: U.S. Government Printing Office.

U.S. House of Representatives
1984   *Hearings on Human Rights in Cuba.* Washington, D.C.: U.S. Government Printing Office.

U.S. News & World Report
1980a   For Cubans: Hospitality and Hostility. May 19.
1980b   For Most Cubans, U.S. a Happy Haven. September 1.
1980c   Dispersing Cubans Easier Said Than Done. June 2.
1980d   And Trouble With Cuban Refugees Too. August 18.
1984   Castro's 'Crime Bomb' Inside U.S. January 16:27.
1987   The Trials and Errors of Edwin Meese. August 3.

U.S. President's Special Review Board
1987   *Review of the President's Special Review Board.* Washington, D.C.: U.S. Government Printing Office.

U.S. Senate
1987   *Office of Government Ethic's Review of the Attorney General's Financial Disclosures.* Washington, D.C.: U.S. Government Printing Office.

Winn, Peter
1980   Is the Cuban Revolution in Trouble? *The Nation.* June 7:682–85.

Womack, John Jr.
1980   The Revolution Tightens Its Belt. *The New Republic.* May 31:19–23.

Woolner, Ann
1987a   Pat Swindall's Conversion. *Fulton County Daily Report.* February 9.
1987b   Cuban Detention 'A Disgrace.' *Fulton County Daily Report.* January 20: 1–4.

IV

Crimes of State Omission

Overview

Crimes of state omission come in many forms and varieties. The contributions in this section present analyses of various kinds of state omissions that harm innocent persons and threaten the well-being of other vulnerable populations. In the first contribution, "Old Wine, New Bottles, and Fancy Labels: The Rediscovery of Organizational Culture in the Control of Intelligence," Stuart Farson examines the overlapping worlds of organizational culture, organizational deviance, and organizational reform. Farson provides an analysis of the McDonald Commission of Inquiry into Royal Canadian Mounted Police (RCMP) wrongdoing. Specifically, he studies past and present legislative reform efforts to alter the criminal behavior of the RCMP and its Security Service in the context of future new laws, new organizational structures, and new control mechanisms. Too optimistically perhaps, Farson believes that the lesson may have been learned that a strategic as opposed to a case-oriented approach to intelligence gathering could "not only increase organizational efficacy in dealing with [real] security threats, but may also reduce the abuse of civil liberties of particular individuals and groups by eliminating them from the targeting decision agenda." Thus far, however — despite the establishment of new mechanisms for ensuring political knowledge and accountability, and despite the oversight and review mechanisms which were put in place — "the control of wrongdoing has remained ever elusive."

In the next contribution, "When the State Fails: A Critical Assessment of Contract Policing in the United States," John Wildeman examines both the legal abuses and the legal circumventions vis-á-vis the privatization of many of the law enforcement functions of the state. Wildeman provides an overview of the historical and contemporary developments in the growth and practice of contract policing. He concludes "that the exponential growth in contract policing has been accompanied by a diminution of civil liberties and rights such as privacy, confidentiality, and due process as well as by a vast and largely unrecognized increase in the power of the capitalist state."

In "Contradictions, Conflicts, and Dilemmas in Canada's Sexual Assault Law," Ronald Hinch argues that although the state created the impression with Bill C-127 that it had found a compromise between feminist and patriarchial interests in the prosecution of Canadian rape cases, the fact remains that the compromise "does little to alter the patriarchial or class nature either of the law itself or of law enforcement." Moreover, with respect to specific changes in the sexual assault laws, he points out that contradictory sections, in effect, cancel each other out in the four areas he examines: the abolition of the exemption from prosecution granted married men, the abolition of the penetration requirement, the definitions of sexual assault, and the admissibility of reputational evidence. In his analysis, Hinch provides an examination of "feminist criticism of the old law and the state's response to that criticism" as well as "an assessment . . . of the ways in which the state's response can be shown to be protective of patriarchial and class interests." Looking toward the future, Hinch suggests that specific legal reforms regarding sexual assault must be linked to other challenges to patriarchial and class distinctions.

In the final contribution to this anthology, "The Informal Economy: A Crime of Omission by the State," Stuart Henry demonstrates the relationship between a "free market" economy and street criminality. He argues that "some people's participation in informal economic activity can be traced to government policies, and therefore, such state-organized activities can be held co-responsible for their crimes." Henry reasons that "by excluding some people from a legitimate share of the wealth they create, governments force marginalized sections of the population to participate in informal economies wherein some people are introduced to opportunities for criminal activity which harms both themselves and others." Henry concludes that because government policy can be developed so as not to force some economic activity underground, failure to do so may be construed as a crime of omission by the state. His analysis of state crimes of omission implies—as do most of the chapters in this book—that confronting and reducing state criminality in general would have the spin-off effect of reducing other forms of crime (street crime in particular). In other words, aside from the direct harm inflicted by state criminality, there is also the indirect criminogenic nature of state crimes of omission.

7

Old Wine, New Bottles, and Fancy Labels: The Rediscovery of Organizational Culture in the Control of Intelligence*

A. Stuart Farson

Introduction

Between the mid-1970s and early 1980s, intelligence organizations of several liberal democracies came out of the shadows and entered the public spotlight for the first time in their histories. This change in circumstance was initiated by revelations in the media of extensive and deliberate deviance, revelations which led in turn to major public investigations. In the United States, the Rockefeller, Pike, and Church Committees focused attention on the Central Intelligence Agency (CIA) and Federal Bureau of Investigation (FBI) (Rockefeller, 1975; Pike, 1976; Church, 1976). In New Zealand, the report of the Chief Ombudsman concentrated on the Security Intelligence Service (Powles, 1976). In Canada, the role of federal and provincial police forces was the subject of the McDonald and Keable Commissions (McDonald, 1976; Keable, 1976). And in Australia, Justice Hope examined the entire security and intelligence community (Hope, 1976). Among English-speaking democracies, only Britain escaped a major investigation of its services.[1]

These investigations led to common arguments for reforming the ways in which intelligence agencies are controlled and made accountable. Frequently, such proposed reforms were couched in terms of a "delicate balance" existing between the rights of citizens to enjoy individual liberties and the obligations of the state to preserve its integrity and security (Pitfield, 1983). The schemes gave great priority to the appearances of democratic order. New statutory mandates were provided, new mechanisms for ensuring political knowledge and accountability were established, and oversight and review mechanisms were put in place, but the control of deviance has remained elusive.

This era of reform also encouraged the development of a new sub-area of the now-blossoming study of intelligence. The "control of intelligence," as this neophyte may be called, is in large part dominated by political scientists and constitutional lawyers, and the result is a very traditional form of analysis. With each new revelation of deviance, there is a tendency to return to the old well for familiar solutions. Not surprisingly, these solutions have been theoretically driven rather than empirically motivated.

Most literature on the control of intelligence adopts an outsider's perspective to the problem of organizational impropriety, a perspective that emphasizes changing organizational structures. In so doing, the literature focuses attention on methods of political and administrative control (establishing responsibilities and modes of accountability and oversight, etc.), restructuring the division of labor between elements of the security and intelligence community, clarifying lines of coordination and communication, identifying clear patterns of authority, and setting limits on organizational autonomy and individual discretion. Although some attention has been paid to the question of whether the perception and attitudes of persons employed by agencies accused of having behaved improperly need to be changed, little thought has been given to the relationship between structure and attitude, or to the order in which they should be tackled.

Writers eager to adopt an internal perspective argue that structure and attitude are artifacts of organizational culture, and some authors warn that changing these artifacts without confronting the underlying assumptions will not lead to successful change. For example, Edgar Schein has suggested that "the organization will simply revert to its prior way of operating. If a group has had enough of a history to develop a culture, that culture will pervade everything" (Schein, 1985:33).

It can be argued that criminological expertise and organizational theory may prove useful in understanding how to effect better control of intelligence organizations. This chapter looks at the reform of Canada's security intelligence function over the last decade, and illustrates that a major shift has taken place in how control is established. Initially, the government placed great emphasis on developing new rules and procedures. More recently, after finding that these rules were not being followed, it has explored ways of changing the nature of organizations charged with doing security and intelligence work.

The analysis which follows suggests four major points. First, solutions to the problem of organizational deviance are unlikely to be successful if they are based entirely on effecting external control of organizational structures. Second, attempts to change an organization's culture may have beneficial results if they are coupled with a new normative design. Third, the case-oriented approach to intelligence gathering sometimes associated with police work may not only encourage the abuse of civil liberties of people who do not constitute legitimate threats to the security of the state, but such an approach may also lead to a failure to spot and target or allocate appropriate funds to existing or developing threats. And fourth, a more strategic approach to intelligence gathering may not only increase organizational efficacy in dealing with security threats, but may also reduce the abuse of civil liberties of particular individuals and groups by eliminating them from the targeting decision agenda.[2]

Organizational Culture

Edgar Schein (1985:x – xi) recently suggested several important reasons for studying organizational culture, two of which are particularly relevant to this chapter. First, Schein argues that organizational culture is firmly intertwined with leadership. To him, leadership is the *sine qua non* for creating and changing organizational culture and is something quite different from management. Second, he suggests that the field of organization studies is becoming more interdisciplinary and must, therefore, be understood from an interdisciplinary perspective.

Three important themes recur in the literature concerning organizational culture. The first, concerned with deviance within organizations, has focused on the conflict between means and ends and has tried to explain why individuals or groups break clearly defined organizational rules. In an early work concerning a study of aircraft engineering, Bensman and Gerver (1963:597) noted that using a bolt tap to secure screws (the most serious crime imaginable) enabled personnel to maintain public values while performing actions necessary to achieve public or private ends. This was responsible for a form of "institutionalized schizophrenia":

> Individuals act and think on at least two planes, the plane of the public ideology and the plane of action. They shift from plane to plane, as required by their positions, their situations, and their means-ends estimations. In a sense, it is a form of double-think and double-think is the major result of the means-ends conflict.

Bensman and Gerver's analysis demonstrated the importance of organizational culture in controlling deviance. Instead of relying on formal law enforcement methods, factory foremen and inspectors used informal control mechanisms to limit the use of taps to strictly necessary situations. This led the authors to a new definition of crime where:

> A 'crime' is not a crime so long as its commission is controlled and directed by those in authority towards goals which they define as socially constructive. A violation of law is treated as a crime when it is not directed and controlled by those in authority or when it is used for exclusively personal ends (Bensman and Gerver, 1963:598).

They concluded that it was the ends and interests of those responsible for rule enforcement that led to a notion of discretionary license or, more precisely, to the definition of "socially permissible crime" and the degree and severity of punishment. It should be noted that such rule enforcers (i.e., middle managers and inspectors) are those most in a position to influence the organizational culture, and they also have the most to lose from formal application of law enforcement standards.

Interest in police culture and its relationship to organizational reform is longstanding (see Manning, 1971; Van Maanen, 1973, 1974; Sherman, 1978). As long ago as 1973, Van Maanen (1973:416) concluded that "the police subculture . . . will probably exist in even the most reformed of departments. To change the police without changing the police role in society is as futile as the labors of Sisyphus."

Such a statement is in line with the important conclusion reached by David Bayley (1975:377) in his broad-reaching analysis of the relationship between policing and political development in Western Europe. Bayley noted that not only were police systems uniquely national in character, but "their distinctive features [were] relatively impermeable in the face of wars, revolutions and major social and economic transformations. The distinctive characteristics of these police systems have shown remarkable stability over time."

The importance of this relationship (between organizational culture and organizational deviance) has been a major component of recent literature on the public police (Ericson 1981a, 1981b, 1982; Manning, 1977b, 1979; Punch, 1981; Shearing, 1977, 1981) as well as literature on what is frequently referred to as the "political police" (Brodeur, 1981, 1983; Turk, 1981). Building on the work of Bensman and Gerver, Shearing (1981) draws attention to the hypocrisy of police work in a study of municipal policing in Canada. He concludes that police officers respond to two sets of values—those reflected in the formal rules of due process and those reflected in the informal rules of police subculture. This, he argues, allows the police to obey the rules of due process and at the same time "keep the streets clean" through behaviorial means. The former set of rules is for appearances, and the latter is for effecting behaviorial change.

In an empirical study showing how Canadian police use a variety of rules from different sources, Ericson (1981a, 1982) takes Shearing's argument a step further. Extending a line of argument initially developed by McBarnet (1976, 1979, 1981), he illustrates how the formal rules (the criminal law) become enabling devices for police work and for the provision of appearances. But the criminal law (or the "Ways and Means Act," as it is sometimes referred to in police parlance) is a two-edged sword. It can also be used to hoist the police on its own petard. For this reason, the police also make extensive use of internal disciplinary rules. These rules, Ericson points out, provide an aura of control and professionalism while leaving those in charge with wide interpretive latitude. Using the work of Manning (1971, 1977b, 1980a), Ericson (1981b) shows how the police in Canada use informal, unarticulated "rules of thumb" or "recipe rules" developed by the police subculture as bases for action. He (1981b:102) concludes with a warning note:

> Certainly, changing a few rules to give greater appearances of procedural regularity will do nothing to change the present order of things, and it may well strengthen the tendencies one was seeking to alter. A wealth of socio-legal research, as well as research in other governmental and industrial organizational settings . . . instructs us that new reforms and the rules that are supposed to bolster them are typically incorporated into existing practices and frequently strengthen the practices.

Turk's work on political policing (1981) also attempts to assess the impact of reform. In addition, it sets out to clarify the meaning of deviance for this type of policing and to identify its structural sources. Turk makes the important observation that, of the two forms of political police deviance—demonstrable violations of legal rules and blameworthy failures in achieving organizational goals — public attention has been drawn to the former, and little has been said of the latter. The reason for this is easy to see but hard to understand: Legal rule breaking has a habit of coming to the surface, but the latter does not. Legal deviance tends to become visible through official investigations, but organizational goals do not. In agencies where secrecy is the norm, organizational goals are seldom revealed even when they are internally known and understood — which, Turk points out, is not always the case. To Turk, organizational deviance in political policing is a function of the need to satisfy overt and covert external demands without risking undeniable failure. In true conundrum fashion, he suggests that the "fundamental source of deviance *in* political policing is the deviance *of* political policing" (1981:120). His analysis of the potential success of proposed remedies for both sorts of political policing deviance is as somber as Ericson's is for public policing deviance. He argues that recommendations concerning open public control, radical political change, legal reforms, goal redefinition, and personnel management are likely to have little or no success. Only organizational change and closer monitoring are likely to reduce legal deviance, and only separating functions is likely to affect organizational behaviorial deviance. Ericson concludes that:

> No clear path to controlling the controllers is yet to be seen. Perhaps respect for the ideals of real democracy and social justice, elusive as they are, can somehow be made a serious concern of those who monitor, operate, and employ political police. Those holding such hope are true idealists, for to rely upon the honour of those who purport to defend a society means . . . to trust in the capacity of the defenders to transcend instead of merely reflect its inadequacies" (1981:123).

A second important theme concerns organizational improvement and leadership (see Deal and Kennedy, 1982; Kilmann, 1984; Schein, 1985; Peters and Waterman, 1982; Peters and Austin, 1985; Sathe, 1985; Tichy, 1983; Wilkins and Ouchi, 1983). With a few notable exceptions (e.g. Walker, 1986) most of this literature is concerned with the private sector. By far the most significant impetus for it was the dramatic success of Japanese business (Ouchi, 1981; Pascale and Athos, 1981), largely at the expense of American companies. This genre is epitomized by Peters and Waterman's *A Passion for Excellence* (1982), which focuses on what organizations can do for themselves and specifically avoids external-to-organization influences. This book dramatically challenges accepted principles of American business. Established rules for improving efficacy are shown to be wrong, and strategic planning is found to be a false god. Developed initially in the postwar period to improve budgetary control and provide an integrated theory upon which corporate functions and strategy could be based, strategic planning came to be seen as counterproductive. Most significantly, it works against the positive aspects of corporate culture by dehumanizing them. The planning process actually deadens strategic thinking (Porter, 1987).

The third relevant theme within the literature concerns metaphors, signs, tropes, and so on. This literature is important not only because it informs how subcultural rules are formed and transmitted (Martin, Feldman, *et al*, 1983; Martin and Powers, 1983; Schall, 1983), but because it emphasizes the participation of the police (Manning, 1977, 1980). In a recent study, Shearing and Ericson (forthcoming) take matters a step further with their analysis of police stories. They suggest that the police are not rule-guided "cultural dopes," but active participants in a process. The stories police officers pass on to one another are open-ended in character. The listener is not a passive recipient. On the contrary, he is encouraged to consider a range of possible actions and to improvise accordingly. In this way, the story acts as a guide—not an instruction—for action.

It may be argued from all this that the application of formal control standards has both positive and negative effects. Tightening formal standards limits the capacity of organizational leaders to achieve their objectives. Loosening formal standards has three important effects. First, it allows a greater degree of less serious "crime" to occur. Second, it permits informal control mechanisms to play a major role in limiting deviance to less serious areas. And finally, it arguably allows organizations a greater opportunity to fulfil their mandates.

An important focus of this chapter is the fact that the current balancing act in the intelligence area does not take into account the need to draw a balance between formal and informal methods of organizational control. This, it may be argued, is largely due to a failure to understand the reciprocal relationship that exists between propriety and efficacy. Emphasis is placed on the application of formal mechanisms that are geared to control impropriety from the outside. Hypothetically, this may lead to unintended consequences. Rather than creating a balance between the interests of the state and those of individuals, this emphasis may simply redress the balance by improving the protection of civil liberties. This in itself may have important negative consequences for such liberties in the longer run.

The following analysis concerns events that have taken place in Canada over the last decade or so, starting with the McDonald Commission of Inquiry into the practices of the Security Service of the Royal Canadian Mounted Police (RCMP). This inquiry exposed severe weaknesses in both the formal, external controls over the RCMP and in the informal controls of its Security Service. The next section examines the period between the publication of the McDonald Commission report and the enactment of new legislation, demonstrating the influence of the legal culture and illustrating its solution to the problem. Following that are revelations by the oversight mechanisms and the media indicating that—despite new laws, new organizational structures, and new control mechanisms—matters changed very little. Finally, the analysis concentrates on the work of the Osbaldeston task force. Here it is argued that attention was finally focused on the problems of organizational culture and how to solve them.

Background

The McDonald Commission of Inquiry came about almost by accident (Sallot, 1979). In March 1976, a former RCMP officer who was on trial for bombing the private residence of a Montreal businessman while a member of the force, testified that he had done "much worse" as a member of the Security Service. Under the protection of the Canada Evidence Act, Robert Samson admitted that he and members of the Montreal and Quebec provincial police forces had broken into the offices that *L-Agence-Presse Libre du Québec* (APLQ) shared with the Movement for the Defence of Political Prisoners of Quebec (MDPPQ) and stole thousands of documents.[3]

An inquiry by the Quebec Attorney General led to charges against three officers from the RCMP, the Quebec Provincial Police, and the Montreal City Police. Each pleaded guilty to authorizing a search without a warrant. Matters might have stopped there had it not been for an article in the *Vancouver Sun* (for which John Sawatsky would win the Michener Award for public-service journalism).[4] This article revealed that Samson had acted under the direction of senior officers and that a coverup of methodical illegal activity existed to the highest ranks of the RCMP. Soon after the police officers were sentenced, Solicitor General Francis Fox advised the House of Commons (*Debates,* June 17, 1977:6793) that he had "repeated and unequivocal assurances" from the RCMP that the APLQ incident was "exceptional and isolated" and that the Force's directives clearly required the actions of all members to be within the law.[5] Within a month of this statement, however the Solicitor General was forced to acknowledge that the opposite was true. It now appeared (*Debates,* July 6, 1977:7365) that certain members of the RCMP "could well have used methods or could have been involved in actions which were neither authorized nor provided for by law" in discharging their responsibility to protect national security, and the Commissioner of the Force now recommended a public inquiry into the national operations and policies of the RCMP Security Service.

This sudden about face from two unconnected events. In meetings with officials representing the Crown's Law Officers two disgruntled former members of the RCMP Security Service who believed that they had been wrongfully dismissed, provided damning information which indicated that Samson's revelations were just the tip of the iceberg. They opined that it was part of their job to perform activities of a questionable nature and that they had done no worse than numerous other members of the force.[6] But perhaps more threatening for federal authorities was the establishment in 1976 by the Government of Quebec of its own commission of inquiry—the Keable Commission.

Problems with the Old Wine

As might be expected, the Commission of Inquiry that was established had a decidedly legal turn of mind. Its chair, David McDonald, was a justice of the Supreme Court of Alberta, and the other two commissioners were lawyers. Besides confirming the break-in and theft of documents from the APLQ and MDPPQ, the Commission catalogued (McDonald, Vol.1:101) an extensive list of illegal acts that it referred to as "institutionalized" within the RCMP.[7] Importantly, the Commission also confirmed that there was a lack of political accountability: Ministers simply did not want to know (or did not want to let on that they knew) what the Security Service was doing.

Although the central problem facing the Commission was to explain why members of the Service had behaved illegally and improperly, a considerable amount of time was devoted to the issue of what the organization could do to prevent the recurrence of such behavior. In developing a response to this problem, the Commission started from two premises. First, the commissioners assumed that there was a danger in relying too heavily on what they called "watchdog" or "policing" control mechanisms.[8] Such mechanisms, they thought, could produce rigidity in the organization and apathy in individuals, and might lead some members to circumvent the rules. Second, they challenged the notion on which such controls were based. People who committed impropriety were not necessarily rotten apples. They could be exemplary citizens (McDonald, Vol. 2:695).

Like criminologists who examine organizational deviance, the Commission perused the issue of the relationship between ends and means. They found that members of the Service provided three rationales for justifying the means used. First, there were certain circumstances under which special means were required. Second, under such circumstances such actions were not based on a guilty mind. And third, such actions were done at the command of superior orders.[9] As a result the commissioners concluded (McDonald, Vol. 2:698) that:

The reasons for committing wrongdoings are complex and have at least as much to do with 'systems' failures—that is, failures in the systems of law, management, and governmental relationships affecting the Security Service—as they do with human failings. This conclusion leads to another: that to rely *solely* on control mechanisms which 'police' behavior or require approval for action from some organization or individual outside the agency would lead to a system of controls which is less effective than it could be. We, therefore stress a variety of approaches: some admittedly are of a watchdog type, but others aim at reducing or eliminating the characteristics within an organization that lead 'good' people to act improperly or illegally.

They noted that a major disadvantage of these latter approaches was the fact that they could not be implemented quickly. These approaches concerned the modus operandi of senior management, leadership style, personnel policies, legal advice, internal auditing, and internal security. Many of them were premised on earlier thinking and other recommendations to government. Critically important to these approaches was the need to incorporate civilian specialists in research and analytical capacities.

During the early years of the Cold War, a number of studies recommended innovations in recruitment and training for the Service (Rivett-Carnac, 1947; McClung, 1955). A particularly important study was conducted by Mark McClung, a senior civilian researcher in 1955. McClung's report considered the establishment of a security organization separate from the Force as ideal, but McClung did not propose such a system on the grounds that it was not politically attainable. Instead, he argued against upgrading the Special Branch (then part of the Criminal Intelligence Branch) and for a split into a "two-team organization" comprised of a Special Branch and an Internal Security Service (ISS). The Special Branch would be comprised of regular members of the Force and would have complementing specialties with the ISS in countersubversion, security screening, government and public liaison, and emergency planning. The ISS, on the other hand, would be entirely civilian, with complete responsibility for counterespionage, research, policy development, and foreign liaison.

The logic of this recommendation was based on two premises. First, the Special Branch was not thought to be doing its job and, given the immediate pressures of the Cold War, there was insufficient time for the Branch to shore up its defenses. And second, Canadian police forces could not perform the duties of a security service because of their recruitment, training, and career planning practices (McDonald, Vol. 2:699–70).

The idea of civilianization was extended in the late 1960s by the Royal Commission of Security (Mackenzie, 1969), who believed that an entirely civilian agency should perform the functions of the Security Service in Canada. The commissioners based their argument on three premises. First, they agreed with earlier assessments that the roles of police and security services were markedly different. Therefore, it was inappropriate to base security service recruitment, training, and career patterns on a police model. Second, the RCMP had failed to take the initiatives in this policy area. And finally, placing the security function under the same roof as police work made it harder for both the RCMP and the Security Service to do their jobs. With a touch of clairvoyance, they noted:

> A security service will inevitably be involved in actions that may contravene the spirit if not the letter of the law, and with clandestine activities and other activities which may sometimes seen to infringe on individuals' rights; these are not appropriate police functions (Mackenzie, 1969:20).

On previous occasions, the RCMP had been able to fend off the winds of change, but this time it was obliged to compromise. Prime Minister Trudeau (*Debates*, June 26, 1969:10636–37) agreed to leave the Security Service within the Force, but he instructed the RCMP Commissioner to ensure that it would be "increasingly separate in structure and civilian in nature" and would incorporate new and more flexible recruiting, training, and career planning policies.

Drawing upon evidence provided by ministers and senior officials of the Force and a thorough analysis of RCMP files, the McDonald Commission (McDonald, Vol. 2:673–74) made a point of noting that the RCMP had made a concerted effort to avoid implementing the Prime Minister's policy:

> For the better part of the last decade, the successive Commissioners of the Force and their Senior managers who were not part of the Security Service have endeavoured to ignore the policy statement whenever possible. When circumstances forced them to deal with the statement, they have tended to misinterpret it by concentrating on the "increasingly separate in structure" aspect of the policy, showing insufficient concern for what has become to be called "civilianization" of the Security Service.

In one respect, however, the Service did become more civilian in nature. That was in the appointment of John Starnes as the first civilian Director General. His testimony before the Commission (McDonald, Vol. 2:680) shows the limited success he had in achieving either broader civilianization or structural separation. He was able, however, to employ the Bureau of Management Consulting (BMC) to undertake a study of organization and classification. Its report (BMC, 1973:10) stressed a need for the "professionalization of the organization" and concluded that:

> While there must be knowledge and understanding of, and empathy with, the processes of social change in law enforcement officers, the prime orientation is the maintenance of law and order. We see such an orientation in security officers as being counter productive to the effective functioning of security operations.

The BMC made a number of important recommendations for change. These included: centralizing policy and program control while decentralizing execution; using management by objectives theory to revamp the planning process; flattening out the pyramidal management system by reducing the number of supervisory levels; improving internal and external training programs; upgrading entry selection criteria; and improving morale by such mechanisms as basing promotion on merit rather than length of service. The BMC's most controversial recommendation, however, was to improve the effectiveness of managerial controls by increasing the autonomy of the Service in terms of both its operational and administrative resources (McDonald, Vol. 2:682 – 83; BMC, 1973:83–89).

In addition to the extensive list of legal deviance, the McDonald Commission also found what Turk has called "blameworthy failures to achieve organizational objectives." As a result, Commission staff conducted an extensive analysis of the Service's organizational structure, staff, and internal workings. Thirty-eight off-the-record, clinical interviews were conducted with "movers and shakers" within the Service in order to identify concerns about the organization's management and culture. An important finding revealed by these interviews (McDonald, Vol. 2:687) was the high degree of dissatisfaction experienced by civilian members of the Force. One described the second-class status allotted to civilians as "administrative apartheid." The Commission concluded that this state of affairs was intolerable and dangerous, arguing that it made the organization vulnerable to leaks and penetration (McDonald, Vol. 2:688).

The Commission came to view the problem of treatment towards civilians and the Force's resistance to change in terms of the RCMP's organizational culture. Many witnesses described the process of recruitment into RCMP and subsequent training and career patterns in terms of a "religious order." New members entered the order at a young age at the lowest level and experienced a sort of "initiation rite" at the training center in Regina. For the rest of their time with the Force (a thirty-five-year pension scheme discouraged leaving), they were bound by an extensive and well-defined set of disciplinary rules. The net effect was to build loyalty — not to the police profession — but to a militaristic organization and to encourage distrust in outsiders and their values. The Commission concluded that the sum of these factors and their special emphasis within the Force made the RCMP vastly different from any other government department or agency (McDonald, Vol. 2: 689–90).

In an attempt to resolve the twin issues of effective performance and lawfulness, the Commission saw two elements as being both essential and difficult for the RCMP to accept. These were the development of structures and procedures which would ensure that the agency was under political control and direction, and management, recruiting, and personnel policies that were appropriate to a security intelligence (McDonald, Vol. 2:754). The fact that these elements of change would be difficult for the RCMP to accept, coupled with the RCMP's failure to implement the Prime Minister's directive, led the Commission to call anew for the separation of the Service from the Force.

The Commission believed that a particular management style was needed within the new agency. They agreed with Justice Hope that the agency head should not only possess high capacity and probity but be perceived by persons in government and public alike to possess such qualities (Hope, *Fourth Report*, para.385). They also favored a team approach to decision making, with senior members drawing upon wide and varied experience outside of investigative work (McDonald, Vol. 2:703–4). They believed that a leadership style relying on obedience was inappropriate for a security intelligence agency. Obedience to leadership had to give way to a team approach because getting things done often meant working with people in situations where there was no reporting relationship (McDonald, Vol. 2:732–33; BMC, 1973:38).

On the subject of personnel policies, the Commission agreed that the new agency should hire more people with university degrees, particularly those from such disciplines as administration, economics, languages, and law. In addition, the agency should look for people with particular characteristics: the capacity to work in an organization about which little is known; discretion; emotional stability; a keen sense of, and support for, democratic principles; maturity; no exploitable character weakness; patience; political acumen; and tolerance (McDonald, Vol. 2:711). In order to widen the recruitment base, the Commission recommended recruiting not just from the bottom up but through temporary transfers from government and by attracting people from academic institutions and the private sector.

The Commission also recommended against the generalist career model. To discourage job changing simply to achieve promotion, they recommended reducing the number of job levels within the organization. This, they argued, would allow individual members to stay in positions longer yet still receive pay increases. In addition, they suggested that there should be a number of senior positions where administrative duties were not required, thus allowing incumbents to develop specialized knowledge (McDonald, Vol. 2:719–720). To strengthen communication in general, the commissioners recommended that there be only one category of employee, intelligence officers. And to strengthen the sense of community, the Commission advocated doing away with separate eating and social facilities (McDonald, Vol. 2:734).

The New Bottle

Between the receipt of the Commission's final report and its publication, the government set up two administrative groups. The first, called the "Concept Group," developed a legislative framework for a Security Intelligence Service. The second, known as the Security Intelligence Transitional (SIT) group, looked after the transition of parts of the Security Service from the RCMP.[10] According to a former Liberal cabinet minister, the purpose of this legislation was to effect separation, not to impose civilianization, which was considered a second stage.[11] Certainly, no attention to matters of organizational culture were attended to by either the Special Committee of the Senate, which examined the first run at the Act (Bill C-157) or the House Committee, which examined the later version (Bill C-9). Nor did either of these bodies attempt to assess whether there were threats to Canada's security.[12]

The legislation established a new nonpolice agency called the Canadian Security Intelligence Service (CSIS), which was limited in its mandate to collecting information and intelligence about activities that constituted threats to the security of Canada (CSIS Act: S.12–20). The organization was given no power to counter or deter such threats,[13] nor were any peace officer powers provided.[14] Nevertheless, the overall capacity of the legislation was enabling in that it legalized activities that had hitherto been unlawful. Not only did it increase the range of investigations that were allowed, but it permitted CSIS agents to obtain intrusive warrants at a lower threshold level than had been required under RCMP procedures.[15]

A complex but largely watchdog control system was put in place. Although it is not necessary to go into elaborate detail here about what this system consisted of,[16] two key points should be made. First, the system of controls was countervailing in design. On every occasion where organizational autonomy or individual discretion was provided, off-setting modes of accountability and control were put in place. And second, the CSIS Act established three levels of oversight and review. The office of Inspector General was established to review the Service's activities and monitor its compliance with operational policies. Insofar as the Inspector General was located outside the Service but within the Solicitor General's ministry and obliged to provide certificates to the Minister, he was intended to be very much the Minister's eyes and ears on the Service (CSIS Act: S.30[2]). The second level of review is the Security Intelligence Review Committee (SIRC), a body designed to be independent of government and responsible to Parliament. Its essential function is to review the performance of the Service with its duties and functions (CSIS Act:S.38). The third and final level lies with specially designated judges of the Federal Court who are obliged to review all warrant applications for intrusive investigations (CSIS Act:S.21–28).

The CSIS Act confirmed the RCMP's continued role in security and intelligence work in two ways. First, it did not touch a number of security functions that the Force had historically provided; consequently, these remained with the RCMP. And second, Part IV of the CSIS Act specifically gave the Force the responsibility for dealing with security offenses. This has only kept the RCMP in the enforcement end of political policing but has allowed the Force to continue its intelligence gathering role, particularly in the counterterrorism area.

The Rediscovery of Organizational Culture

Sirc's Role

Since its inception, the SIRC has published four annual reports and conducted a number of special studies. Though ostensibly a review committee of the agency's propriety, the role of the committee has been interpreted more widely.[17] In its first annual report, the committee questioned the Service's recruitment and training policies and gave notice that it intended to make them high-priority matters. Ninety-five percent of RCMP Security Service members had apparently transferred to CSIS (SIRC, 1984 – 85:10). In an interview after the report's release SIRC chairman Ron Atkey said that the committee was concerned that CSIS was merely "old wine in a new bottle" and "the same old group with a different label" (Malarek, 1985:M1). The committee also expressed concern about another matter that bore heavily on the question of organizational culture. Through their analyses of CSIS performance during two important incidents—the terrorist attack on the Turkish Embassy and the threat to bomb the Toronto Transit system—SIRC established that CSIS had not been able to get access to Canadian Police Information Centre (CPIC) data (SIRC, 1984–85:13). Despite the fact that more than ninety-five percent of CSIS personnel were former members of the RCMP, CSIS was not considered a police organization by the CPIC Advisory Committee (CPICAC). The CPICAC had therefore denied CSIS access to its terminals.[18]

SIRC's second report covered much of the same ground. This time, however, the committee members were bolder in their statements. They were now "disappointed that the progress towards civilianization has been so slow." While they were pleased that the process of recruiting and training new intelligence officers was generally working well, they noted important deficiencies. There were not enough women or francophones being recruited, and (very importantly) there were too few lateral transfers of highly qualified people into the middle and senior levels of management (SIRC, 1985–86:5). Furthermore, SIRC noted an unwillingness to bring in outsiders among "many within CSIS, particularly in senior management" (*Ibid*:6).

To get to the root of the problem, SIRC launched a full research study into personnel recruitment, training, and development.[19] Not surprisingly, SIRC based its analysis on those sections of the McDonald Commission report which had explored the deficiencies of the RCMP's organizational culture.[20] The most damning findings were that CSIS was still using a "bottom-up" approach to recruitment, it still did not have an employee assistance program to help individuals with personal problems, and it had serious communication and morale problems.[21] In all, SIRC made twenty-three recommendations,[22] two of which are of particular importance for the purposes of this chapter. The first (SIRC, 1986:85) was a recommendation to "encourage entry into operational areas of the Service of a limited number of individuals at senior levels through direct entry, secondments and promotion from non-operational areas within CSIS."

Interestingly, this got translated in their annual report (SIRC, 1985 – 86:14) to a more general recommendation to "recruit additional personnel from outside the Service to middle-management positions," a statement which can be quite misleading. The last recommendation was for "CSIS Senior Management [to] build a culture in the organization that stresses a philosophy that its people are its most important resource" (SIRC, 1986:87).

It is significant to note that this recommendation was based directly on the philosophy of excellence advocated by Peters and Waterman.[23] The recommendation was trivialized in the annual report to "greater efforts [should] be made to improve communication between senior management and employees" (SIRC, 1985–86:15).

Besides being a review body, SIRC also acts as an administrative tribunal to hear complaints. In 1985 and 1986, some 470 complaints (87.5% of all complaints) were filed concerning a lack of bilingualism in the Service by CSIS members themselves. Largely as a result of this, SIRC was instructed by the Solicitor General to conduct a special study into the problem. Eventually published in June 1987, the report established the existence of anti-French Canadian and anti-Catholic sentiments within the Agency. There was, in the measured words of the report (SIRC, 1987:1), a "culture gap,"[24]

> . . . not enough real commitment to the government's official languages policies and not enough real understanding of the Francophone culture that shapes the thinking of one in four Canadians. Despite good intention at the top and legitimate pressures from staff, CSIS too often acted like an essentially Anglophone institution with French-language capability as a troublesome frill.

More importantly, the report pointed a finger at the real problem:

> In staff relations, a communications gap separated management and staff. I could be blamed partly on transition, which forced management to make snap decisions founded more on intuition than on well-understood policy or systems. But the problem went deeper, to habits of secrecy and and nostalgia for an hierarchical command structure.

This point had not been missed by the Ottawa *Citizen*. An editorial (Anon., 1987a) had earlier suggested that CSIS's linguistic nonperformance was evidence of its own operational weakness. It argued that the new Service was intended to overcome the RCMP's failure to provide useful intelligence to the Trudeau government about the Front Libération du Québec (FLQ) in Quebec during the October Crisis of 1970. Instead, the *Citizen* (Anon., 1987b) argued, "we see the service failing to meet even the minimal standards set by the Official Languages Act. That in itself is a failure of intelligence—and could be a sinister breach of the nations's security."

Another important fact established by SIRC was that a network of freemasons existed within CSIS. This network operated in the upper echelons of the Service and in such "crucial sectors" as personnel. Surprisingly, however, SIRC did not find it necessary to pursue the covert influences of freemasonry on the Service. Instead, SIRC satisfied itself with the acknowledgement that "there is no doubt in our minds that an 'old boys' net' of RCMP veterans exists within the Service" and the conclusion that SIRC recommendations would prevent discrimination against Francophones and other minorities within the Service (SIRC, 1987:15).

SIRC's third annual report returned to familiar themes. The police/nonpolice dichotomy was raised again. CSIS headquarters still did not have a CPIC terminal. Given that thousands of police cruisers now had terminals on their dashboards, SIRC concluded that the delay was clearly an indication of a turf battle. The police were simply not prepared to treat CSIS as an equal partner (SIRC, 1986–87:15). More importantly, SIRC now expressed concern that CSIS and the Crime Intelligence Branch of the RCMP were duplicating efforts in the counterterrorism area (SIRC, 1986–87:27). Old chestnuts like the organization not using its open source unit enough were broached again. The standard of research and the type and quality of researchers within CSIS led SIRC to the conclusion that a case-oriented approach of police work still dominated the Service (SIRC, 1986–87:12–13). Implicit in this conclusion was the notion that the actions of intelligence officers were being determined by information received by the system, not specifically or strategically sought by it.[25] It was apparent that CSIS had not moved beyond the counterespionage approach to the new level of mind game required by counterintelligence work.[26]

SIRC, also posed new questions with a familiar ring. Does CSIS, they asked

> protect the national interest as effectively as possible? Is it efficient —in terms of both management goals like financial integrity and policy goals like 'civilianization' and official bilingualism? (SIRC, 1986–87:5)

SIRC was still concerned about the number of people in CSIS with police backgrounds. Even after the "bridgeback scheme" (which al-

lowed former RCMP officers to leave civilian service security work and
to return to the RCMP to do non-security work) had expired (July 16,
1986), 83% of CSIS employees were still bringing the memories and habits of the RCMP to work with them (SIRC, 1986–87:43). Adding insult
to injury was the number of former police officers recruited as intelligence officers by direct entry. Of all new intelligence officers, 34% had
originated by direct entry. Of this number, 91% came from police backgrounds (81% from the RCMP). This was more than a bone of conten-
tion for SIRC. It was also a source of aggravation, frustration, and morale problems for other recruits because 98% of these direct entry
personnel had come in at the highest nonmanagement level (SIRC,
1986–87:43–44).

SIRC might have gone on simply producing an annual round of
criticisms had it not happened that SIRC's first major area review coin-
cided with the arrest of a CSIS informer. The review concerned the
smallest of CSIS's operational activities, countersubversion.[27] Because
of a perceived threat to civil liberties revealed by the large number of
active files, the review concluded that the countersubversion role
should be divided among CSIS' other two branches—with Counter-Intelligence dealing with foreign influences and Counter-Terrorism handling risks of violence (SIRC, 1986–87:40).[28] The arrest in question involved Marc Boivin, a union strike organizer who had been an informer
for CSIS and the RCMP for fifteen years. Most of this time, he had been
instructed to collect information on the labor movement and persons attempting to influence it. His arrest (on criminal charges relating to a
conspiracy to bomb hotels) occurred as the result of information given
by CSIS to the *Sûreté du Québec* on June 4, more than three weeks before
SIRC's annual report was released (SIRC, 1988:5–9).

The Independent Advisory Team's Role

SIRC's report and Boivin's arrest led the Solicitor General to set up
an Independent Advisory Team (IAT) under former Chief Clerk to the
Privy Council Gordon Osbaldeston.[29] This task force was charged with
addressing problems arising from CSIS' policies concerning recruitment, training and development, personnel management, and targeting—and with assessing the possible adverse effects of countersubversion efforts on civil liberties (*News Release*, July 22, 1987). But most
important of all, the task force was asked to develop an action plan for
change. The need for change was reinforced by the resignation of the
agency's director and the "retirement" of certain senior staff after a revelation that CSIS had provided false information in an application for a
crucial wiretap.

According to Osbaldeston, the major difference between his IAT and the many studies that had gone before it was the fact that the IAT took it as a given that CSIS must be civilianized (Diebel, 1987). In this regard, the IAT felt obliged to observe that the civilanization had lost whatever meaning it once had. As a result, they reconstituted it in terms of the broader question of people and organizational change. To accomplish this, they observed in marvellous circumlocution that "the Service must modify its culture, and with it, its mix of people." (IAT, 1987:10)

The IAT's report identified four important prerequisites for change: effective leadership; effective human resource management; integrated recruitment, training, and career development; and a re-modelling of the corporate culture to enhance esteem and encourage different values (IAT, 1987:11). The IAT did not take an individual-problem approach to its mandate but rather a holistic view. It noted (IAT, 1987:22) that any serious study of the countersubversion function "soon leads one to the entire targeting process and thereby illuminates most of the weaknesses in the Service's corporate culture." In this regard the IAT noted that the security intelligence framework,

> though nominally in place, has not functioned as was intended. The priority setting role of this framework has never really been exercised. The blend of skills and talents needed to support the targeting process, investigation and analysis is not adequate" (IAT, 1987:22).

In addition to problems with CSIS' corporate culture, the IAT discovered problems with the corporate culture of the larger security and intelligence community. Not only was CSIS being driven by operational prerequisites, but so too was the Secretariat within the Solicitor General's Department. Furthermore, there was no agency-secretariat-inter-departmental committee process by which annual threat assessments could be developed and intelligence priorities could be approved by Cabinet. Although the Solicitor General was now accountable for the legal side of the process, he was not fully integrated into the governmental policy process (IAT, 1987:27–28).

In terms of an action plan, the IAT prepared a public report with thirty-four recommendations and private codicils.[30] These recommendations covered a wide range of issues: increasing the Director's visible role within the agency, making changes in the planning process, eliminating the Counter-Subversion Branch, improving the Solicitor General's involvement in the policy process, and creating mechanisms for increasing pride in CSIS and increasing the morale of CSIS employees. In the final analysis, however, the IAT report did not say why most of the changes were necessary or what would happen if they were not carried out.

Conclusion

This chapter has been concerned with police deviance but not the sort of deviance normally discussed in the criminological literature. This is not the deviance of the bad apple or the rotten barrel, nor even deviance with intent. It is deviance more akin to Turk's "blameworthy failures to accomplish organizational objectives." In this case, it is perhaps deviance of the subconscious routinely applied.

The cultural response of CSIS in the 1980s to the idea of 'civilization' was inherently similar to that of the RCMP in the 1950s. Despite legislative changes, business was largely conducted as usual. Although there was an influx of new blood, it came in largely at the bottom of the organization. And although some old managers moved on, new ones were drawn primarily from the ranks of the old Service. The central ideas of CSIS were as reflections of past generations, and the McDonald Commission's dream of a more intellectual approach to intelligence gathering remained a dream. Most of the old wind had simply been decanted into a new bottle with a fancy label.

It may be argued that attempting to deal with the scandals of the present (which have a habit of repeating themselves) without dealing with the fundamental cultural factors of the past is like blowing into the wind. For example, eliminating the Counter-Subversion Branch and relocating its functions to Counter-Intelligence and Counter-Terrorism may well reduce the noticeable amount of abuse of lawful advocacy and dissent, but it will do so for the wrong reasons. It will do so because the function is squeezed for resources and overtaken by other priorities, not because hearts and minds within the organization have changed about who should be watched and countered.

On the other hand, the implications of not 'civilianizing' CSIS constitute a grave threat to both civil liberties and national security. This is particularly true in a world where terrorist groups do not play by accepted rules nor live within recognizable boundaries, but instead use third-party states to play out their own national dramas. The case-oriented approach to intelligence gathering as historically practiced by the Security Service of the RCMP represents but one level of intelligence collection. A far higher level is that of proactive, strategic intelligence, which starts not with the "nominal" list of suspects so familiar to reactive police work, but with regular strategic analyses of what constitutes current and potential threats and an assessment of the risks specific threats pose. This approach requires a different cultural mix of people, with skills drawn from a wider variety of intellectual and ethnic backgrounds, than have traditionally been present in the RCMP.

Although it is, of course, impossible to control against all types of intelligence failure, the likelihood of such failure is arguably greater when there is a reliance on the more reactive, case-oriented approach. And when failures do occur, the lessons for civil liberties are clear. The failure of the intelligence arms of the RCMP and Quebec police forces to alert their respective governments to the limitations of the FLQ threat in the Fall of 1970 and then advise them on the nature of the conspiracy — to say nothing of finding the hostages — not only caused the government to overreact by imposing the War Measures Act, but it provided the police with an opportunity to settle old scores. Later, this failure caused the federal government to instruct the Security Service to keep them better informed. The subsequent unlawful acts and the practices not authorized by law that were identified by the Duchaîne, Keeble and McDonald Commissions may be seen in light of this instruction.[31]

Domestic intelligence collection emphasizing a strategic (rather than case-oriented) approach may prove less haphazard, better disciplined, and more closely confined in its targeting. In a strategic environment, critical decisions concerning the allocation of resources could be based on current risks and opportunities, not driven by past operational practices. In this way, targeting could also be based on more finite criteria — i.e., an obligation to assess whether a person or group constitutes a *current* risk — not just on whether a group or individual had historically constituted a threat in someone's mind's eye.

But even though increased organizational efficacy in dealing with security threats reduces certain threats to civil liberties, organizations dominated by the strategic mind are not necessarily free of potential problems.[32] The work of intelligence — strategic or otherwise — will likely always include grey areas where personnel, for a variety of reasons, are disinclined to be controlled. This may mean, for example, that domestic intelligence agencies would merely become better at rationalizing and accounting for their targeting decisions, not more skilled at deriving them judiciously. This implies that particular care must be taken in the pre-event approval and monitoring of targeting decisions.

In democratic societies, who the state watches (and how) is properly a political decision that requires the involvement of democratically elected, publicly accountable political masters. Without changes to the organizational culture of CSIS and a move toward a more strategic approach to intelligence gathering, one might expect future revelations to indicate that CSIS has continued to conduct business as usual. But legislative reforms of the 1980s and the government's concern over the Boivin affair suggest that matters may now be moving on the right track. It remains to be seen, however, whether the Canadian government will be satisfied with the appearances of reform or will have the necessary will to ensure that those appearances are backed up by substance.

It is hoped that the five-year review of the CSIS Act Parliament is about to undertake will do more than see that the legislation's *i*'s and *t*'s are properly dotted and crossed. This could be a time for examining the broader picture, for checking that political masters are taking a properly active part in the essential decision-making processes, and that oversight bodies are concerned with issues of efficacy as well as propriety. For, as we have seen, the control of intelligence is very much a two-edged sword. Control of impropriety without considering organizational efficacy is as dangerous as ensuring intelligence effectiveness without reflecting on its impact on civil liberties.

Notes

*The author would like to thank Michael Brogden for encouraging him to write the original paper, Margaret Beare and Clifford Shearing for sharing their insights, and Richard Ericson, Peter Manning, and Peter Russell for commenting on an earlier version of this paper. The author wishes to acknowledge the financial assistance of the Solicitor General of Canada provided through Independent Research Grant #1700-22. The opinions expressed, however, are those of the author's and should not be taken in any way to represent the opinions of the Government of Canada. Moreover, this chapter was written before the author became the Director of Research of the House of Commons on the Review of the *Canadian Security Intelligence Service Act* and the *Security Offences Act*. An earlier version of this chapter was presented at the Annual Meeting of the American Society of Criminology, "State and Crime," Chicago, 9–12 November 1988.

1. Britain did not, of course, escape from controversies and scandals concerning security and intelligence matters. The defection of Burgess, Maclean, and Philby — and the revelation that Sir Anthony Blunt, the Surveyor of the Queen's Pictures, was a long-time Soviet agent — led to a search for "moles" that has been described as a national obsession. The Profumo affair of 1963 continues to this day to titillate the British predilection for sexual scandal. What remains to be explained is how consecutive British governments have been able to avoid wide-scale public inquiries of their intelligence agencies.

2. Ken Robertson (1987) has argued that an effective intelligence agency is less likely to be dangerous to civil liberties than one operating under conditions where there is a lack of clarity over the threats facing a particular society and the purposes for which information is collected and used. The argument presented here is based on different premises. Robertson asserts that legislators and the executive branch have failed to provide proper guidance. This chapter suggests that a particular approach to intelligence gathering is not only inappropriate because it is inefficient but also potentially dangerous to civil liberties. Our solutions are necessarily different. His concern the political process; ours concern the ideas that go into that process.

3. Because of a restraining order on press coverage the APLQ incident was not reported until after Sampson's trial had been completed. For coverage, see: *Montreal Star,* (April 1st, 1976).

4. John Sawatsky's article appeared in the *Vancouver Sun* on 7 December 1976. It is interesting to note that Canadian Press refused to carry the story and that not one member of the Parliamentary Press Gallery reported a subsequent planted question in the House of Commons (Sawatsky, 1980:279).

5. All three officers received an absolute discharge on 16 June. The lawyer for the RCMP officer claimed that all three officers had acted from the best of motives.

6. The two former officers in question were Donald McCleerly and Gilles Brunet. According to Sawatsky (1980:221), their private security company had become the prime suspect after it was revealed that Sampson had been under their command in the RCMP. McCleery had been fired from the force in December 1973 for allegedly having improper associations with people close to the Montreal underworld. He argued that such contacts were a necessary element of his job and that questionable practices were widespread. He and Brunet told of barn burning, the theft of documents, and "participation and assistance to the CIA in offensive activities in Canada." See also: Lewis (1981:29). The CIA activity in question is presumed to concern the explosion and fire at the Cuban trade mission in Montreal in 1972. The section on relations with foreign intelligence agencies was expurgated from the McDonald Commission report.

7. The activities included: illegal mail opening, arson, intimidation of potential informants, unlawful surreptitious entries, illegal wiretaps, civil trespass, unlawful use of confidential information, disruptive tactics, theft of dynamite, traffic offenses, use of false identities, and so on. Lewis (1981:26) reported that as many as 200 Mounties might be charged.

8. Control systems of the watchdog type tend to pay more attention to the propriety of organizations than to their operational effectiveness or efficiency.

9. The argument of superior orders was used by constables and commissioners alike. One former RCMP commissioner testified that he had been told

what was necessary and what ought to be obtained. He noted that one would have interpreted it as an instruction or a wish but had he refused he would not have been Commissioner very long (McDonald, *Transcripts*, Vol. 87: 14358).

10. The former was never formally announced. It was lodged in the Privy Council Office and headed initially by Michael Pitfield. The other worked out of the Ministry of the Solicitor General of Canada. It was formally announced on the day the McDonald Commission was released and was known as the Security Intelligence Transitional (or SIT) Group (Confidential interview, member of the Liberal Cabinet, Houses of Parliament, 22 September 1988).

11. Confidential interview, House of Parliament, 22 September 1988.

12. Both committees spent a considerable amount of time defining what the threats were. Neither took more than parts of a session or two to develop either a quantitative or qualitative assessment of the identified threats.

13. These powers had been provided to the RCMP Security Service under Cabinet Directive 35, dated 27 March 1975.

14. CSIS employees were, however, given (ambiguously, one must add) protections similar to those that would be available to peace officers under the law (*CSIS Act*, S. 20).

15. The CSIS Act, for example, allows mail opening, which was hitherto illegal. The Act also provides for access to confidential health records and access to confidential federal government records. In addition, Section 16 empowers CSIS to collect information and intelligence about the capabilities, intentions, and activities of foreign states, persons, and corporations. The threshold for initial investigations is "reasonable grounds" to "suspect," while that for an intrusive investigation warrant under the Act is simply "reasonable grounds" to "believe" that a threat exists. Police investigations under the Criminal Code require "reasonable *and* probable" grounds to believe that a criminal offense has been committed. It should be noted, however, that the *CSIS Act* eliminated Section 16 of the *Official Secrets Act*, which had allowed the Solicitor General to issue a warrant to intercept or seize communications where he was "satisfied by evidence on oath" that such interception was (i) necessary to prevent or detect subversive activity, (ii) detrimental to the security of Canada, or (iii) for foreign intelligence purposes.

16. For a detailed analysis of the system of controls, see: Farson, 1985.

17. SIRC has consistently referred to its "oversight" role, whereas the *CSIS Act* refers only to "review." SIRC justified oversight on the following basis (SIRC, 1985–86:3): "Oversight is the word used in both the United States and the United Kingdom to mean monitoring and evaluation of security intelligence operations. Because it is a well established term in the intelligence community, we also use it despite the risk of ambiguity arising from its other meaning as a

failure to notice." John Starnes (1987), a former Director General of the RCMP Security Service, has disputed this interpretation of the legislation, arguing that Parliament would have used the term if it had meant for SIRC to have the power. Sternes further suggested that SIRC's day-to-day oversight has been harful to the Service. Morale has been lowered, and operational investigations have suffered.

18. This police/nonpolice dichotomy has frequently been put down to bureaucratic turf wars between the RCMP and CSIS. In confidential interview a Canadian municipal police chief suggested that CPICAC may also have been influenced by non-RCMP members of the committee. His past experience with the Security Service left much to be desired. He suggested that "those cowboys" needed to earn their (i.e., the municipal policemen's) trust first.

19. Expurgated copy of SIRC (1986) obtained under Access to Information File No. 1463-1/87 TD-004. The research team interviewed 165 CSIS members, all new Intelligence Officer training recruits, several senior managers, CSIS' training staff, certain members of the security and intelligence community, and "other experts."

20. This is not surprising, particularly because SIRC used the consultant who had worked for the McDonald Commission.

21. The expurgated version of the report does not explicitly indicate the severity of morale problems. It may be deduced, however, from the amount of material that has been removed from Section VI.6, "Morale and Communication"; the fact that positive comments on the subject are not included; the statement that "To raise morale . . . CSIS management should . . . "; and the recommendation that "CSIS Senior Management build a culture in the organization that stresses a philosophy that its people are the most important resource" (see page 81 of the report). The morale problem has, however, been confirmed by confidential interviews with former intelligence personnel and other sources.

22. Only eight of these made it to SIRC's annual report.

23. The report (SIRC, 1986:79) quotes from a section of *In Search of Excellence* that suggests how the average Joe and Jane can be turned into winners.

24. In testimony to a Senate-Commons committee the Official Languages Commissioner put it more strongly, suggesting that CSIS was linguistically in the "Stone Age" (Anon, 1987a:1). Apparently, his evidence was based on some 1,700 complaints, many of them from CSIS employees in Quebec (Anon, 1987b:A8).

25. See: Manning (1980:85–92) for a discussion of the limitations of the case-oriented approach.

26. The simplest way to distinquish between these two levels is to think of the targets involved and the methodologies used. On the lower level, the methodology emphasizes possible suspects. Thus, the starting point tends to

be intelligence from friendly agencies and operational intelligence aimed at embassy personnel. At the higher level, intelligence research constitutes the starting point. It is used to develop hypotheses as to what foreign intelligence service will do—and where, when, and how. Operational intelligence is then used to develop targets.

27. In evidence before a Standing Committee on Justice and the Solicitor General, the Director of CSIS estimated that less than five percent of *agency* resources were allocated to countersubversion (*Minutes*, No. 4, 11 December 1986:48). SIRC (1986–87:35) estimated that ten percent or slightly more of *operational* resources was more accurate.

28. Interviews with a former senior member of the Canadian security and intelligence community indicate that CSIS not only inherited the RCMP personnel but also their functional responsibilities and geographic distribution. Because the Service could offer agents little incentive to move, personnel in certain branches of the Service sometimes remained in locations where the threat they were meant to be dealing with was limited or nonexistent. This apparently resulted in make-work projects—sometimes of a dubious nature—while other areas remained understaffed. The problem was eventually partly addressed by early retirement incentives.

29. In addition to being Secretary to the Cabinet, the Chief Clerk is Canada's senior civil servant.

30. Confidential interview with IAT staff member, Ottawa, 20 October 1988.

31. For comments on the Duchaine and Keeble Commissions on this point, see: Brodeur (1981:149–151).

32. For a detailed analysis of some of the consequences—both intended and unintended—of proactive strategic intelligence, see Marx (1988).

References

Anon
1987 Fortier Says Spy Service in Linguistic Stone Age. *Citizen*. April 30.
1987 CSIS Can't Hear Sounds of Danger. *Citizen*. May 4.

Bayley, David H.
1975 The Police and Political Development in Europe. In *The Formation of Nation States in Western Europe*, ed. by Charles Tilly. Princeton, NJ: Princeton University Press.

Bensman, Joseph and Israel Gerver
1963 Crime and Punishment in the Factory: The Functioning of Deviancy in Maintaining the Social System. *American Sociological Review*. Vol. 28:588–98.

BMC
1973   D.A.W. Richards and J.M.R. Piche. RCMP Security Service Organiza-
       tion Review. *Introductory Report*. Project 5–510. Ottawa: Bureau of Manage-
       ment Consulting.

Brodeur, Jean-Paul
1981   Legitimizing Police Deviance. In *Organizational Police Deviance: Its Struc-
       ture and Control:* 127–160, ed. by Clifford D. Shearing. Toronto: Butter-
       worths.
1983   High Policing and Low Policing:Remarks about the Policing of Political
       Activities. *Social Problems*. Vol. 30:507–520.

Church
1976   Senate Select Committee Intelligence Activities. *Final Report: Books 1–5*.
       Washington, DC: Government Printing Office.

CSIS Act
1983–84   32nd Parliament, 32–33 Elizabeth II, 2nd Session. *Canadian Security
       Intelligence Service Act*.

Deal, T. E. and A. A. Kennedy
1982   *Corporate Culture*. Reading, PA: Addison-Wesley

Debates
1969–88   House of Commons. *Debates*.

Diebel, Linda
1987   Canada's Spy Agency is Back in the Shop for a Refit. *Montreal Gazette*.
       September 19.

Duchaîne
1970   *Rapport sur les Évenements d'octobre 1970*. Quebec: Ministère de la Justice.

Ericson, Richard V.
1981a   *Making Crime: A Study of Detective Work*. Toronto: Butterworths.
1981b   Rules for Police Deviance. In *Organizational Police Deviance: Its Structure
       and Control:* 83–110, ed. by Clifford D. Shearing. Toronto: Butterworths.
1982   *Reproducing Order: A Study of Police Patrol Work*. Toronto: University of To-
       ronto Press.

Farson, A. Stuart
1985   Countering the Security Threat in the 1980's: McDonald's Legacy and
       the Need for Effective and Efficient Control. Paper prepared for the Secu-
       rity Intelligence Review Committee's Research Seminar: Canadian Secu-
       rity Intelligence in the 80's. Meech Lake, Ottawa. October 11.

Hope
1976   Royal Commission on Intelligence and Security. *Reports*. Canberra: Aus-
       tralia Government Printing Office.

IAT
1987a   Independent Advisory Team. *People and Process in Transition.* Ottawa: Solicitor General of Canada.
1987b   Own Davey and Jim Laplante. Working Paper. *The Issues Surrounding Subversion: Detailed Observations, Findings and Recommendations.* Ottawa: Independent Advisory Team.

Keable
1981   *Rapport, de la Commission d'enquête sur des opérations policières en territoire québécois,* Quebec: Ministère de la Justice.

Kilmann, R. H.
1980   *Beyond the Quick Fix: Managing Five Tracks to Organizational Success.* San Francisco: Jossey Bass.

Lewis, Robert
1981   Black Marks for Scarlet Coats. *Maclean's.* Vol. 94, No. 36 (September 7): 21–29.

MacKenzie
1969   Royal Commission on Security. *Report.* Ottawa: Ministry of Supply and Services. (Reprinted 1979.)

McBarnet, Doreen
1976   Pretrial Procedures and the Construction of Conviction. In *The Sociology of Law,* ed. by P. Carlen. Keele, England: Department of Sociology, University of Keele.
1979   Arrest: The Legal Context of Policing. In *The British Police,* ed. by S. Holdaway. London: Edward Arnold.
1981   *Conviction: Law, the State and the Construction of Justice.* London: Macmillan.

McDonald
1981   Commission of Inquiry Concerning Certain Activities of the Royal Canadian Mounted Police. *Second Report* (two volumes). Ottawa: Ministry of Supply and Services.

McDonald Transcripts
Commission of Inquiry Concerning Certain Activities of the Royal Canadian Mounted Police. Unpublished.

Malarek, Victor
1985   95% of CSIS Staff Veterans of the RCMP. *Globe and Mail.* June 11.

Manning, Peter H.
1971   The Police Mandate, Strategies and Appearances. In *Crime and Social Justice in American Society,* ed. by J. Douglas. Indianapolis: Bobbs-Merrill.
1977a   Rules, Colleagues and Situationally Justified Actions. In *Colleagues in Organizations: The Social Construction of Professional Work,* ed. by New York: Wiley.

1977b   *Police Work*. Cambridge, MA: MIT Press.
1979   The Social Control of Police Work: Observations on the Culture of Policing. In *British Police*, ed. by S. Holdaway. London: Edward Arnold.
1980a   *The Narc's Game: Organizational and Informational Limits on Drug Law Enforcement*. Cambridge, MA: MIT Press.
1980b   Metaphors of the Field: Varieties of Organizational Discourse. *Administrative Science Quarterly*. Vol. 24:660–671.

Martin, Joanne, Martha S. Feldman, Mary Jo Hatch and Sim B. Sitkin
1983   The Uniqueness Paradox in Organizational Stories. *Administrative Science Quarterly*. Vol. 28:438–453.

Martin, Joanne and Melanie E. Powers
1983   Truth or Corporate Propaganda: The value of a Good War Story. In *Organizational Symbolism*, ed. by Louis R. Pondy, Peter J. Frost, Garath Morgan and Thomas Dandridge. Greenwich, CT: JAL Press.

Marx, Gary T.
1988   *Undercover: Police Surveillance in America*. Berkeley, CA: University of California Press.

Minutes
1984–85 House of Commons. Standing Committee on Justice and Legal Affairs Committee. *Minutes of Proceedings and Evidence.*
1986–88 House of Commons. Standing Committee on Justice and Solicitor General. *Minutes of Proceedings and Evidence.*

New Zealand
1976   Chief Ombudsman. *Report: Security Intelligence*. Wellington: A. R. Shearer, Government Printer.

News Release
1987   Gordon Osbaldeston to Lead Independent Advisory Team on CSIS. *News Release*. Ottawa: Solicitor General of Canada. July 22.

Ouchi, W. G.
1981   *Theory Z*. Reading, PA. Addison-Wesley.

Pascale, R. T. and A. G. Athos
1981   *The Art of Japanese Management*. New York: Simon & Schuster.

Peters, T. J. and R. H. Waterman
1982   *In Search of Excellence*. New York: Harper & Row.

Peters, Tom and Nancy Austin
1985   *A Passion for Excellence: The Leadership Difference*. New York: Random House.

Pike
1976   House Select Committee on Intelligence, *Report: United States Intelligence Agencies and Activities*. Washington, DC: Government Printing Office.

Pitfield
1983a   Special Committee of the Senate on the Canadian Security Intelligence Service. *Delicate Balance: A Security Intelligence Service in a Democratic Society.* Ottawa: Ministry of Supply and Services.
1983b   Special Committee of the Senate on the Canadian Security Intelligence Service. *Minutes of Proceedings and Evidence.* Ottawa: Ministry of Supply and Services.

Porter, Michael
1987   The Case for Rethinking Strategic Planning. *Globe and Mail.* June 6.

Punch, Maurice
1981   Management and Control of Organizations: Occupational Deviance, Responsibility and Accountability. Inaugural Lecture. Nijenrode, Leiden: Stenfewrt Kroese.

Punch, Maurice (ed.)
1983   *Control in the Police Organization.* Cambridge, MA: MIT Press.

RCMP
1947   C.E. Rivette-Carnac. *Reorganization: Special Branch Headquarters and Divisions.* Ottawa: RCMP.

1955   Mark McClung. *Memorandum on Organization of the Internal Security Service.* Ottawa: RCMP.
1956   *Memorandum on the Organization of the Internal Security Service Submitted by Mark McClung.* Ottawa: RCMP.

Robertson, Kenneth G.
1987   Intelligence, Terrorism and Civil Liberties. *Conflict Quarterly.* Vol. 7: 43–62.

Rockefeller
1975   Commission on CIA Activities Within the United States. *Report to the President.* Washington, DC: Government Printing Office.

Sallot, Jeff
1979   *Nobody Said No: The Real Story About How the Mounties Always Get Their Man.* Toronto: James Lorimer & Company.

Sathe, V.
1985   *Culture and Corporate Realities.* Homewood, Ont: Irwin.

Sawatsky, John
1980   *Men in the Shadows: The RCMP Security Service.* Toronto: Doubleday.

Schall, Maryan S.
1983   A Communication Rules Approach to Organizational Culture. *Administrative Science Quarterly.* Vol. 28:557–581.

Schein, Edgar H.
1985 *Organizational Culture and Leadership*. San Francisco: Jossey-Bass Publishers.

Shearing, Clifford D.
1977 *Real Men, Good Men, Wise Men and Cautious Men*. PhD Dissertation. Toronto: University of Toronto.

Shearing, Clifford D. (ed.)
1981 *Organizational Police Deviance: Its Structure and Control*. Toronto: Butterworths.

Shearing, Clifford D. and Richard V. Ericson
n.d. Police Culture: Towards a Tropological Theory of Action. Unpublished paper.

Sherman, Lawrence W.
1978 *Scandal and Reform: Controlling Police Corruption*. Berkeley: University of California Press.

SIRC
1985–1986 Security Intelligence Review Committee. *Annual Report: 1985–86*. Ottawa: Ministry of Supply and Services.
1986 Security Intelligence Review Committee. *Eighteen Months after Separation: An Assessment of CSIS' Approach to Recruitment, Training and Related Issues*. Ottawa: SIRC.
1986–1987 Security Intelligence Review Committee. *Annual Report: 1986–87.* Ottawa: Ministry of Supply and Services.
1987 Security Intelligence Review Committee. *Closing the Gap: Official Languages and Staff Relations in the Canadian Security Intelligence Service*. Ottawa: Ministry of Supply and Services Canada.
1988 Security Intelligence Review Committee, *Section 54 Report to the Solicitor General of Canada on CSIS's Use of Its Investigative Powers with Respect to the Labour Movement*, Ottawa: SIRC.

Starnes, John
1987 Intelligence Committee Report Marred by Cant. Ottawa. *Citizen*. August 19.

Tichy, N. M.
1983 *Managing Strategic Change*. New York: Wiley.

Turk, Austin T.
1981 Organizational Deviance and Political Policing. In *Organizational Police Deviance: Its Structure and Control*, ed. by Clifford D. Shearing. Toronto: Butterworths.

Van Maanen, John
1973 Observations on the Making of Policemen. *Human Organization.* Vol. 32:407–418.
1974 Working the Street: The Developmental View of Police Behavior. In *The Potential for Reform of Criminal Justice,* ed. by H. Jacob. Beverly Hills, CA: Sage.

Walker, Wallace Earl
1986 *Changing Organizational Culture: Strategy, Structure and Professionalism in the US General Accounting Office.* Knoxville: University of Tennessee Press.

Wilkins, A. L.
1983 Organizational Stories as Symbols which Control the Organization. In *Organizational Symbolism,* ed. by Peter J. Frost, Garath Morgan and Thomas Dandridge. Greenwich, CN: JAL Press.

Wilkins, A. L. and W. G. Ouchi
1983 Efficient Cultures: Exploring the Relationship between Culture and Organizational Performance. *Administrative Science Quarterly.* Vol. 28:468–481.

8

When the State Fails: A Critical Assessment of Contract Policing in the United States

John Wildeman

During the 1970s, much was written about the "privatization" of the governmental functions of the capitalist state, functions such as health care, refuse collection, road and highway repair, and even corrections and rehabilitation (O'Connor, 1973; Spitzer and Scull, 1977; Draper, 1978). In the 1980s, privatization of services which were once the monopoly of the state proceeded apace with the implementation of the Reagan doctrine (See U.S. Department of Justice, 1985.) This chapter attempts a critical assessment of contract policing—the privatization of the social control and law enforcement functions of the state. The analysis raises the question of whether this development represents a decline in the state's responsibility and effort to protect the civil rights and liberties of its citizens. If such a decline in civil liberties did exist, it would paradoxically be based on the actual increase in state control resulting from the rapid growth of contract policing. So far, there has been relatively little empirical investigation of this critical issue.

The argument that privatization of the state's law enforcement function is an integral dynamic of capitalist development has been advanced frequently in the literature (Spitzer & Scull, 1977; Shearing and Stenning, 1981; O'Malley, 1988; Platt, 1988). O'Malley (1988:82) sums up this argument as it was first advanced by Spitzer and Scull:

> As monopoly capitalism expands, so too does the demand for provision of politico-legal functions which are not, or cannot, be effectively provided by the state. Corporations therefore increasingly are resorting to contract or internal policing: a substitution of state-operated political functions.

More than a decade earlier, Spitzer and Scull argued that the relationship between the expansion of private policing and the development of capitalist economic systems is in large measure the consequence of the need of capital to rationalize control over production and labor itself. They saw the emergence of profit-oriented police services in the private sector as an integral part of "the extension of capitalist control over the labor process and the rationalization of productive activity" (Spitzer and Scull, 1977:18).

A Paradox: Public Police and Private Growth

Modern contract policing in the United States began in the late nineteenth century, with the most significant decades being the 1880s and 1890s. The second half of the nineteenth century saw a rapid expansion of capitalist industrial development fueled by a massive influx of immigrant labor. This influx was in turn accompanied by widespread labor unrest and efforts to organize the masses of immigrant laborers. In response, the capitalist sector stimulated the explosive growth of private security. In the subsequent struggles, the use of private security guards (often no more than hired thugs) to combat unionization efforts became standard practice. The infamous Pinkerton Detective Agency and the Burns Detective Agency stand out as the capitalist sector's most effective and repressive tools in the early struggle to dominate and control labor.[1]

In 1893, however, federal employment of private security in any capacity whatsoever was prohibited by passage of the so-called Pinkerton Law (27 Statute 591, 5 U.S. Code 53, enacted March 3, 1893): "Hereafter no employee of the Pinkerton Detective Agency, or similar agency shall be employed in any Government Service. . . . " But today the employment of private police by the private sector continues to be the most essential weapon in the fight for control over labor (Brandes, 1976). Public police are rarely called upon to provide the manpower, technology, and expertise required to control labor organizing and militancy.

A few observations are in order regarding the state's increasingly ineffective control of crime in the 1970s and 1980s and its comparatively large funding increases for federal, state, and local law enforcement bodies and institutions. Even as the capitalist state extracts ever-increasing tax revenues from citizens with the pledge of police protection, corporate and street crime rates continue to escalate. Private citizens, neighborhood groups, and (more significantly) multinationals and other large corporations in the banking and finance, retail, insurance, manufacturing, and construction industries are spending more and more on contract policing.

Several statistics on police expenditures and employment for eighty-eight large U.S. cities attest to the massive increases in law enforcement expenditures by government (U.S. Department of Justice, 1986). In nominal dollars, there was a thirty-seven-fold increase in spending for police services between 1938 and 1982. This means that, adjusted for inflation, Americans spent five and one-half times more in 1982 than they did in 1938 for law enforcement. On an annual per capita basis, police expenditures (adjusted for inflation) quadrupled between 1938 and 1982 — from seven to twenty-eight dollars per person. Furthermore, the number of police employees doubled in the years between 1954 and 1972. From 1972 to 1982, police employment nationwide remained fairly steady, but it has been slowly and steadily climbing since 1982. The police share of city budgets has also steadily increased — from eight percent in 1940 to fourteen percent in 1980.

Criminal justice expenditures on all levels of government totaled a record $46 billion in 1985, and the largest portion of this total, $22 billion, was allocated to law enforcement. In other words, Americans paid $22 billion dollars for federal, state, and local police protection in 1985 (Sourcebook of Criminal Justice Statistics 1986). These monies paid for the full-time employment of 693,245 men and women. In the country at large, 52.8 people per 10,000 population are employed in our criminal justice systems. And yet, by any official measure — Uniform Crime Reports, the National Crime Panel, or various studies of the Bureau of Justice Statistics — our crime rates continue to rise.

The growth of private policing in the United States, has been even more dramatic and rapid than the growth of the public police. Contract police are surrogates for legitimate, sworn agents of state control. In 1970, the number of private police employees was roughly the same as the number of public police employees. Since 1970, however, private police have grown to outnumber public police by more than two to one (Gallati, 1983; Cunningham and Taylor, 1983; U.S. Department of Justice, 1984; Platt, 1988). Thus, we may conservatively estimate the number of private police employed either full- or part-time in the United States at approximately 1.5 million.

In dollars and cents, the business of contract policing is lucrative indeed. In 1977, the "private security service market" was valued at $2.7 billion. By 1986 (less than ten years later), contract policing was valued at $7.9 billion. Furthermore, demand for security services has been projected to increase at a 9.1% annual rate, reaching a value level of $12.3 billion by 1991 (Freedonia Group, 1987).

How do surrogate police fill the gap left by the failure of public police to provide effective police protection and investigative activities? Do contract policing arrangements realize social and individual justice in the absence of public accountability? Does contract policing actually (and paradoxically) *increase* state control? These are questions of deep concern because our privacy, freedom, and security are at stake.

Contract Policing and Social Justice

One of the principle objections to the very concept of contract policing is that private police are just that—private. They do not work for law enforcement institutions supported by taxpaying, voting citizens. Contract police constitute a police power beyond the direct control of the state, procedural law, and the democratic process in general. In the long run, contract policing — particularly the employment of off-duty public police by private firms and interests—undermines the public interest. Some commentators see in private police the potential beginning of a slow transition to a totalitarian police state, a sort of Law Enforcement Intelligence Unit (LEIU) on a vast national scale (O'Toole, 1978; Kakalik & Wildhorn, 1972).

Founded in 1956, the LEIU is essentially a private club whose members are officers of urban police forces across the country. LEIU members conduct secret investigations on behalf of corporations and other private interests under the protection of their status as private police acting as members of a private security firm. As contract police, LEIU members are not bound by the legal restrictions governing the behavior and activities of public law enforcement agents. Shrouded in the cloak of a private membership organization, LEIU members are free to engage in activities that would clearly be illegal if they were engaged in by public police Thus, the LEIU has been described as a quasi-secret police intelligence organization acting without legal authority. An example of an activity that would clearly be illegal if engaged in by public police is the sharing of intelligence files on private citizens. Despite such practices, the LEIU has received generous grants and close cooperation (principally through data sharing) from the Justice Department.

Thus, the LEIU and many other contract police organizations are able with impunity to sidestep legal issues bearing on the protection of citizens' privacy and confidentiality. Furthermore, because these are private firms, citizens cannot demand legal access to their intelligence files, as is the case with the intelligence files of public police (such as the FBI). For private citizens, this is the worst of both worlds: invasion of privacy and confidentiality with no possibility of reviewing the accuracy or inaccuracy of intelligence files compiled by the contract police organization. Nor can citizens even know with whom this intelligence information has been shared (for example, credit rating institutions, insurance firms, banking enterprises, and other private detective firms). Of course, not all contract police have the same goals, resources, and status as the LEIU. Nevertheless, hundreds of thousands of private police are either retired law enforcement officers or, more commonly, active officers moonlighting while off-duty.

Two Scenarios

In the first scenario, private interest groups and organizations (i.e., shopping malls, corporations, neighborhoods) hire and use off-duty public police. Such personnel are basically serving a public agency and a private employer at the same time, though in different roles and functions. In the second scenario, public police use the services of contract police (i.e., the Department of Justice using the data files of the LEIU). Both scenarios constitute very real threats to the civil liberties of citizens in a democratic society, but the first obviously constitutes the greatest threat. In this case, the powers, experience, and training of the public police—all paid for by taxpayers—are made available on a contractual basis to the private sector and are thus used with a great deal less scrutiny, review, supervision, and legal control than that which stems from procedural law.

These questions have not escaped the attention of journalists. In a front-page *New York Times* article in February 1989 criminologist Mark Moore of Harvard said that "private financial relationships with public agencies undermine the notion of a public police force with equal protection for all." (The same article cites the work of Albert Reiss of Yale and Clifford Shearing of Toronto, both of whom have conducted limited empirical investigations of the private hiring of public police.) In Florida, the police departments in Miami and St. Petersburg have programs that match sworn officers with private employers, and the departments charge a fee to meet the overhead costs of the matching service. This whole issue calls up the conflict of interest on the part of public police in private employ.

Aside from the limited research of criminologists such as Reiss and Shearing, the empirical question has not been investigated. In a study of thirteen police departments in medium-sized jurisdictions (the largest department was Boston, with 1,946 sworn officers) Reiss (1988:2) reports that:

Despite the fact that today many departments not only condone but actively arrange off-duty assignments for their officers, there had been, before the research reported here, no examination of the different organizational arrangements used to manage extra-duty work or of their associated benefits and problems.

Reiss also identifies three management models: the Officer Contract model, in which each officer finds his own secondary employment; the Union Brokerage model, in which the police union finds paid private work for its members; and the Department Contract model, in which the police department contracts directly with private employers.

We simply do not know how many public police across the nation are hired out to private concerns or under what arrangements. Nor do we have any data on how this increasingly common practice results in invasions of citizens' civil rights. An empirical investigation to answer these questions would call for massive funding on the federal level as well as cooperation on local levels. All we know with certainty is that using public authorization to legitimate private police work runs the risk of state authority insuring private interests over public goals. Nigel South, of the Center for Criminology at Middlesex Polytechnic in England, recently examined the growth and significance of the private security industry in Great Britain, the United States, Canada, and Europe. Although South's analysis addresses the issues of public accountability, private security, and civil liberties, it does not report primary data on the actual extent and institutional organization of contract policing in these countries (South, 1989).

It has also been pointed out that public police (active or retired) employed by the private sector are able to cover up their illegal investigative behaviors and techniques with facility and ease (Marx, 1986). This is because they are well acquainted with the ways in which their brethren in the public sector go about discovering these illegal investigations and bringing them to light.

The main pool from which private security firms recruit and hire personnel is the public police on the federal, state, and local levels. The private use of secret agents by multinational corporations and the wealthy, for example, depends heavily upon the recruitment of agents from the federal intelligence community. Tens of thousands of these agents have gone into contract policing over the years. No longer motivated by patriotism but rather by profit and private interest, these agents are not bound by their law enforcement oaths as public servants. In fact, senior police administrators constitute the major reservoir of talent for leadership, supervisory, and command positions in the contract police industry. Under the administrative leadership of this elite segment of contract police is the group referred to in private security lingo as the "mercenaries" — the roughly ninety percent of the industry's personnel who are guards, watchmen, or patrolmen.

American society has been described as being on a "surveillance binge." For every bugging device used by agents on all levels of government, it is estimated that three hundred are used in the private security sector. Most often, these electronic devices are in the hands of former or active public police employed by private security firms (Hougan, 1978). Most police departments do not have the budgets to purchase sophisticated intelligence-gathering devices and other electronic surveillance tools. Large contract police firms, on the other hand (being successful capitalist enterprises), do have the funds to acquire these technologies and train personnel to use them — often in violation of laws protecting citizens' rights to privacy. As a result, contract police firms have the best of both worlds: they hire men and women whose police training has been paid for with public tax monies, and they have the capital to purchase sophisticated policing instruments (again, policing instruments that are often used indiscriminately in violation of civil rights). Finally, contract police organizations do not have to pay for information and other intelligence data gathered by public police at the taxpayers' expense when this information is given to private firms.

Contract policing has expanded well beyond the original industry objective to see to the security and protection of private property. Contract policing today is evolving into more of a business operations function. The industry's leading monthly, *Security: The Magazine for Security Decision Makers*, proclaimed in a recent editorial that "today's readers describe themselves in terms [such as] support services, facilities management, administrative operations . . . " (Lydon, 1987:13). Translated, these descriptive phrases refer to the intelligence functions of data gathering, surveillance, and interagency information transfer. These functions are often free from the restrictive, closely defined limitations circumscribing the range of behaviors legally available to public police. The result is incursions into citizens' rights to confidentiality and privacy.

Marx (1987) notes that the profit sharing which often results from successful private police operations can be a powerful stimulus to circumventing the safeguards that the law provides citizens of civil society. The incentive of a great deal of money earned from a successful sting operation, for example, can unglue the most ethical private policeperson. This incentive (or, more accurately, temptation) does not exist for public police. Profit sharing in the solution of crimes or the breakup of crime syndicates is not part of the law enforcement tradition in the United States. A sworn officer may hope only for a citation and points toward promotion. An analogy may be drawn to a bounty hunter who is well rewarded for capturing a horse thief and a Texas Ranger who, upon doing the same thing, receives no special honorarium for his work. Contract police can legally perform many operations that public police are forbidden by law from performing. A confession of guilt beaten out of a suspect by a private policeperson is admissible evidence in a court of law, while a confession similarly obtained by a sworn agent of the state is not admissible (Marx, 1987).

What exactly are contract police legally empowered to do while on duty on private property? A contract cop working at a mall, department store, or amusement park can detain, coerce, or otherwise intimidate a person in ways legally forbidden to public police. Contract police have a considerably wider range of authority in these situations than public police. In short, contract police on patrol on any private property to which the public is granted access for commercial reasons can legally act in ways that are strictly prohibited for public police. It should be remembered that contract police are private citizens under the law, and private citizens are legally free to act towards other private citizens in ways sworn officers are not.

This is not to deny the fact that security managers in the contract police sector often find themselves in difficult legal binds. On the one hand, if they fail to provide effective protection to their customers, patrons, and employees, they are liable to be sued for damage resulting from this policy. On the other hand, if they provide overly aggressive, untrained, or poorly supervised security guards[2] who overtly and obviously violate the rights of patrons, customers, or employees,[3] they are also open to suits.

These considerations lead us to the inescapable conclusion that our need for contract police in America (a need that springs from the development of late-twentieth-century capitalism) results in a very real and serious threat to civil liberties. The state has failed, it seems, in two ways. Not only has it failed to protect us materially, but—and this is our primary argument— it has failed to protect our constitutionally guaranteed rights and freedoms.

Contract Police and the Social Control Power of the State

A common argument holds that the rise of contract policing in America reflects a breakdown in our criminal justice system and a decline in citizens' regard for the law — an example of Durkheimian anomie

(O'Toole, 1978; Cunningham and Taylor, 1984). This argument leads to the conclusion that the increasing prevalence of contract policing is a clear sign of the decreasing power of state control, a sign of the erosion of the social control power of the state. A similar conclusion holds that the growth of private security "spreads out" and dilutes the power of the state, thereby inhibiting the growth of centralized, totalitarian police control. Consequently, the rise of contract policing may be taken by some as a welcome sign of the democratization of social control. Thus, the reasoning goes, the failure of the state and state law enforcement institutions is a failure to protect us individually and collectively against one another. This failure has lead to the proliferation of contract policing and the rise of a more democratic, "people power" type of social control outside the direct reach of the central power of the state. This is a dubious argument for what appears to be an untenable position.

A more persuasive argument holds that the increasing numbers of contract police firms and their employees — and the operations of contract police — leads to a massive increase in the social control power of the state. Those who use this argument do not view the criminal justice system as inadequate or failing. Rather, they see contract policing as a natural complement or maidservant to the state, permitting even more effective and efficient law enforcement. Thus, "private security makes an invaluable contribution to the public weal. Its absence would be disastrous to law and order, and the operation of the criminal justice system. It constitutes the largest available untapped, unstructured, dormant resource for the prevention and control of crime" (Lipson, 1975:vii). This dovetails with the public image presented by the chief spokespersons for the private security industry: Without contract policing, white collar and street crime would overwhelm us. Cooperation between public and private police is such that private police constitute a subtle, almost crypto-official arm of the state. The only difference is that contract police are less constrained by legislation and the courts.

The line between these two social control institutions is fuzzy. The technology of one is the technology of the other. The subculture of contract police is shared by the subculture of public police, and vice versa. Their "working personalities" and perceptions of the world are similar, and their domain assumptions regarding human nature are identical. On paper, the two are distinct institutions, deriving their legitimacy and authority from different legal and social sources; in practice, however, they are one. Contract police are simply the paraprofessionals of public police.

One example (there are many more) of the virtual unity of focus and organizational cooperation between public and private police is an annual award of up to ten thousand dollars for "the greatest scientific contribution to police work." Who sponsors this award? It is jointly organized, judged, and awarded by two deeply patriotic and archtypical capitalist organizations: American Express and the International Association of Chiefs of Police. The first is a multinational corporation that began as a contract policing concern and the second is an association of public police chiefs.

Reichman (1987) refers to the institution of contract police as "tiny theatres of private control that supplement the more extensive and centralized state social control apparatus." The two are virtually one in reality, with interlocking networks of surveillance and shared intelligence. The forces of social control converge in this fuzzy terrain, and the end result is a quasiofficial extension of the intelligence and surveillance powers of the state, unfettered by the need to conform to the rigid, precise limitations of constitutional law. The links may be tangled and the cooperation at the interface between the two may not always be smooth; nevertheless, those links and the sharing of attitudes, data, and techniques are all very real.

Opponents of this interpretation make much of the antipathies and mutual criticisms that sometimes mark everyday interactions between public and private police. For example, sworn officers often complain of a lack of professionalism, an openness to corruption, and a proneness to ineptitude in the contract police they work with (Cunningham and Taylor, 1984). This complaint is, of course, very real and constitutes the human element of social and organizational interaction throughout society as a whole when professionals work with those who are not as well-trained and supervised.

It is sometimes easier to gain a perspective on the familiar through the lens of the unfamiliar. For example, to better grasp the fact that the social control power of the state in America is extended and strengthened by the growth of private policing, it might be helpful to see how private policing clearly extends the social control function in a nation-state quite different from our own in terms of culture, traditions, and history.

The Peoples' Republic of China's *Beijing Review* reports (with apparent pride) that security services in China have created a new market in recent years. Three new contract police firms have been established in Beijing, one of which is the Beijing Electronic Security Services Company, whose employees are

> mostly retired policemen and ex-servicemen. . . . All guards sent
> by the company dress in dark blue uniforms (a copy of the uni-

forms of public police officers throughout China) and are armed with cudgels and walkie-talkies. . . . It plans to set up a broadcasting station to keep in contact with the public security bureau and assist public security policemen in maintaining order (Wang, 1988:28).

These developments represent a further extension of the totalitarian control of the communist regime and of the social control apparatus of the Chinese state. Is it not the same in the United States with regard to the social institutionalization of contract policing?

Since 1978 and the end of the Mao era, in a series of faltering steps, China has been very gradually "opening to the world" under the leadership of Deng Xiaoping. It was Deng who began to relax formal state and party control in order to promote economic growth. The traumatic events in the spring and summer of 1989 will surely arrest this momentum temporarily. No one knows for sure, but indications are that this Chinese version of *glasnost* will eventually be resumed after leadership power struggles have worked themselves through and a Chinese version of democracy is ultimately implemented. Part of this Chinese *glasnost* involves a cautious and gradual (but growing) limitation of the centralized state's broad and oppressive powers of social control over Chinese citizens. The leadership's harsh crackdown following the Tienanmen Square occupation and democracy rallies, however, brought a temporary halt to this democratization process.

It is curious that the phenomenon of contract policing should begin to emerge (and presumably expand rapidly in the near future) at this particular point in the history of postrevolutionary China. This seems to suggest that the same or analogous thing may be happening in our own country. Contract policing in the United States has flourished in response to the courts' progressive limitations and careful definitions of the police powers of the state. Contract policing thus neutralizes the legal limitations and restrictions on the capitalist state's powers of social control in the areas of surveillance, intelligence gathering, data sharing, and even physical coercion.

The same phenomenon can be seen in socialist China and in capitalist America. We are witnessing contract police organizations reinforcing and extending the social control powers of the centralized state. The private and public sectors are no longer two distinctly separate entities in the arena of social control. But how could it be otherwise, given the overwhelming and stifling power of state control—either capitalist or socialist—in the latter decades of the 20th century?

Conclusion

This chapter has considered in some detail the relationship between state responsibility for social order and private arrangements to secure order — that is, contract policing. It has examined the relationship between public and private forms of social control, an arena fraught with contradictions and ambiguities. We have addressed the question of whether privitizing the state's social control function represents a decline in the state's responsibility to protect the civil rights and liberties of citizens and whether such privatization represents an increase or decrease in the state's power. Our conclusion is that the exponential growth of contract policing has been accompanied by a diminution of civil liberties and rights such as privacy, confidentiality, and due process as well as by a vast and largely unrecognized increase in the power of the capitalist state.

There are many reasons for the startling increase in the social control powers of centralized states, capitalist as well as socialist, in the twentieth century. Some of these reasons are easily recognized, but others are more subtle. Either way, the developing global political economy suggests that the current trend toward contract policing will continue into the twenty-first century. What can be done about this social process is an entirely separate issue.

Notes

1. The five largest private security firms in the United States today (accounting for more than half of the revenue earned by the entire industry) were founded in the late nineteenth century and have all at some point been involved in the struggle against organized labor. These five firms are the Pinkerton Agency, William J. Burns International Detective Agency, the Wackenhut Corporation, Walter Kidde and Company's Globe Security Systems, and Wells Fargo Guard Services (primarily a rent-a-guard and armored car service).

2. Streeter vs Sullivan, Suprème Court of Florida, May 21, 1987.

3. Latek vs K Mart, Supreme Court of Nebraska, Feb. 27, 1987.

References

Brandes, S. D.
1974 *American Welfare Capitalism*. Chicago: University of Chicago Press.

Cunningham, W., and Taylor, T.
1983   Ten Years of Growth in Law Enforcement and the Private Security Relationships. *Police Chief.* Vol. 50, No. 6:28–40.
1984   *Crime and Protection in America: A Study of Private Security and Law Enforcement Resources and Relationships.* Washington, D.C.: National Institute of Justice.

Draper, H.
1978   *Private Police.* Harmondsworth, England: Penguin Books.

Freedonia Group
1987   Security Indicators: Trends and Forecasts for Determining Loss Prevention Needs. *Security: The Magazine for Security Decision Makers.* Vol. 24, No. 9 (September):18.

Gallati, R. R. J.
1983   *Introduction to Private Security.* Englewood Cliffs, NJ: Prentice-Hall.

Hougan, J.
1978   *Spooks: The Haunting of America – The Private Use of Secret Agents.* New York: William Morrow.

Kakalik, J. S. and S. Wildhorn
1972   *Private Police in the United States.* 5 vols. Santa Monica, CA: The Rand Corporation.

Lipson, M.
1975   *On Guard: The Business of Private Security.* New York: Quadrangle.

Lydon, K.
1987   Who Makes Security Decisions for U.S. Business? (editorial). *Security: The Magazine for Security Decision Makers.* Vol. 24, No. 9 (September):13.

Marx, G. T.
1986   The Iron Fist in the Velvet Glove: Totalitarian Potentials Within Democratic Structures. In *The Social Fabric,* ed. by J. Short. Beverly Hills, CA: Sage.
1987   The Interweaving of Public and Private Police in Undercover Work. In *Private Policing,* ed. by Shearing and Stenning. Newbury Park, CA: Sage.

New York Times
1989   When Private Employers Hire Public Police. February 26:1.

O'Connor, J.
1973   *The Fiscal Crisis of the State.* New York: St. Martin's Press.

O'Malley, P.
1988   Marxist Theory and Marxist Criminology. *Crime and Social Justice.* Vol. 29:70–87.

O'Toole, G.
1978   *The Private Sector: Rent-a-Cops, Private Spies and the Police-Industrial Complex.* New York: Norton.

Platt, T.
1988   U.S. Criminal Justice in the Reagan Era: An Assessment. *Crime and Social Justice.* Vol. 29:58–69.

Reichman, N.
1987   The Widening Webs of Surveillance: Private Police Unraveling Deceptive Claims. In *Private Policing,* ed. by Shearing and Stenning. Newbury Park, CA: Sage.

Reiss, Albert, Jr.
1988   Private Employment of Public Police. *National Institute of Justice Reports.* July/August, No. 210:2–6.

Shearing, C. and Stenning, P.
1981   Modern Private Security: Its Growth and Implications. In *Crime and Justice – An Annual Review of Research,* Vol. 3, ed. by M. Tonry and N. Morris. Chicago: University of Chicago Press.

South, Nigel.
1989   *Policing for Profit: The Private Security Sector.* Newbury Park, CA: Sage.

Spitzer, S., and A. T. Scull
1977   Privatization and Capitalist Development: The Case of the Private Police. *Social Problems.* Vol. 25, No. 1:18–29.

U.S. Department of Justice
1984   The Growing Role of Private Security. Washington DC: Bureau of Justice Statistics.
1985   *The Private Sector and Prison Industries.* Washington, D.C.: Bureau of Justice Statistics.
1986a   *Sourcebook of Criminal Justice Statistics,* 1.1 – 1.6. Washington, D.C.: Bureau of Justice Statistics.
1986b   Police Employment and Expenditure Trends. Washington, D.C.: Bureau of Justice Statistics.

Wang, Liau
1988   New Security Services in Beijing. *Beijing Review.* Vol. 30, No. 31 (August 1–7):28.

9

Contradictions, Conflicts, and Dilemmas in Canada's Sexual Assault Law

Ronald Hinch

In 1982,[1] the Canadian state was faced with a dilemma. For more than a decade, feminist critics had been alleging that Canadian rape laws were anti-woman and should be changed. The state's dilemma was to find a way to reform the law so that it would appear to satisfy feminist demands but at the same time leave the patriarchal and class nature of Canadian society unscathed.

Needing a solution that would appear to satisfy everyone, the state passed Bill C-127. According to the government, this Bill marked a major step forward in recognizing the legal rights of women. Some commentators (see Still, 1983) went so far as to argue that it went too far, that it gave unwarranted credibility to feminist criticism.

A somewhat different interpretation is presented here. Consistent with analyses of similar reform measures in the United States (Feild and Bienen, 1980:153-206; Caringella-MacDonald, 1988) and Britain (Adler, 1987), it will be argued here that the reforms implemented via proclamation of Bill C-127 have had minimal impact on criminal justice processing of rape complaints. Although the state has created the impression of a compromise between feminist and patriarchal interests, this compromise does little to alter the patriarchal or class nature either of the law itself or of law enforcement.

This interpretation is grounded in the analysis of law reform offered by William J. Chambliss (1986; Chambliss and Seidman, 1981). According to Chambliss, the state's dilemma is how to offer solutions to conflicts without significantly altering the structural cause of the conflict. In capitalist societies, this means solutions that appear to resolve conflicts between capital and labor while leaving the basic contradictions between them unresolved. In patriarchal societies, it means finding solutions that appear to resolve conflicts between men and women while leaving the contradictions of patriarchy unresolved. In societies which are both patriarchal and capitalist, solutions must leave both structures intact while giving the appearance of reform.

The analysis proceeds with an examination of feminist criticism of the old law and the state's response to that criticism. Finally, an assessment is presented of the ways in which the state's response can be shown to be protective of patriarchal and class interests.

Conflicts Inherent in the Old Rape Law

The feminist struggle to reform rape laws has been a long, hard-fought battle. Feminists of different political persuasions[2] (Griffin, 1971; Brownmiller, 1975; Clark and Lewis, 1977; Smart, 1977; Kasinski, 1978a, 1978b; Mackinnon, 1982; Adler, 1987; Gunn and Minch, 1988) have fought in various ways to bring an end to sexist rape laws. Although each school identifies a different source for the problem, all agree that rape laws have historically been anti-woman. In the struggle against sexist rape laws, these feminists have identified problems not only with the definition of rape, but also with law enforcement. It is through examining these problems that the larger concerns over patriarchy and class become clear.

Defining Rape

In the eyes of feminists, a number of problems plagued the definition of rape in the Criminal Code of Canada (CCC) as it stood before 1983. Not only did the law exempt married men from being prosecuted for raping their wives, it also placed too much emphasis on the sexual nature of the offense and too little on the violence involved.

Until 1983, Section 143 of the CCC[3] said that rape occurred when a man had unconsented sexual intercourse with a woman who was not his wife. This definition left any woman who had been raped by her husband unable to prosecute him.[4] According to Brownmiller (1975), this legal immunity originated in ancient times. In early human societies, women sought protection from all other men by surrendering sexual access to one man, who would protect her from other men if she provided him with exclusive and virtually unlimited sexual access. According to this line of thought, the exemption from prosecution given married men under the CCC was simply an extension of this ancient right. Although some feminists disagreed with Brownmiller regarding the origins of the exemption for men who raped their wives, all were outraged that it still existed and wanted it removed.

Before 1983, the offenses of rape, indecent assault on a male, and indecent assault on a female were all classified under the sexual offenses section of the CCC. This classification presented feminists with a number of problems. First, the distinction between rape and indecent assault was based on the assumption that incidents involving vaginal penetration by a penis were more violent than other forms of unconsented sexual contact because the vagina had been penetrated. Feminists argued that this was muddied thinking. Other forms of forced sexual touching could be just as dangerous and life-threatening as rape. The level of violence, not the level of sexual intimacy, was the real issue. Therefore, they argued, the criminal code should make distinctions based on the level of violence, not the level of assumed sexual intimacy. In a related concern, those feminists intent on demonstrating legal equality of the sexes saw it as blatantly unequal to have homosexual rape treated as a less serious offense than heterosexual rape. These feminists maintained that homosexual rape could be just as violent as heterosexual rape and represented no less a loss of sexual autonomy. The law should therefore treat male and female victimization under the same section of the code and with the same degree of seriousness.

The Problem with Law Enforcement

Feminists further argued that the enforcement of rape laws, even when the victim was not married to the accused, was generally based on male-centered conceptions of the nature of sexual relations between men and women. For example, Clark and Lewis (1977) reported that many complaints of rape were disbelieved by the police if no evidence of resistance—bruises, torn clothing, and so on—was available. It was as though, without this evidence, women could be assumed to have consented. Little consideration was given to the possibility that some women might not resist out of fear for their safety or the safety of others.

Further, Clark and Lewis (1977:91, 123) found that women with disreputable sexual or social histories effectively lost their right to seek legal recourse. Women who were drunk when reporting incidents to the police, or women known to be alcoholics, drug users, on welfare, as well as former or current mental patients and prostitutes—all of these women had difficulty convincing police that they had been raped. Approximately ninety-eight percent of these women had their complaints of rape classified as unfounded by the police. Clark and Lewis called these women "women who can't be raped" or "open territory" victims.[5]

Feminists took particular exception to previous studies (see, for example, Amir, 1971) suggesting that victims precipitated attacks by engaging in behavior they should have known would lead to sexual contact. Feminists attacked the concept of victim precipitation, claiming that it blamed the victim for the behavior of the offender. Application of the concept meant that only "good" women—women who met the appearance and behavior standards of "respectable women"—could be raped. Significantly, Clark and Lewis found that professional women, who most closely met these standards, were the least likely to encounter problems with the way police handled their complaints. They were the most likely to be believed and the least likely to have their complaints termed unfounded.

The courts also came under attack for their low conviction rates. Feminists claimed that the low rate of conviction in rape cases was caused by two factors. First, the penalties for rape were too severe: The possibility of life imprisonment for rape contributed to lower conviction rates. That is why, as Snider (1985) pointed out, women's groups presenting briefs to the parliamentary committee who studied the issue prior to passage of Bill C-127 argued for lower penalties. These groups did not want the threat of severe punishment inhibiting the possibility of conviction. Second, the practice of allowing the defense to question a victim's credibility by introducing reputational evidence resulted in placing the victim on trial: She had to prove her innocence in order to prove the offender's guilt. Even though the admission of reputational evidence had been restricted to a certain degree before 1983, it was still common for defense lawyers to challenge a victim's credibility by presenting evidence to discredit her. The defense could make it appear as though the victim was either lying about her own role—that she really did give consent—or that she shared the blame for what happened.

In a related matter, some feminists were angered at the Supreme Court of Canada's 1980 ruling in the Papajohn case. In that case, the court ruled that a defendant who had an honest but mistaken, though reasonable, belief in consent could not be convicted of rape. For feminists, this ruling represented one more application of patriarchal conceptions of sexual relations between men and women. It meant that, even if a victim had not given consent, the accused could go free if he interpreted her actions as implying consent. After all, said the feminists, within patriarchal ideology a woman is expected to at least initially resist all sexual encounters. This initial resistance is assumed to be an indication that she wants to be conquered. It is a test of a man's masculinity to change her no to a yes. In the logic of patriarchy, the initial no, and sometimes even subsequent no's really mean *not yet*. The man is expected to persist, to conquer, to convince the woman to have sex with him. If a certain woman resists more strongly than others, it is an indication that she does not "give in easily," or that she "likes it rough." Such a woman calls for more persistence, perhaps even force. When a woman stops saying no and offers no further resistance, patriarchal logic assumes she is saying yes.

A few feminists, especially the Marxian feminists (Kasinski, 1987b; MacKinnon, 1982; Schwendinger and Schwendinger, 1983) were concerned that law enforcement practices favored some men more than others. They argued that men from lower socioeconomic groups, working-class men, were far more likely to be arrested, prosectued, and convicted than men from higher socioeconomic groups. Although Marxian feminists recognized the need for law reform, they were pessimistic that reforming the rape laws would make a significant change in either the patriarchal or class-biased nature of law enforcement.

Generally speaking then, feminists argued that a new law was needed. The law they envisaged would be structured so that:

1. The marital privilege would no longer exist.
2. The level of violence would be used to determine the seriousness of the act.
3. The victims previous sexual conduct and social reputation would not be admissable as evidence.
4. The 'honest but mistaken belief in consent' defense would be abolished.
5. The penalties would be lowered to encourage conviction.

Snider (1985) has shown that feminists were not the only ones seeking changes in the law. Various state control agents—most notably the police, other enforcement agents (i.e., provincial Attorneys-General), and organizations representing criminal lawyers—used the parliamentary committee hearings for Bill C-127 and its predecessor, Bill C-53, to voice their concerns. The Canadian Association of Chiefs of Police and the Attorneys-General argued pro-control positions. Among other things, they wanted to eliminate rules of evidence that favored the accused. They also wanted tougher penalties than those sought by women's groups. In general, these groups wanted "to bring more people under the control of the criminal law . . . for a longer time period" (Snider, 1985:344).

The Criminal Lawyers' Association argued that the proposed law went too far in restricting the rights of the accused and recognizing the rights of the victim. They resisted provisions in the law which would restrict the rights of the accused to question a complainant's credibility by examining her sexual history and reputation. They wanted, according to Snider, "a liberalising law, allowing defendants full legal rights and increased chances of acquittal" (1985:344).

The New Law

At first glance, it would appear that feminists got most of what they wanted. Bill C-127 made the following changes:[6]

1. The offense of rape was abolished along with the two indecent assault offenses.
2. Married men are no longer able to claim exemption from prosecution on the basis of a marriage contract.
3. The trio of sexual assault offenses replacing the charges of rape and indecent assault are distinguished by the amount and type of violence used.[7]
4. It is no longer necessary to prove vaginal penetration to prove that a serious attack has occurred.
5. The introduction of reputational evidence is forbidden by Section 244.7.

The question that needs to be answered is this: How effective have these changes been in meeting feminist demands for change?

The Result

Appearances are deceiving. It should be noted that some of the changes feminists sought were not incorporated into the law. For example, law enforcement agencies got the tougher penalties they wanted; the less severe penalties favored by feminists were rejected. Furthermore, the infamous Papajohn decision allowing the defense of 'honest but mistaken belief in consent' was retained in the new law as Section 244.4. How this will affect conviction rates in the long run remains to be seen, but preliminary findings indicate little difference in conviction rates (Renner and Sahjpaul, 1986; Sahjpaul and Renner, 1988).

If the areas in which feminists did not get what they sought are problematic and raise questions about the nature of law reform, then the areas where the law appeared to give in to feminist demands raise even more fundamental questions. The failure to achieve certain feminists goals, such as the abolition of the 'honest but mistaken' defense, may actually undermine what appears to be feminist victory. The discussion here centers on the following issues:

1. The formal abolition of marital privileges versus the reality of inequality in marriage
2. The formal abolition of the need to prove penetration versus the practical need for corroborative evidence
3. The formal recognition of levels of violence used versus the reality of poorly defined offenses
4. The formal restrictions on reputational evidence versus the reality of the exceptions to the rule
5. The problem of class

The Marital Privilege

The formal abolition of the marital privilege surely marks a significant ideological milestone. It is a clear recognition that partial progress has been made toward removing some of the more blatant, formal mechanisms of patriarchal control. Men can no longer claim legal exemption from prosecution for raping their wives.

However, several factors undermine this formal abolition. First, ideologically, the change from rape to sexual assault means that men can still escape prosecution for raping their wives. In a passionate defense for retaining the name rape, Cohen and Backhouse (1980) argued that it was meaningless to change the name if the act remained. They argued that a stronger ideological statement would be to retain the name. This is most obvious in the case of marital rape. Cohen and Backhouse suggest that charging married men who force sexual intercourse with their wives with rape is a stronger ideological statement of an end to marital rape privileges than charging them with sexual assault. The latter label seems to carry fewer negative connotations.

Second, it should be pointed out that, under the old law, it was possible for married women to charge their raping husbands with indecent assault or even common assault. Even before the law changed in 1983, it was also possible for married women to make allegations of abuse via rape a part of divorce proceedings. Thus, it was and is simplistic to assume that married women who were raped by their husbands had no legal recourse. This is not to suggest that these options implied the same degree of seriousness, or ideological impact. They did not. The point is, women were not without legal recourse, however inadequate that recourse might have been.

Third (and most significantly) it is a well-established fact that married women are reluctant to charge their husbands with assault. The legal right to charge husbands with assault (common or sexual) does not guarantee that married women have access to this right. Although evidence indicates that married women are increasingly willing to make their victimization public, it is also clear that not all of them wish to criminalize their husbands. There is also evidence indicating that social pressures still exert influence on women not to make their victimization public. The literature of wife abuse makes this point very clear. Many, perhaps most, abused women remain reluctant to come forward because they fear they will not be believed. They fear that others will believe they brought the attacks on by their own behavior, that they could have prevented the attacks by being more understanding of and more responsive to their husbands' needs, moods, and whims. Although the law makes it clear that married women have legal recourses, those recourses are sometimes blocked by social conditions which remain as solidly patriarchal as ever and isolate women within the family.

Fourth, legal recourse does not assure married women that they are safe from character assassination. Section 246.6 explicitly states that evidence of prior sexual contact between the accused and the victim is admissable without restriction. It is not difficult to imagine how defense lawyers could use this to attack a woman's character, to make it appear as though she were trying to get even with her husband for some other problem. Sahjpaul and Renner's (1988) study of court processing of sexual assault under the new law indicates that defense lawyers are still challenging the credibility of victims in court. The bottom line is that marital privilege remains supported as much by social convention as it does by the law.

Finally, some research indicates that economic dependence on a husband is the most important factor leading to a married woman's decisions not to report being raped by her husband (See Schwendinger and Schwendinger, 1983:197 – 221; Russell, 1982). This means that the right to charge husbands with sexual assault may be a hollow right. It is of little consequence when fear of economic loss or ruin prevents a woman from reporting the abusive behavior of her husband.

The Penetration Requirement

The penetration requirement was abolished for two reasons. First, it was abolished to make it easier for police to bring charges in cases where the victim alleged penetration but supporting evidence was not available. Second, its abolition was intended (along with the abolition of the rape charge and the creation of three sexual assault charges defined in terms of levels of violence) to transfer emphasis from the sexual nature of the act to the violent nature of the act.

Before 1983, police frequently abandoned cases when supportive evidence of penetration, when alleged, could not be found. Such evidence can be lost in various ways including a time delay before reporting an incident or taking a bath or shower before reporting an incident. Thus, the abolition of the penetration requirement (and the corroboration rule) was supposed to make the work of the police easier. Because it would no longer be necessary to prove penetration to bring a charge of sexual assault, it would be easier, technically, for police to lay charges in cases where evidence of an attack existed but no evidence of penetration.

Research on police enforcement practices after the law was amended in 1983, however, found police reluctant to continue investigation when a victim alleged penetration but little or no corroborative evidence was available (See Hinch, 1988a, 1988b). For example, the police continued to ask for corroborative medical evidence, and when such evidence was unabailable or proved inconclusive, police generally discontinued investigation. In some cases, police asked victims to submit to polygraph tests. If a polygraph proved inconclusive or indicated that a victim was lying, the matter was usually dropped. A victim's refusal to submit to a polygraph also sometimes resulted in termination of an investigation. Thus, it is not at all clear that abolishing the penetration requirement has solved the problem. Some complaints in which penetration is alleged continue to be dismissed for lack of corroborative evidence.

It is also not clear whether abolishing the need to prove penetration has decreased the emphasis on the sexuality of the event. It is still common for the news media, both electronic and print, to report incidents as *rape*. Neither can it be ignored that the new offenses are all labeled *sexual* assaults. While this label clearly separates them from other types of assaults, it still leaves their sexual character front and center: It is their sexual character which separates them from other assaults. Thus, the claim that transfering these offenses to the offenses against the person section of the criminal code and abolishing the need to prove penetration somehow reduces the sexual nature of the act loses credibility. These amendments may place greater emphasis on the levels and types of violence involved, but it is not clear that they have altered either the legal or the popular image of the event as a sex crime.

Poor Definitions

Even before the amendments became effective, there was concern that the definition of sexual assault under the new act was inadequate (Lowenberger and Landau, 1982), and commentators continued to question the lack of definition in Section 246.1 (Landau and Lowenberger, 1983; Hinch, 1985, 1988b). Questions have been raised not only about the implications in terms of police enforcement, but also in terms of judicial decision making.

One study indicates that during the first two years of enforcing the new law, police frequently used the old legal names when labeling offenses in their reports (Hinch, 1988a, 1988b). The labels 'rape,' 'indecent assault on a male,' and 'indecent assault on a female'—as well as labels which merged the old with the new (sexual assault on a female, for example)—were found with sufficient frequency to raise questions about whether the police are fully cognizant of the significance intended by the changes. Given the absence of definitions in the new law, old definitions seem to have been retained.

Effectively, the police became the first-line definers of what constitutes a sexual assault. Again, research indicates a certain degree of inconsistency in definition. In his study of police practices, Hinch (1988a, 1988b) reports that some incidents involving touching of women's breasts or buttocks are interpreted as sexual assaults, while other (sometimes very similar) incidents are processed as either common assaults or noncriminal events. In one case, a man in his thirties "French kissed" a preteen girl while they were sitting on a bed. He also tried to lie down and get on top of the girl. The police report concluded that, because he did not touch the girl in any area which would constitute sexual touching, not only was the incident nonsexual, but no assault of any kind had taken place. While the police studied did not always dismiss such complaints as unfounded, they nonetheless showed considerable reluctance to proceed with certain investigations, especially when little or no violence was evident, or when the victim and the offender knew one another.

Also noteworthy is Sahjpaul and Renner's (1988) conclusion that considerable undercharging occurs. That is, offenses which could be charged as sexual assault with a weapon or aggravated sexual assault are sometimes charged with the lesser offense of sexual assault. This fact lends credibility to the claim that the lack of definition in the law leads to the trivialization of some events. (See Hinch 1988a).

The courts have had similar difficulties in deciding what constitutes sexual assault. In 1984, a New Brunswick court ruled (in *R. vs Chase*) that unconsented touching of the breasts constitutes common assault, not sexual assault. In making the ruling, the judge equated women's breasts with men's beards as secondary sexual characteristics. Further appeal to the Supreme Court of Canada, however, saw this decision overturned. The Supreme Court ruled that unconsented touching of women's breasts constituted sexual assault.

The problem is not limited to determining which areas of the body are considered sexual. The police and some courts have reasoned that the intent of the offender to commit a sexual assault must also be considered. In some cases, it has been necessary to substantiate not only that a sexual area has been touched without consent, but that the offender had a sexual intention in touching that area. For example, Hinch (1988b) reports an incident in which a woman and her daughter were bumped from behind while standing in line at a grocery checkout. The woman was touched in the area of the buttocks, and the little girl in the area of the chest and genitals. After questioning the victims, the offender, and several witnesses, the police concluded that the offender had not intended his actions as sexual touching, but rather as friendly gestures. Similar judgments have been rendered in the courts.

In *R. vs Cook* (1985), a British Columbia court made a ruling which comes very close to accepting the notion of victim precipitation. According to the court, in certain situations a victim's actions could imply consent. The court ruled that after "initial mild sexual touching," that was preceded by a "sufficient acquaintanceship," consent to subsequent touching could be assumed. Only after explicit refusal to grant further consent to touching could the incident be termed assault, sexual or otherwise.

The current definition of sexual assault is not one favored by feminists. Feminists favor a definition that would include any unconsented sexual touching. What the state has provided instead is an undefined label which is interpreted by a predominantly male police and judiciary to mean that an offender must have sexual intent—and must not have been mislead by faulty interpretation of his relationship with the victim—in order for an incident to be considered sexual assault. If an offender's interpretation of his relationship with the victim is faulty but sufficient evidence can be produced to suggest that his actions were precipitated by the victim's actions—even though she did not give consent—consent could be implied. In these circumstances, no offense has occurred.

Reputational Evidence

In response to the claim that the old rape laws put the victim on trial, Bill C-127 included new restrictions on the introduction of reputational evidence. Section 244.7 forbids the introduction of "evidence of sexual reputation, whether general or specific ... for the purpose of challenging or supporting the credibility of the complainant." The law, however, is not without its contradictions. For example, Section 246.6

allows the introduction of evidence related to the complainants prior
sexual activity when it (1) involves evidence of prior sexual contact with
the accused, (2) "rebuts evidence of the complainant's sexual activity or
absence thereof that was previously" introduced by the prosecution, (3)
is evidence aimed at establishing "the identity of the person who had
sexual contact with the complainant on the occasion set out in the
charge," or (4) is evidence of sexual activity between the victim and persons other than the accused which took place on the same occasion for
which the accused is standing trial and which "related to the consent
that the accused alleges he believed was given by the complainant."
Ranson (1982, 1982b) and Hinch (1985, 1988a, 1988b) have argued that
these restrictions coupled with Section 244.4 (permitting the defense of
honest but mistaken belief in consent) continue to allow the victim to be
placed on trial.

   These restrictions on the admissibility of reputational evidence
have been ruled unconstitutional by at least one Canadian court. In
1984, a Newfoundland court ruled (in *R. vs. Coombs*) that those sections
of the CCC which restrict the introduction of reputational evidence violate the rights of the accused to a full defense. Others have joined the
Newfoundland court in offering this opinion. The Canadian Civil Liberties Association (See Fagan, 1987) has also criticized the current law's
restrictions on the admissibility of reputational evidence, arguing that
the restrictions violate the rights of the accused to a fair trial. Thus,
these restrictions are coming under the same kind of attack as similar
legislation in the United States (Sagarin, 1977; See also Feild and Bienen, 1980:153–206). The Supreme Court of Canada has yet to rule on
this issue.

   Sahjpaul and Renner (1988:511) conclude that little has changed in
the way defense lawyers attempt to discredit victims during cross examination in court. They argue that "the defence strategy of using neg-
atively toned questions and of attacking the victim's credibility, by implying that she is lying . . . along with the questions on consent . . . put
[the victim] under considerable personal attack." Sahjpaul and Renner
also indicate that prosecutors are often guilty of forcing a victim to give
an emotional account of the incident. This contributes to a potentially
dangerous situation for the victim. It reinforces the stereotype that only
victims who show strong emotional responses were truly raped.

   Problems, however, are not confined to the courts. The courts deal
only with cases supplied by the police, and not all complaints received
by the police result in arrest or court appearance. Studies of police processing of sexual assault complaints since the new law came into effect
suggest a reduction in the rate that complaints from those victims Clark

and Lewis (1977) labeled 'open territory victims' are concluded unfounded, but little difference in the final outcome of complaints from these women (Hinch, 1988b). Their complaints are still less likely than complaints from respectable women to result in a charge, and they are still two or three times more likely than other women to have their complaints effectively concluded unfounded.

For example, in 1983, a fourteen-year-old girl arrived home claiming that she had been raped. The police report gave prominence to several factors. First, it noted that the girl, who was on probation, had arrived home after her court-imposed curfew. Second, the girl had previously been a resident of a juvenile institution. Third, the girl's mother claimed that the girl had been having sex since she was eleven. Fourth, she did not get along well with her mother, who was uncertain about the truthfulness of her story. After speaking only to the girl and her mother, the police officially concluded the complaint *cleared otherwise*[8] with a notation by the investigating officer that he believed the girl was lying. In this case, it appears that the girl's juvenile record, sexual history, and poor relationship with her mother were used to discredit her.

Similar results were evident when victims had been hitchhiking or drinking, or when they were believed to be using drugs. None of the hitchhiking victims had their complaints classified as founded, and only one of nineteen complaints from women noted on police reports to be intoxicated when sexually assaulted had her complaint concluded with a charge. Most were effectively dismissed as unfounded.

It should be noted that, before implementation of Bill C-127 in 1983, police were concluding fewer complaints from open territory victims as unfounded. In 1970, 97% of such cases were dismissed as unfounded (Clark and Lewis, 1977); in 1982, 38% were (Hinch, 1988b). Thus, it would appear that forces other than changes in the law had been producing changes in the way the police processed complaints from these victims. Nevertheless, despite the decreasing gap, and despite changes in the law, open territory victims are still more likely than other female victims to have their complaints effectively dismissed as unfounded.

To be fair, it must be acknowledged that many of the intoxicated women were said to be too drunk to give police sufficient evidence to proceed. Some could not describe their attackers, and others were not sure whether they had been attacked. Thus, in some instances, police reluctance and inability to bring charges may be understandable. It is hard to bring a charge when an offender cannot be identified, or when a victim is unable or unwilling to say if she had been attacked.

Nonetheless, in two cases insult was added to injury when female sexual assault victims were charged with being drunk in public. In another incident, an intoxicated offender who grabbed a woman's breast as she left a small truck was charged with being drunk in public, but not with either common assault or sexual assault. The implication is that being victimized while intoxicated does not constitute legal victimization, and unconsented sexual touching while intoxicated does not constitute violation of the law. Only the act of being intoxicated in a public place is illegal. Would this logic apply to intoxicated bank robbers?

It is not at all clear that the revised CCC is effective at preventing a victim's reputation from becoming an issue during either police investigations or court proceedings. The bottom line here is that women who do not behave as so-called respectable women are expected will encounter more difficulties with the police and the courts. It must never be forgotten that the image of respectability is both a class-based and patriarchal conception of woman's role in society.

The Problem of Class

Even though the law now makes it clear that employers who force sex acts upon employees by threatening them with job loss, etc. can be prosecuted for sexual assault, nothing in the law alters the class bias in law enforcement. The fact that women with good reputations—that is, women meeting the criteria of 'good' specified by middle-class society — have more credibility with the police and the courts implies that women from lower socioeconomic classes still face an uphill battle in being heard (Clark and Lewis, 1977; Hinch, 1988a, 1988b).

Paradoxically, lower-class men, although less so, will still continue to be overrepresented among offenders known to the police. Gunn and Minch found that 47% of the known offenders in their study were unskilled laborers (1988:80). Clark and Lewis (1977) found an even higher proportion of skilled and unskilled laborers and other working class men among known offenders. Nothing in Bill C-127 addresses this over-representation.

Conclusion

This chapter set out to counter the notion that Canada's sexual assault law marked a significant step forward in the struggle to make rape and sexual assault laws less patriarchal. Even though the Canadian state amended its statutes to give the appearance of responding to cries of sexism, it is apparent that little real change has occurred. Specific features of the law and its enforcement remain as patriarchal today as they were before January 1983. Where sections of the law appear to meet feminist demands for change (in Section 244.4, for example, which restricts the introduction of reputational evidence) other sections (Section 244.4, for example, which allows the 'honest but mistaken' defense, and Section 246.6, which allows the introduction of evidence relating to prior sexual history between the accused and the victim) contradict and render the change ineffective. These contradictory sections—as well as the actions of the police and courts in enforcing the law—effectively retain the patriarchal character of Canadian criminal law. Patriarchal values and practices are evident in all four of the areas this chapter examined: the abolition of exemption from prosecution granted married men, the abolition of the penetration requirement, the definition of sexual assault, and the admissability of reputational evidence.

Furthermore, Bill C-127 did little or nothing to alter the fact that certain groups of women receive less protection from the law. Such is case for women from lower socioeconomic backgrounds who cannot demonstrate their 'respectability' as easily as can women from higher socioeconomic backgrounds. The class-based nature of the law and its enforcement remains intact.

What these observations mean for the future is uncertain. Although feminists dissatisfied with the outcome of Bill C-127 will no doubt continue to lobby for changes, the prospect for effecting change via law reform is not good. Future law reforms are likely to be similarly twisted and distorted in order to maintain the status quo with respect to patriarchal and class relations.

On the other hand, to allow the state and the forces of patriarchy and class to do as they will without resistance would be even more disastrous. The outcome in this particular case may not have been what was hoped for, but the struggle to make the law and its enforcement more responsive to women's needs cannot be measured by the success or failure of a single law reform measure. The struggle to reduce or eliminate patriarchal and class rule is far too complex to be measured solely by the outcome of Bill C-127.

Those who sought and continue to seek change must not be content to focus exclusively on law reform. They must also work for change in other areas of social life. Women are victims of more than sexual assault. Therefore, limiting discussion to only those laws which affect women as victims of a particular type of crime is unnecessarily restrictive. The laws governing sexual assault must be viewed in the context of all laws affecting women. These laws must also be viewed in the context of the total complexity of contemporary social life. As long as patriarchy exists, women as a group will be at a disadvantage compared to men as a group. As long as class relations remain intact, women (and men) from lower socioeconomic groups will continue to be at a disadvantage compared to women (and men) in higher socioeconomic groups.

The objective in seeking law reform is not simply to change that specific law. Nor is it the objective to force lawmakers and enforcers to meet the specific demands in a given area—for example, sexual assault. Although these are immediate and necessary objectives in the reform process, they are not the only or even most important ones. The primary objective is to use the struggle for law reform as part of a larger struggle for reform, or reconstruction, of the entire society. It is not just the law which must be changed, but the entire society, complete with its patriarchal and class distinctions. Only by changing the entire society is it possible to escape the vicious circle of reforms designed to give the appearance without the reality of change.

Notes

1. The legislation, Bill C-127, which cleared the House of Commons in August 1982, was preceded by two earlier attempts at amending the rape law. Bill C-52 was introduced in 1978, but died on the order paper after an election was called. Bill C-53 was introduced in 1981. It sparked much heated debate and was eventually withdrawn. After removal of some controversial sections, especially on child sexual abuse and pornography, Bill C-53 resurfaced as Bill C-127.

2. It is to be acknowledged that feminist argument is not monolithic: there are numerous feminist theories of law. See: Boyd and Sheehy (1986) for a more thorough examination of the varieties of feminist scholarship. Unless otherwise stated, the word feminist is used here as a generic, all-inclusive term.

3. All references to the Criminal Code of Canada are taken from Heather (1983).

4. While there was no possibility of legally charging their husbands with rape, married women could have charged their husbands with lesser offenses such as indecent assault or assault. Although my own research comparing police processing of sexual assault before and after the law changed (Hinch, 1988a; 1988b), turned up only one incident in 1982 in which a woman raped by her husband charged him with assault, the fact remains that the technical possibility existed, and apparently was used, however rarely, for women to charge their husbands with criminal offenses resulting from their husbands' attempts to rape them.

5. According to Clark and Lewis (1977:123), "open territory" victims include " 'promiscuous' women, women who are 'idle,' 'unemployed' or 'on welfare,' living 'common law,' 'separated' or 'divorced' . . . 'drug users'; 'alcoholics,' or 'incorrigible'."

6. This list of changes is not intended to be exhaustive. Rather, it is offered as a list of the more significant changes that appeared to satisfy feminist demand for change. In each case, however, it will be shown that the appearance is far from then reality.

7. The new sexual assault charges are specified as: Sexual Assault, Sexual Assault with a weapon or causing bodily harm, and Aggravated Sexual Assault.

8. The official conclusion of this case is not in compliance with the rules governing the use of the "cleared otherwise" category. A complaint may be cleared otherwise if it meets two conditions. First, an offender must be identified. Second, there must be some fact (such as the refusal of the victim to press charges) beyond police control preventing them from laying a charge. In this case, no offender was identified, and there is no indication in the police report that the victim would have refused to press charges.

References

Adler, Zsuzsanna
1987 *Rape on Trial*. London: Routledge and Kegan Paul.

Amir, M.
1971 *Patterns of Forcible Rape*. Urbana, IL: Univ. of Chicago Press.

Boyd, Susan B. and Elizabeth A. Sheehy
1986 Canadian Feminist Perspectives on Law. *Journal of Law and Society*. Vol. 13, No. 3 (Autumn):283–320.

Brownmiller, Susan
1975 *Against Our Will: Men, Women and Rape*. New York: Simon and Schuster.

Caringella-MacDonald, Susan
1988 Marxist and Feminist Interpretations on the Aftermath of Rape Reforms. *Contemporary Crises* 12, 122–144.

Chambliss, William J.
1986 On Lawmaking. In *The Social Basis of Law*, ed. by S. Brickey and E. Comack. Toronto: Garamond Press.

Chambliss, William J. and Robert Seidman
1981 *Law, Order and Power*. New York: Addison Wesley.

Clark, Lorenne and Deborah Lewis
1977 *Rape: The Price of Coercive Sexuality.* Toronto: The Women's Press.

Cohen, Leah, and Constance Backhouse
1980 Putting Rape in its Place. *MacLeans.* Vol. 93. No. 26 (June 30):6.

Fagan, Drew
1987 Drop Sex-History Law, Civil Rights Lawyer Asks. *Globe and Mail.* January 15:A19.

Feild, Hubert S. and Leigh B. Bienen
1980 *Jurors and Rape.* Toronto: Lexington Books.

Griffin, Susan
1971 Rape: The All-American Crime. *Ramparts.* Vol. 10, No. 3 (September): 26–35.

Gunn, Rita and Candice Minch
1988 *Sexual Assault: The Dilemma of Disclosure, The Question of Conviction.* Winnipeg: The University of Manitoba Press.

Heather, D. R. H.
1983 *Snow's Annotated Criminal Code: 1983 Annual Edition.* Toronto: Carswell Company Ltd.

Hinch, Ronald
1985 Canada's New Sexual Assault Laws: A Step Forward for Women? *Contemporary Crisis.* Vol. 9, No. 1 (March):33–44.
1988a Inconsistencies and Contradictions in Canada's Sexual Assault Law. *Canadian Public Policy.* Vol. XIV, No. 3 (September):282–294.
1988b The Enforcement of Canada's Sexual Assault Law: An Exploratory Study. *Atlantis.* Vol. 14, No. 1 (Fall):109–115.

Kasinski, Renee Goldsmith
1978a The Rise and Institutionalization of the Anti-Rape Movement in Canada. In *Violence in Canada*, ed. by Mary Alice Beyer Gammon. Toronto: Methuen Publications.
1978b The Social Control of Women. In *Law and Social Control in Canada*, ed. by W. L. Greenaway and S. L. Brickey. Scarborough: Prentice Hall Canada Ltd.

Landau, Reva and Lois Lowenberger
1983 Rape Law Still in Crisis. *Broadside.* Vol. 4, No. 8:4.

Lowenberger, Lois, and Reva Landau
1982 A Rape by Any Other Name. *Broadside.* Vol. 3, No. 9:3.

MacKinnon, Catherine A.
1982 Feminism, Marxism, Method and the State: An Agenda for Theory. *Signs.* Vol. 7, No. 3.

Ranson, Joanne
1982a   Past Sexual History: The Victim on Trial. *Kinesis.* November.
1982b   Consent and Honest Belief in C-127. *Kinesis.* October.

Renner, K. Edward, and Suresh Sahjpaul
1986   The New Sexual Assault Law: What has Been its Effect? *Canadian Journal of Criminology.* Vol. 28, No. 4 (October):407–413.

Russell, Diana
1982   *Rape in Marriage.* New York: Macmillan.

Schwendinger, Julia R., and Herman Schwendinger
1983   *Rape and Inequality.* Beverly Hills: Sage Publications.

Sahjpaul, Suresh, and K. Edward Renner
1988   The New Sexual Assault Law: The Victim's Experience in Court. *American Journal of Community Psychology.* Vol. 16, No. 4:503–513.

Smart, Carol
1976   *Women, Crime and Criminology: A Feminist Critique.* London: Routledge and Kegan Paul.

Snider, Laureen
1985   Legal Reform and Social Control: The Dangers of Abolishing Rape. *International Journal of Law.* Vol. 13: 337–356.

Still, Larry
1983   The New Rape Laws. *The Vancouver Sun.* January 13.

10

The Informal Economy: A Crime of Omission by the State

Stuart Henry

This chapter will begin by clarifying what I take to be state crime and go on to show how, by failing to limit accumulation of private wealth at its source, capitalist governments are responsible for creating the conditions of demand and supply that support the growth of informal economies. By excluding some people from a legitimate share of the wealth they create, governments force marginalized sections of the population to participate in informal economies wherein some people are introduced to opportunities for criminal activity which harms both themselves and others. In short, this chapter argues that some people's participation in informal economic activity can be traced to government policies and, therefore, such state-organized activities can be held co-responsible for their crimes.

Crimes by State Omission

Before considering crimes by state omission, it is crucial to specify what is meant by state crime and why it is an appropriate subject for our analysis. As Ballard (1936) pointed out long ago, the state is not the government (a group holding power), but a structure through which government acts. Nor is the state a unitary association having the ultimate power of coercion; that it appears so is a manifestation of the association of those holding power. Rather, as Jessop (1982) argues, the state is a relatively autonomous plurality of institutions through which various social forces struggle for use of its various apparatuses and agencies. Similar to Renner's (1949) view of law, the state is but an empty, colorless framework until it is given meaning by those who claim its capacity for domination. However, as a framework, it shapes and channels those laying such claim, and it both limits and focuses that exercise of power while simultaneously enabling those who exercise it (Giddens, 1984).

Government is a coalition of social and class forces, but is not the only one to access the state nor the only one to be penetrated by it. This implies that government policy, which is an agenda for harnessing state instituions and apparatuses, both shapes and is shaped by those competing interests within the state. Consequently, the state alone cannot cause harm, nor can it commit crime. To argue this is to accede to gross reification. Only those forces that capture state power can do this, and thus it is to governments — their policies and co-producing, social and class-based interests — that we must look in any analysis of crime by the state. Moreover, any analysis that begins with the assumption that the state is a unitary dominating force fails to recognize the inherent contradictions within it. As Jessop (1982) argues, such analysis fails to recognize the potential for the struggle within the state to both reaffirm and undermine class power. Thus, the appropriate focus for this analysis is government policy — enacted, interpreted, and enforced by government in the name of the state.

Similar caution is necessary in defining government crime. It is now accepted that the term *white-collar crime* is an inappropriate general category because it fails to address the structural organizational level (Coleman, 1985). More preferable is the definition derived from Clinard and Quinney's (1973) distinction between occupational and organizational crime. In their definition, the term *organizational crime* refers to crime committed by those in legitimate positions within an organizational structure for the benefit of the organization. It is not enough that such crime be identified only by existing criminal law. On the whole, that law not only assumes intentional actors and symmetrical power relations between individuals (Coleman, 1982), but it was written by class contemporaries of the powerful.[1] As a result, such bourgeois law systematically protects corporate interests, even if this is through the inadvertent preference for compliance systems of control over those of deterrence (Reiss, 1983), or through what Braithwaite (1986:12–13) says is a "profound class bias in the way the laws are often administered" such that corporate offenders, "if they get to court at all, are punished less severely than traditional criminals." For these reasons, Sutherland (1949) recognized that any attempt to confront crimes by corporations must start from the view that an act is a crime if it is punishable by any administrative body with the power to exercise punitive sanctions. Others have expanded these early definitions so that, not only can legitimate corporate entities, through their agents, be responsible for crime, but so too can agencies of government through their public office holders and elected representatives.

However, radical commentators who have recognized govern-ment crime have seen it as the product of agencies rather than of gov-ernment policy as a whole. For example, The American Friends Service Committee (1971:10) stated that "actions that clearly ought to be la-belled 'criminal' because they bring the greatest harm to the greatest number, are in fact accomplished officially by agencies of government." Others (Balkan et al, 1983:186) similarly describe government crimes as "committed by officials and government organizations." McCaghy and Cernkovitch (1987:351, 404) define government crime as "organiza-tional crimes committed by members of governmental agencies for the purpose of furthering political or bureaucratic goals, or protecting po-litical or bureaucratic interests," and they go on to argue that "the more crucial government crimes do not concern mere money but are activities that jeopardize fundamental civil rights through gross abuses of power." Moreover, it has been well documented (Douglass and John-son, 1977; Becker and Murray, 1971) that these crimes typically include illegal surveillance, infiltration and sabotage of alternative organiza-tions, political bribery and corruption, election rigging, and foreign espionage.

Although it is important for both individual and collective viola-tors to be held accountable, an enlightened view must take account of the harms committed on a population or segment of that population by government policy making as a whole, rather than simply by the covert operations of its constituent officers and agencies. Just as a corporation might be held liable for an official policy that results in the indiscrimi-nate dumping of toxic waste, so should a government be held respon-sible for harms resulting from a policy of concealment of information whose general knowledge would have resulted in protective measures being taken by the population. An example would be the concealment of information about radioactive leaks on the grounds that publication of such knowledge was not in the interest of national security.

However, it is argued here and elsewhere (Box, 1983; Kramer, 1984) that it is not enough to define state criminality as merely crimes of commission. An adequate analysis of state criminality must also in-clude crimes of omission as well as commission. Kramer (1984:18), for example, defines corporate crime as:

> Criminal acts (of omission or commission) which are the result of deliberate decision making (or culpable negligence) by persons who occupy structural positions within the organization as cor-porate executives or managers. These decisions are organizational in that they are organizationally based—made in accordance with

the operative goals (primarily profit), standard operating procedures, and cultural norms of the organization—and are intended to benefit the organization itself.

So too at the governmental level, for unless corporations are made responsible for the unintended consequences of their actions, then it is possible for decision making to be compartmentalized such that those in lower hierarchical positions, or in contracted agencies, will be employed to achieve corporate goals by whatever means they choose (Henry, 1985; Katz, 1979; Conklin, 1977). Likewise with agencies of government, such as the CIA's hiring of organized crime syndicates to carry out its more unsavory activities. However, it is not just government agencies that can commit crime through culpable negligence, but also government policy as a whole. Indeed, the very ability of an administration to blame the criminal actions of its agencies on overzealous implementation of policy rather than on the policy itself (as in Iran-Contra, for example) is an instance of institutionalized culpable negligence.[2]

An adequate definition of government crime, then, must include policy that results in unintended but avoidable acts of harm to its citizens or those of other nations. Put simply, if a drunk driver can be guilty of negligent homicide, so too can an ideologically "intoxicated" government whose policies directly or indirectly result in loss, injury, or death. Thus we can define state crime as the material or physical harm on its citizens, a subgroup of citizens, or citizens of other nations resulting from the actions or consequences of government policy, mediated through the practice of state agencies, whether these harms are intentional or unintentional.

Taxation, Welfare and the Creation of Dependency:
Crimes of Exploitation

One of the many policies subject to critical reassessment by the preceding definition is the policy of distributive justice. Should members of a society be free to accumulate wealth according to their individual merit, and based on prior claims to ownership of private property, irrespective of the harmfulness of their consequences for those less able to compete, or even those less successful at the competition? Should they instead subordinate individual claims to a general good? Alternatively, should individuals be limited by government regulation to accumulating only that which does not deprive another co-producer or consumer of a proportionate share of the created wealth, based on the amount that the accumulator would accept as fair were their positions reversed? Taking the latter, Rawlsian (Rawls, 1971; Barry, 1973) philosophy of distributive justice together with our definition of government crime would mean that the inaction of government in allowing some to exploit others in their accumulation of a disproportionate share of private wealth would be a crime because it would be condoning deprivation of the powerless by the powerful.

It may be argued that the redistributive taxation system relieves government of culpability. However, this only compounds the crime. A redistributive taxation system does not prevent disparities of wealth; worse, it encourages the illusion of their legitimacy. Moreover, it is an ineffective method of redistributing wealth, because there is no necessary correlation between those who are taxed and those who receive welfare benefit, with the result that those taxed feel unjustly penalized. Those accumulating wealth (because of government failure to limit their acquisitions at source) are mislead into the belief that taxable income is their private property. Furter, a government taxation and redistribution system not only harms those accruing the benefits of wrongfully accumulated wealth, but it fails to connect the amounts deducted as tax to those who shared in creating the wealth in the first place, thus harming them also. Contrast this with a system under which co-producers share in profit bonus schemes and own company stock, one where there is no perceived sense by owners and managers that they are losing *their* wealth to an undeserving poor![3]

Arguably, redistribution of taxed income creates further harm insofar as beneficiaries became dependent on welfare, and to the extent that they are misled into believing either that this support is their right, or worse do not feel entitled to it, and feel deprived of a perceived sense of independence or of the will to be self-supporting. If they were receiving the proportion of wealth that they are being deprived of as co-producers and consumers, they would rarely need welfare benefits in the first place.

Finally, the government is committing a further crime if, having established a state of welfare dependency, it then withdraws the support system that it has created. This forces those who, as a result of the governments original inaction to control exploitation, have to compete in an arena which is further uncontrolled and unprotected from exploitation. This is precisely what happens in some aspects of the informal economy.

The Informal Economy as a Creation of the State

One area wide open to such exploitation is the informal, irregular, or underground economy. The very structure of capitalism generates its own historically specific types of informal economies as a result of its failure to ensure the fair distribution of wealth. Ferman and Ferman (1973:5) were the first to demonstrate this in a seminal article in which arguing that the very origins of irregular economies "lie in structural conditions and processes in the larger society, and cannot be divorced from them." The authors claim that modern capitalist industrial society encourages such economies by creating structural inequalities based on class, ethnic, and cultural segregation. In addition, economic specialization, protectionist trade unions, and professional associations coalesce so that some goods and services are not widely available or are too expensive for those with low or nonexistent incomes. The direct result is that a market is created outside of the formal, regular economy for cheap goods and services. According to Ferman and Ferman (1973:17), "once regular patterns are established they provide training and opportunity for those members of the community who choose to earn their livelihood this way and are supported by a population that has few viable alternatives for the purchase of goods and services."

A more recent contribution which views the informal economy as a coalition of governmental action and capitalist social structure comes from Linda Weiss (1987:218), who argues that "the underground economy appears less as a phenomenon of crisis than as a political creation, in a sense that its conditions of existence—as a pervasive, routine and institutionalized presence — are significantly shaped by the state." Using Italy as a case in point, Weiss demonstrates that the state (by which she means succeeding Italian governments), with its high level of underground economic activity, has deliberately fostered small capital by giving small, formal companies privileges, and this has encouraged many small employers to move part of their production underground in order "to retain the privileges and benefits that attach to firms of small size" (Weiss, 1987:224). At the same time, Weiss argues, the state endorses the expulsion of married women from the official work force and limits their access to legitimate employment, forcing them into invisible underground economy labor, and it also resists the regulation of outwork in order to reaffirm women's auxiliary and domestic role. Thus, the patriarchal structure of Italian society is reinforced through a combination of state (or, more precisely, government) policy and its facilitation of informal economies.

It has also been argued that government taxation policies have an indirect effect in creating informal economies. Gutmann (1977:26), an advocate of *laissez faire* capitalism, says that "the subterranean economy . . . is a creature of income tax, of other taxes, of limitations on the legal employment of certain groups and of prohibitions on certain activities." He argues that the redistributive economy and the welfare state, growing employment protection legislation, and sex and racial equality legislation are actually creating the grounds for capitalist employers to go outside the system, employ workers off-the-books, and so facilitate the irregular economy. The problem of high levels of government involvement is particularly acute in times of high inflation: "Inflation redistributes income from income earners to government as tax payers are pushed into higher tax brackets; squeezed taxpayers in turn try to push part of the cost of inflation onto the government by getting off-the-books income" (Gutmann, 1989:29).

These arguments suggest that (1) capitalist inequalities create the conditions for informal economies, (2) interest groups seeking protection against such inequalities intensify the growth of informal economies, and (3) government policies (ostensibly designed to protect various groups from the harshness of economic inequality or even to maintain fair competition) also foster informal economies. Of course, the tacit Mertonian assumption behind all of these arguments is that social structures exclude some people from the commonly shared goals of material wealth, and that those excluded will reject their exclusion and seek to increase their share of wealth through alternative, illegitimate means, most notably by establishing a series of trading relationships or hidden economy outside of the formal economy.

One result is that the political economy of western capitalism,[4] rather than being a unified whole dominated by a capitalist free market economy and a facilitative state, is, as Jessop (1982) has argued, much more fragmentary and contradictory. As I have shown elsewhere (Henry, 1988), western industrial societies are multiplex economies containing a range of qualitatively different, conflicting and coalescing subeconomies under the over-arching domination of capitalism. These constituent economies of capitalism are not discrete or separate entities, but overlapping and interrelated—each with its own discernable identity and each sharing common features with the wider structure of which they are a part. What these diverse informal economies have in common is certainly difficult to describe without first specifying the total societal context. For advanced western capitalist societies in times of relatively full employment, informal economies seem to share the following characteristics: They are (1) concealed from the state accounting system and largely unregistered by its economic and criminal measurement techniques, (2) small-scale, (3) labor-intensive, requiring little capital, and (4) locally based, with trading taking place through face-to-face relationships among friends, relatives, or acquaintances in a limited geographical area. Beyond this, characteristics such as whether altruistic or avaricious, autonomous or parasitic, legal or illegal, whether

using cash or kind as a medium of exchange, are less generally applicable. These are, in fact, criteria used by commentators to distinguish
different constituent sub-economies. For these reasons, it is very difficult to be precise about where one sub-economy ends and another begins. What is certain, however, is that participants to one constitutent
sub-economy will likely experience some of the activities of the others,
depending upon their place in the opportunity structure and their economic and social resources.

The Myth of Informal Economy as Mutual Aid

It is certainly true, as Stack (1974), Lowenthal (1975), and Dow
(1977) have argued, that some informal economies exist and function as
mutually supportive networks for their members. However, this view
can ideologically support the movement away from welfare capitalism
because it allows government to demonstrate that levels of state intervention which cause "dependency" are unnecessary, while simultaneously claiming that the contradictions of capitalist inequality are not
as harsh as the official data suggest. Indeed, in their most romantic
form, informal economies are seen as functional to capitalist society by
allowing new businesses to be tried out, showing that workers are not
lazy, and so on. For example, leading government officials in western
capitalist societies have claimed that the irregular economy of off-the-
books work is actually indicative of the spirit of capitalism. In Britain,
both Prince Charles and Prime Minister Thatcher have claimed that the
irregular economy "proves that the British are not work shy." Similarly,
former president Ronald Reagan said that the irregular work done by
illegal aliens employed off-the-books may contribute more to the U.S.
economy through the cut-rate work that they do than they take out in
benefits, because their unregistered status does not allow them to draw
state benefits. He has also suggested that the necessary cut in welfare
services demanded by the budget deficit creates the opportunity for local self-help and mutual aid initiatives, from psychological support
groups to neighborhood housing construction and project management, and from parent-run day care to self-help for the elderly.

The reality of informal economies, however, is very different.
First, those economies based on intimate exchange are penetrated and
co-opted by capitalist market economies. Second, the intimate exchange model is not the typical form that irregular economic activity
takes. Recent research shows that, more typically, the irregular economy is characteristically entrepreneurial and based on negative rather
than positive reciprocity.[5] Indeed, evidence suggests that those with the

most resources and a structurally sound economic position are most likely to succeed, to the exclusion of those with lesser means — the young, retired, poor, and unemployed (Alden, 1981; Henry, 1982; Pahl, 1984, 1987). Importantly, the illicit nature of much irregular work means that there is often little or no control over safety, considerable exploitation and discrimination, and no product protection for consumers.

From Irregular Work to Crime

The consequences of being forced out of the regular economy into the irregular economy are also contradictory. Numerous studies have shown that on a personal level, unemployment often results in a psychological syndrome of denial followed by dejection. For some, however, the informal economy offers an apparent escape. It offers various opportunities for trading (or "swapping") goods and services and for doing useful work. But importantly, the overlapping of informal economies shading off into illegality means that some of these opportunities are likely to be illegitimate. If one buys goods in an illegitimate context, some of what is bought is likely to be the product of serious crime. The items purchased may simply be bulk purchases or wholesale goods, but they may also be goods stolen from legitimate workplaces or the products of burglary or breaking and entering (Henry, 1978). Increasingly, they may also involve illicit substances (Simon and Witte, 1982; Mattera, 1985; Headley, 1988).

An individual's decision to take part in trade involving illegal goods and services is the result of an interactive process with newly acquired members of the hidden-economy trading network. People come to the decision to commit an illegal purchase with more or less openness, more or less willingness, and more or less affinity or aversion. Although people are free to make choices in this context and are not compelled to act in any particular way, past experience of perceived rejection by the formal, regular economy, and rejection or alienation from its supposed welfare safety net, may provide sufficient justification to neutralize any initial moral qualms. Indeed, what tips the balance of choice and leads to the initial decision to take part in illicit activity may depend quite literally on how open and willing a person already is. It may depend as much on how the excluded and marginalized see their irregular work as furthering their new identity as welfare recipient or unemployed. Alternatively, any reluctance to commit an act may slowly be worn away by the persistent requests of those with whom the individual has been forced to form friendly relations. Gradually, the welfare recipient or unemployed person may come to identify with their new associates, trusting their judgments and adopting their justifications for participating in unlawful behavior. In addition to the Nationales for Committing Illicit Activity, these new associates may provide the necessary role performances and skills sufficient enough to transform the next request of the potential participant to participate from another refusal into a first-time participation. In Sutherland and Cressey's (1960) terms, these friends may finally tip the balance to provide personal biographies with an excess of definitions favorable to rule violation. Still, it is the individual who chooses rather than the differential associations per se that result in willingness to participate. The difference is that by now their circumstances and friends, their wider sociocultural heritage, and personal biographical experiences have narrowed the focus to an "either-or" issue from what was once an unlikely possibility.

In these circumstances, the decision to try irregular trading once may come as a great release. It certainly changes the whole meaning of the situation. No longer is the person dependent solely on past meanings about illegal trading or on second-hand constructions communicated to them through the media, political commentators, or even the words and actions of friends who already participate. They now have created space for further decisions based on their *own* experience, while simultaneously making more available a repeat performance at the same or a future date. If experience of the activity is negative, they may be unwilling to try it again, having satisfied themselves and their persuaders that they know what it is and do not personally like it. However, if the experience is sufficiently neutral or attractive, they may be willing to try such work, trade, or purchases again—to intensify the experience or simply because, when they tried it before, nothing particularly unpleasant happened. After a succession of increasingly favorable experiences, they may be prepared not merely to try the behavior again but to actively seek it out. Increasingly, the experience becomes a part of the individual's new identity as a member of the informal economy.

At this stage, negative pronouncements about tax evasion and illegality and consequences of trading in the underground economy made by representatives of the regular or redistributive economy are likely only to have reinforcing effects. Clearly, governments can pass legislation which outlaws many informal economy activities. Those engaged in irregular work (and their employers) can be prosecuted and sanctioned under federal tax laws. Similarly, those who participate in hidden-economy pilfering and trading are subject to theft laws. Whether they will actually be processed through the state criminal justice system depends on how far the wider capitalist economy is able to put informal economies to its use (Henry, 1987). However, attempting to undermine the informal economy through derogatory mislabeling and by the attribution of motives carrying negative connotations is, at this stage, a very uncertain enterprise. To suggest to those with positive experiences of the informal economy that participants in such activities are dishonest, solely interested in pecuniary rewards incommensurate with efforts, and cannot be trusted is unlikely to ring true. Such suggestions will not result in rejection of the activity because participation has resulted in an affiliation with the informal economy and has given these people a social place. At this point, an individual's experience of irregular economy trading as not only harmless but helpful, is then pitched against bureaucratic criticisms of these informal activities. Such criticisms are rendered hollow against the actual experience of irregular work and hidden-economy trading as an enjoyable, communal, and socially rewarding means of obtaining otherwise unavailable goods and services. The more people experience the reality, the more contempt accrues for those who decry it.

Two consequences of this initial entry into irregular economic activity can undermine the capitalist economic system. The first (and more general) consequence is that the formal or regular economy can be challenged in numerous ways so that cheating is seen as something everyone does, as part of the real way society works. Ironically, the media's attempt to condemn irregular-economy activity as tax evasion simultaneously highlights the fact that all levels of society are engaged in these activities, even its moral standard bearers. When doctors are found to be siphoning off clients from their practices into private care or defrauding medicare with fictitious claims for nonexistent patients, then the informal economy starts to "eat away at the moral fabric of society. Very soon the line between fiddling and outright theft becomes blurred. . . . A nation on the fiddle is usually a nation in financial and moral trouble. After all when everyone else is fiddling you tend to go along" (Walmsley, 1980).

The undermining of the wider capitalist system by informal economies is a fear that has also been recognized and expressed by governments. In Britain, the Public Accounts Committee of the House of Commons has said, "There is a real danger of tax evasion spreading beyond the limits of the present black economy" (Walmsley, 1980). The committee chairman said that "if people see others breaking the law without any chance of being caught it could affect tax payers who might say, if it's good for them, lets see if we can break the law in some other way." And a former chairman of the British revenue service said that "it is eroding what you might call the integrity of tax paying generally." In short, then, the very public condemnation of informal economic activity alerts others to its existence and serves to attract new participants who might have either remained outside or remained ignorant of its existence—people who feel cheated by a society that claims to control such activity but finds that some of its very figureheads are secretly engaged in it.

The second, more specific, way in which entry into irregular economic activity can result in crime has to do with a further narrowing of opportunity. One such narrowing leads to the availability of more criminal activity. Ironically, just as those squeezed out of the formal economy and welfare system might find a place in the irregular economy, so too are those unable to compete in the irregular economy squeezed into the criminal economy. These people have their opportunities narrowed such that their only choice becomes whether or not to seek participation in illegal activity through its considerable overlap with the criminal economy. Thus, finding minimal opportunities in off-the-books work, the recent entrant to the informal economy might find easier access to the criminal activity of trading in stolen goods or drugs. One group of commentators has argued that this is precisely how young people become involved in and addicted to drugs. The conventional view holds that narcotics cause crime because ways must be found to support the high cost of substances. The policy implication of this view is that cutting addiction will reduce crime. Auld, Dorn, and South (1986) argue, however, that welfare payments are inadequate for the purchase of basic needs such as housing, clothing, heating, and food. In order to meet these needs, people engage in irregular work, and it is through their involvement in this partially illegal irregular economy that they sometimes encounter and come to buy and sell narcotics such as heroin. Thus crime—in the form of illegal trading in goods and services—can be seen to lead to heroin use. Indeed, recent research on the link between crime and drug use in the United States shows that, for many, not only does first crime precede first drug use, but those who have engaged in crime prior to becoming addicted dramatically increase their criminal activity subsequent to addiction. In a review of studies on male narcotics addiction, Speckart and Anglin (1985) conclude that addiction does not so much cause crime as *amplify* income-generating criminal activities. Even more striking was the typical pattern for female addicts: first criminal involvement, first juvenile arrest, first drug use, first narcotic addiction, and first adult arrest (James, 1976; James et al, 1979). Moreover, in a study of female heroin addicts, Mauge (1981) found that those who participated in crime earlier in life were more likely to increase illegal activity than those who had never participated in crime.

Only 13% who had never been arrested increased their criminal activity after initiating heroin use, but 70% of those who were first arrested before using heroin increased their criminal activity. Commenting on the evidence from such research, Anglin and Hser (1987:365) say, "There seems to be a progression from crime and juvenile arrest to drug use to addiction to adult arrest. For the majority of female addicts, crime precedes the onset of first use while drug use maintains and increases later criminal behaviors." This conclusion is similar to that of Speckart and Anglin (1986) for male addicts. Put simply, rather than cause initial involvement in crime, "narcotics addiction is an amplifier of income-generating criminal activities" (Anglin and Hser, 1987:393)

The implications of this evidence are clear. Those who do not experience crime are less likely to become addicted. If they do become addicted, they are less likely to increase their criminal activity as a result. In contrast, those who are first introduced to crime can subsequently move into drug use; once they become addicted, an increase in their income generating criminal activity will follow. The key policy issue seems to be preventing that first involvement in crime. Auld, Dorn, and South (1986:173) pinpoint this exactly:

> A shift in economic policies that reduced the extent to which the irregular economy permeates increasing numbers of inner-city and other areas would reduce petty crime, and with it much heroin use in its presently expanding forms. A direct assault by law enforcement agencies against episodic heroin users, by contrast, would do relatively little to dent the criminal aspects of the irregular economy in which they play only a part.

This takes us back to the beginning — the crucial role of government in shaping the conditions, class relations, and opportunities in capitalist society.

Conclusion

To summarize, governments of capitalist societies fail to control the distribution of wealth at source, which in turn creates inequalities that are fundamental to the reproduction of the capitalist system. To protect themselves from these inequalities and from policies of government neglect or omission, some groups form exclusive organizations that maximize their advantage within system. Both inequalities and interest groups exclude some people from a just share of goods and services. To reduce the harshness of this exclusion, governments introduce redistributive systems. In addition to creating fiscal crises for the state and undermining capital accumulation, these redistributive systems perpetuate inequalities because, instead of relating the reduction of some people's wealth directly to the increase in the wealth of those they exploit, governments objectify the redistribution process. This makes those who are taxed resentful and some of those who receive welfare either ungrateful or dependent. To avoid restrictions, those who are taxed seek employees and services outside the formal system, which creates a demand for irregular work and illicit off-the-books trade. To ameliorate those accumulating wealth and to solve their fiscal crisis, governments cut or means-test welfare programs. This forces many of those relying on welfare to seek survival outside the formal economy and thus supply the very labor and services demanded by those seeking to avoid paying taxes and fulfilling other government regulations. Those excluded and alienated seek support in the variety of informal economies that emerge. However, the unregulated nature of such economies makes it even more difficult for those with limited abilities and resources to survive. As a result, a subgroup is driven deeper into areas where the competition is lower because risks are greater. For many this means participation in crime and illegal trde. In this context, they encounter drug trading and the opportunities to try drugs. For those who try drugs and become addicted, the probability of increasing income-generating criminal activity is high.

Insofar as state crime is the action or inaction of government policy that creates harm, then government's inability and unwillingness to control the distribution of wealth at source has been shown to result, through a complex series of events, in harm. Government policy, therefore, creates the conditions for informal economic activities wherein some people are introduced to opportunities to participate in crime. Once involved, the activity becomes self-justifying and self-perpetuating. Minor crime provides opportunities for drug use, and drug use can lead to addiction, which amplifies involvement in more serious crime. Insofar as government policy can be constructed so as not to force some economic activity underground, failure to do so can be considered a crime of the state of omission.

Notes

1. Even though more recent developments in business statutes have eliminated *mens rea* as a requirement for proof of guilt. See: Hopkins (1981).

2. Iran-Contra is the most recent systematically documented illustration of compartmentalized governmental decision making — in which the Contras were supplied and directed from a covert governmental agency, with no more authority than the general approval to meet the administration's goals, but with relative autonomy as to how these goals were met.

3. It is important to note here that co-producers also assume risk but are concomitantly party to the decisions about the risks to which they elect to subject themselves. As Abel (1982: 702, 710) argues, only the person subject to possible harm knows how much of the risk they wish to absorb and how much to control, and that risk control is best achieved through a cooperative structure in which each person is "able to control the risk to which he or she is exposed" and where people share equally "those risks we collectively choose to encounter."

4. Moreover, the argument does not apply only to capitalism, for it is clear that the bureaucratic structures of socialism are responded to in similar ways and that their formal categories will be circumvented by the construction of unofficial forms of exchange. See: Sampson (1987).

5. For a distinction between the social relational bases of different types of informal economy, see: Gaughan and Ferman (1987).

References

Abel, Richard
1982   A Socialist Approach to Risk, *Maryland Law Review,* 41:695–754.

Anglin, M. Douglas and Yih-ing Hser.
1987   Addicted Women and Crime. *Criminology, 25:*359–97.

Alden, Jeremy
1981   Holding Two Jobs: An Examination of Moonlighting in Stuart Henry (ed) *Informal Institutions,* New York: St. Martin's Press.

American Friends Service Committee
1971   *Struggle For Justice.* New York: Hill and Wang.

Auld, John, Nicholas Dorn, and Nigel South.
1986   Irregular Work, Irregular Pleasures: Heroin in the 1980's in R. Matthews and J. Young, *Confronting Crime,* Beverly Hills: Sage, pp. 166–87.

Balkan, Sheila, Ronald J. Berger, and Janet Schmidt
1983   *Crime and Deviance in America: A Critical Approach.* Belmont, CA: Wadsworth Publishing Company.

Ballard, L. V.
1936   *Social Institutions.* New York: Appleton-Century.

Barry, B. M.
1973   *The Liberal Theory of Justice.* Cambridge, MA: Harvard University Press.

Becker, L. T., and V. G. Murray
1971   *Government Lawlessness in America*. New York: Oxford University Press.

Box, Steve
1983   *Crime, Power and Mystification*. London: Tavistock.

Braithwaite, John
1986   White Collar Crime. *Annual Review of Scoiology 1985*. New York: Annual Reviews Inc.

Clinard, Marshall B. and Richard Quinney
1973   *Criminal Behavior Systems*. New York: Holt, Rinehart and Winston.

Coleman, James S.
1982   *Asymmetric Society*. Syracuse, NY: Syracuse University Press.

Coleman, James W.
1985   *The Criminal Elite*. New York: St. Martin's Press.

Conklin, John E.
1977   *Illegal But Not Criminal*. Englewood Cliffs, NJ: Prentice Hall.

Davis, John
1972   Gifts and the UK Economy. *Man*. Vol. 7:408–29.

Douglas, Jack D. and J. M. Johnson
1977   *Official Deviance: Readings in Malfeasance, Misfeasance and Other Forms of Corruption*. Philadelphia: Lippincott.

Dow, Leslie M.
1977   High Weeds in Detroit. *Urban Anthropology*. Vol. 6:111–28.

Ferman, Patricia R., and Louis A. Ferman
1973   The Structural Underpinning of the Irregular Economy. *Poverty and Human Resources Abstracts*. Vol. 8:3–17.

Gaughan, Joseph P., and Louis A. Ferman
1987   Towards an Understanding of the Informal Economy. *The Annals of the American Academy of Political and Social Science*. 493:15–25.

Giddens, Anthony
1984   *The Constitution of Society*. Oxford: Polity Press.

Gutmann, Peter M.
1977   The Subterranean Economy. *Financial Analysts Journal*. 34:26–27.

Headley, Bernard D.
1988   War Ina 'Babylon': Dynamics of the Jamaican Informal Drug Economy. *Social Justice*. 15:61–86.

Henry, Stuart
1978   *The Hidden Economy.* Oxford: Martin Robertson.
1982   The Working Unemployed: Perspectives on the Informal Economy and
       Unemployment. *Sociological Review.* 30:460–77.
1985   Review of *Corporate Ethics and Crime: The Role of Middle Management* by
       Marshall B. Clinard. *British Journal of Criminology.* 25:70–73.
1987   The Political Economy of Informal Economies. *The Annals of the American
       Academy of Political and Social Science.* 493:137–53.
1988   Can the Hidden Economy be Revolutionary? Towards a Dialectical
       Analysis of the Relations between Formal and Informal Economics. *Social
       Justice.* 15:29–60.
1981 (ed.)   *Informal Institutions.* New York: St. Martin's Press.

Hopkins, Anthony
1981   Class Bias in the Criminal Law. *Contemporary Crisis.* 5:385–94.

James, Jennifer
1976   Prostitution and Addiction: An Interdisciplinary Approach. *Addictive
       Diseases and International Journal.* 2:601–618.

James, Jennifer, Cathleen Gosho, and Robbin Watson Wohl
1979   The Relationship Between Female Criminality and Drug Use. *Interna-
       tional Journal of the Addictions.* 14:215–29.

Jessop, Bob
1982   *The Capitalist State.* New York: New York University Press.

Katz, Jack
1979   Concerted Ignorance: The Social Construction of Cover-up. *Urban Life.*
       8:295–316.

Kramer, Ronald C.
1984   Corporate Criminality the Development of an Idea. In *Corporations as
       Criminals,* ed. by Ellen Hochstedler, Beverly Hills: Sage Publications.

Lowenthal, Martin
1975   The Social Economy of Urban Working Class Communities. In *The Social
       Economy of Cities,* ed. by G. Gappert and H. Ross. Newbury Park: Sage Pub-
       lications.

Mattera, Philip
1985   *Off the Books: The Rise of the Underground Economy.* London: Pluto Press.

McCaghy, Charles H. and Steven A. Cernkovich
1987   *Crime in American Society.* New York: Macmillan.

Mauge, Conrad E.
1981   Criminality and Heroin Use Among Urban Minority Women. *Journal of
       Addictions and Health.* No. 2.

Paul, Ray E.
1984 *Divisions of Labour.* Oxford: Basil Blackwell.

Rawls, John
1971 *A Theory of Justice.* Cambridge, MA: Harvard University Press.

Reiss, Albert J. Jr.
1983 The Policing of Organizational Life. In *Control in the Police Organization,* ed. by M. Punch. Cambridge, MA: MIT Press.

Renner, Karl
1949 *The Institutions of Private Law and Their Functions.* London: Routledge and Kegan Paul.

Sampson, Steve
1987 The Second Economy of the Soviet Union and Eastern Europe. *The Annals of the American Academy of Political and Social Science.* No. 493:120–36.

Simon, Carl P. and Ann D. Witte
1982 *Beating the System: The Underground Economy.* New York: Auburn Publishing Co.

Speckart, George and M. Douglas Anglin
1985 Narcotics Use and Crime: An Analysis of Existing Evidence for a Causal Relationship. *Behavioral Sciences and the Law.* No. 3:259–83.
1986 Narcotics Use and Crime: A Causal Modeling Approach. *Journal of Quantitative Criminology.* No. 2:3–28.

Stack, Carol B.
1974 *All Our Kin: Strategies for Survival in a Black Community.* New York: Harper & Row.

Sutherland, Edwin H.
1949 *White Collar Crime.* New York: Dryden.

Sutherland, Edwin and Donald Cressey.
1960 *Principles of Criminology.* Chicago: Lippincott.

Walmsley, Jane
1980 London on the Fiddle: Part 2. *Evening Standard.* March 18:20–21.

Weiss, Linda
1987 Explaining the Underground Economy: State and Social Structure. *The British Journal of Sociology.* 38:216–34.

V

Epilogue

Resisting State Criminality and the Struggle for Justice

Gregg Barak

In January 1990, I gave a presentation to the Department of Criminology and the Group for Research on the Production of Order at the University of Ottawa which called for the incorporation of state criminality into the formal study of criminology. Members of the audience wanted to know two things. One, how did my call for an expanded definition of crime differ from the calls of Sellin and Sutherland in the 1930s and 1940s or the calls of the Schwendingers and other radical criminologists in the 1970s? And, two, what kinds of contributions could criminologists make to the study of state criminality that other social scientists or even journalists could not make?

In response to the definition of crime question, two points are worth making. First, my desire for incorporation of state crimes is merely a logical extension of the earlier call by criminologists to include the behaviors of white-collar and corporate offenders — behaviors which may or may not be legally defined as against the law, but which, nevertheless, cause harm, injury, and violence — into what was then emerging as the precursor to the study of the "crimes of the powerful." Second, and more significantly I believe there is the factual record that, for the most part, the call in the 1970s by two radical criminologists for the study of systems of exploitation and state criminogenic institutions has not been seriously pursued by criminology.

In response to the question about what criminology can do for the study of state criminality, I believe that chapters in this anthology offer rich examples of the types of theoretically and practically informed analyses that other criminologists can pick up on. Specifically addressed in this volume are insights and ideas that students of crime, criminal justice, law enforcement, adjudication, incarceration, and state control can bring to the study of state criminality — insights and ideas that are conspicuously absent from analyses grounded in disciplines such as political science, history, or journalism. In other words, although only a prerequisite or an introduction to state criminality, this work nevertheless provides macro and micro (as well as macro-micro) criminological analyses of state crimes and state apparatuses. It is precisely these kinds of criminologically informed analyses that hold the potential to reasonably extend various theoretical models of criminality and its control, especially concerning those behaviors involving organizational criminality.

Finally, I believe that the incorporation of state criminality into the study of criminology will offer at least two other dividends. First, it will fill out the totality of the study of criminality, and second, it will underscore the criminogenic relationship between state crimes and other forms of criminality, both in the streets and in the suites.

Resisting State Criminality and the Struggle for Social Justice

Crimes by the state involve violence and property and include such diverse behaviors as murder, rape, espionage, coverup, burglary, illegal wiretapping, illegal break-in, disinformation, kidnapping, piracy, assassination, counter- and state terrorism, bankrupting and destroying whole economies, secrecy, unaccountabilaity, corruption, exporting arms illegally, obstruction of justice, perjury, deception, fraud, conspiracy, and the general violation of both domestic and international laws. They also include behaviors which cause social injury and therefore violate universally defined human rights (e.g., food, shelter, self-determination, etc.).

State criminality and the historical and contemporary abuses by nations against their own and other state's citizenry have been well documented in this anthology and elsewhere. Yet the question remains: How and why have criminologists let such oftentimes horrendous behaviour on the part of states escape their attention and inquiry? Similarly, how is it that both the mass media and politicians seem oblivious at worst—and selective at best—when it comes to the routinization of political repression at the hands of formidable and not so formidable state apparatuses? The answer to both of these questions has to do not only with the political nature of state criminality, but more specifically with the fact that all "modern" crime (state and nonstate) "is merely a specific historic condition, variably present and having variable effects [subject to the] historical continuities and discontinuities in capitalist production and accumulation" (O'Malley, 1987:79).

Whether we are discussing the widespread and systematic reliance on torture in Turkey or large-scale starvation in the Sudan and Ethiopia, the use of poison gas against Kurdish rebels in Iran or the ongoing injuries and avoidable deaths of Palestinians in the Israeli-occupied West Bank, the covert operations of the CIA abroad or the FBI at home (with the authorization established by either *de jure* or *de facto* policies of the national security state)—we must always recognize that we are talking about politically and sociohistorically specific state crime. That is, these acts committed by and/or on behalf of the state and its dominant ruling elites are political crimes essentially because they have been rationalized or justified in order to preserve and maintain the status quo. In this sense, all of these crimes by the state become repressive means directed at the real and imagined enemies of a given state and the associated political and economic arrangements. The problem, of course, remains: How do citizens of a given state and peoples from multiple states intervene into the various state apparatuses of the world for the purposes of controlling both the crimes and the criminogenic nature of state power?

With respect to the United States' capitalist state power, former case officer and agent for the CIA Philip Agee (1988:8) has concluded that the covert and overt activities, for example, of his former organization's role in the political oppression and denial of fundamental human rights in developing nations (especially in Latin America) have always had the primary objective of maintaining "long-range control of the natural resources, the labor, and the markets of other countries." Allegedly, however, this type of intervention was engaged in for the purposes of making the world freely democratic and anticommunist. In the anticommunist political culture of the West, "any popular revolutionary movement that seeks revolutionary change or fundamental radical change in favor of the worker" is equally threatening to the capitalist state (Agee, 1988:9).

In practice, it makes no difference to U.S. imperialist policy whether the victims of state terrorism, for example, are communists, nationalists, populists, or socialists. They all become political victims, subjects of legitimated repression and state criminality, because they have been successfully labeled as Marxists-Leninists or as enemies of democracy and the "free enterprise" system. Hence, the actions taken by the CIA and the local oligarchies (e.g., banking and commercial interests) in Latin America against Juan Bosch in the Dominican Republic or Salvador Allende in Chile — and against the vast majority of rural peasants or of marginalized urban workers—were rationalized through the emotional and political rhetoric of anticommunism used to justify subversive operations abroad. "They are subversive in the sense that from the very beginning, the CIA has used money and control of the people to seek control over the so-called free, pluralistic, democratic institutions of other countries" (Agee, 1988:6).

Perhaps no better examples exist than the specially trained security forces the CIA has established as instruments for political control in such countries as Greece (KYP), South Korea (KCIA), or Iran (SAVAK). These security forces provide some of the nastiest services to be found anywhere, especially when it comes to kidnappings, murders, and assassinations:

> There are, for example, the Guatemalan services that the CIA has worked with hand and glove since the CIA proposed to overthrow the Arbenz government in 1954. Nobody knows for sure how many, but the educated guesses are something between 100,000 and 150,000 have been murdered in that country since that CIA sponsored coup more than 30 years ago. In El Salvador alone, you have something like 70,000 people kidnapped and tortured to death, their bodies thrown along the roads, since the Reagan support program began (Agee, 1988:11–12).

On the other hand, state-supported terrorism of the kind waged by the U.S.-trained Contras in Nicaragua has also resulted in fifty thousand wounded and twenty thousand dead Nicaraguans in less than ten years. But these expressions of state criminality are not limited to the torturing and murder of political enemies; they also include the crimes against self-determination committed by trade policies, for example, that assert adverse economic pressures on political parties, the church, and the press, or by waging disinformation campaigns inside and outside these so-called Third World countries. As former Contra public relations person Edgar Chamorro has noted about the actions and consequences of various disinformation campaigns aimed at the people of Nicaragua:

> Our psychological wars [were] very cleverly oriented to use people or to lie and they [were] very cruel to the recipient. Because there is cruelty not only in rapes, or in assassinations, but also in destruction of the economy, in making people suffer for lack of full electricity and water (Chamorro, 1988:24).

In short, Chamorro argues that the various strategies of low-intensity war (low-intensity conflict) depend on an evolving methodology of permanently looking for ways to hound people.

The arguments implicitly and explicitly developed throughout this book suggest that the reduction of wholesale as opposed to retail forms of state criminality would have a far greater impact on the levels of violence and suffering worldwide — especially since the former are often criminogenic of the latter. Our nontraditional arguments about the legal and nonlegal relationships of the crimes by state omission are particularly salient here. Take, for example, the "crime of homelessness" which results in both crimes by and against homeless people (Barak and Bohm, 1989). This crime of omission by an advanced, post-industrialized, capitalist state consists of laws that do not guarantee and policies that do not provide permanently affordable housing for all residents. The fact that the current social relations of bourgeois legality do not directly, or even remotely, recognize permanent housing as a fundamental human right does not preclude either the struggle for or the eventual development of such a *de jure* or *de facto* right. In other words, human rights exist in both theory and practice, and as such they may be viewed as part and parcel of the historical development in the ever-evolving status of the collective rights of all human beings (Felice, 1989).

With respect to the more general economic, political, and social development of the countries and peoples of Asia, Africa, and Latin America, the role of U.S. intervention through its foreign policy has certainly been a deterrent to the materialization of the rights of Third World people, at least since 1945. And "since the late 1960s, it is unfortunately the United States of all governments in the West that has most consistently opposed the realization of the right of self-determination by the peoples of the Third World and is, therefore, portrayed as an implicable foe of the rights of people" (Falk, 1989:60). The record of the United States, for example, "when it comes to the ratification of the major multilateral human rights instruments [is] one of the very worst . . . among all of the so-called Western liberal democracies" (Boyle, 1989:71).

The omission by the U.S. government to finally ratify the Prevention and Punishment of the Crime of Genocide (opened for signature in 1948) until late 1988 — and the continued failure of the United States to ratify such human rights documents as the Convention on the Reduction of Statelessness (1961), the International Convention on the Elimination of All Forms of Racial Discrimination (1965), the American Convention on Human Rights (1965), the International Covenant on Economic, Social and Cultural Rights (1966), the International Covenant on Civil and Political Rights (1966), the International Convention on the Suppression and Punishment of the Crime of Apartheid (1973), and the Convention on the Elimination of All Forms of Discrimination Against Women (1979)—has certainly contributed to crimes against humanity worldwide (Boyle, 1989). These crimes by state omission or the repressions of the fundamental right to self-determinism have been directly linked to U.S. foreign policy and are, at the same time, responsible for U.S. violations against the basic duty to abide by international law.

Of course, signing any of these documents which identify and attempt to delegitimate those public and private policies, both domestic and foreign, as state crimes against humanity should prove to be a pragmatic obstacle to the development of capitalist accumulation. Such legitimation of this kind of state criminality *vis-à-vis* the internationalization of law would, in effect, outlaw counterrevolutionary terrorism and other forms of state terrorism (i.e., low-intensity conflict) and structural violence that afflict the ill, the underdeveloped, and the poor. It follows, as Falk (1989:68) has stressed, that "the rights of peoples can be understood at its deepest level as a counterterrorist code of rights and duties, especially directed against state terrorism of the sort associated with the foreign policies of leading imperial governments."

Resisting all forms of state criminality in the world today is no simple enterprise because it calls for challenging existing and prevailing ideologies of militarism and paramilitarism. The struggle for world peace and social justice—and the reduction in all forms of crimes by the state—also necessitates a decreasing role in the state political police apparatuses as well as an expanding role in multilateral cooperation among all nation-states. This utopian world vision requires that all peoples of the global community understand that "no problem we face, not the nuclear one, not the ecological one, not the economic one, can possibly be handled, even addressed, on a unilateral national basis" (Ellsberg, 1988:18).

The "end" of the Cold War alludes to the possibility that in the near future the United States will, for example, be able to abandon the postwar foreign policy and ideology grounded in the failures of Wilsonian idealism and inter-war diplomacy, and the construction of a post-1945 world view of isolationism (i.e., staying out of Europe) and interventionism (i.e., economic and geopolitical expansionism wherever else possible). Such an international foreign policy was the product of a leadership that did not trust law or morality or international institutions as the basis for maintaining international security. They were skeptical of the United Nations, they were skeptical of any kind of serious reliance on international law. Judge Cannon and Dean Acheson were the archtypical thinkers with this kind of point of view. They believed that the way to create peace, the only way, was to have superior countervailing military power. And that therefore, the preparation for war, paradoxically, was the basis for peace, and the only basis. So becoming, disarming, or demobilizing, were actually war-provoking postures (Falk, 1988:4).

Needless to say, this Orwellian notion of peace through state-perpetuated warfare (conventional or low-intensity) has certainly been a difficult policy to shake. Only recently, for example (and for a variety of reasons — including apathy and ignorance as well as principle and integrity) were the actions of U.S. interventionism in Nicaragua rejected by the majority of Americans. This rejection by both the American people and an ambivalent U.S. Congress was used, in part, to justify the numerous state crimes carried out on behalf of the Reagan administration, including those which have and have not been acknowledged concerning the Irangate and Contragate scandals. However, the illegal invasion of Panama in the last weeks of 1989 was a popular state crime, sanctioned by eighty percent of the American people.

If dreams of a "peacemaking" criminology and larger visions of a one-world community are to ever materialize, then a significant step in the right direction would be for all states worldwide, especially the super- and medium-power states, to sign on to what has been termed the "third generation of rights" by former UNESCO legal advisor Karel Vasak. The third generation of rights goes further in its attempt to maximize the realization of human rights for all peoples of the world than the first and second generations of rights did. Each generation of structurally evolved rights has been the product of different historical struggles waged by peoples without rights to obtain these rights. With each new historical period, new notions have been expressed with respect to fundamental rights and to whom those rights pertain.

The first generation of rights are referred to as "negative rights" in that they call for restraint from the state. These rights were derived from the American and French revolutions and the struggle to gain liberty from arbitrary state action. These rights may be found in the Civil and Political Rights of the International Bill of Rights. The second generation of rights are referred to as "positive rights" in that they require affirmative action on the part of the state. These rights are found in the Economic, Social, and Cultural Rights of the International Bill of Rights. They emerged from the experience of the Soviet Union and they also resonate in the welfare state policies of the West. Finally, the third generation of rights calls for international cooperation. These rights are evolving out of the condition of global interdependence confronting humanity today. They recognize that human rights obligations can no longer be satisfied within individual states. In other words, the rights of peoples — independent of states — are required for a reduction in state violence, maintenance of world peace, protection of the environment, and global development on a massive scale (Crawford, 1988). Putting human justice into practice by whatever means necessary, and by all types of universal arrangements reached by state and nonstate representatives alike, are prerequisites for reducing all forms of crime, injury, and victimization.

Within the narrower pathways of criminological development and social justice, the coming-of-age or legitimation of the study of state criminality represents one of the fundamental prerequisites for the emergence of an integrated theory and praxis toward the reduction of state and nonstate crime. As suggested by the findings and analyses presented in this book, the theory and practice of state criminology calls for both a structural critique of the state (capitalist or socialist) and a transformation in the prevailing relations of the developing global political economy.

References

Agee, Philip
1988   Remarks presented at the session, The Role of the CIA. Anticommunism and the U.S.: History and Consequences, Institute for Media Analysis Inc., Harvard University, November 11–13.

Barak, Gregg and Robert M. Bohm
1989   The Crimes of the Homeless or the Crime of Homelessness? On the Dialectics of Criminalization, Decriminalization, and Victimization. *Contemporary Crises: Law, Crime and Social Policy.* Vol. 13, No. 4.

Boyle, Francis
1989   The Hypocrisy and Racism Behind the Formulation of U.S. Human Rights Foreign Policy. *Soical Justice: A Journal of Crime, Conflict, and World Order.* Vol. 16, No. 1 (Spring).

Crawford, James
1988   *The Rights of Peoples.* Oxford: Oxford University Press.

Chamorro, Edgar
1988   Remarks presented at the session. The Role of the CIA. Anticommunism and the U.S.: History and Consequences, Institute for Media Analysis Inc., Harvard University, November 11–13.

Falk, Richard
1988   Remarks presented at the session, The Growth of the National Security State. Anticommunism and the U.S.: History and Consequences, the Institute for Media Analysis Inc., Harvard University, November 11–13.
1989   United States Foreign Policy as an Obstacle to the Rights of People. *Social Justice: A Journal of Crime, Conflict, and World Order.* Vol. 16, No. 1 (Spring).

Felice, Bill
1989   Rights in Theory and Practice: An Historical Perspective. *Social Justice: A Journal of Crime, Conflict, and World Order.* Vol. 16, No. 1 (Spring).

Ellsberg, Daniel
1988   Remarks presented at the session, The Growth of the National Security State. Anticommunism and the U.S.: History and Consequences, the Institute for Media Analysis Inc., Harvard University, November 11–13.

O'Malley, Pat
1987   Marxist Theory and Marxist Criminology. *Crime and Social Justice.* No. 29.

Contributors

Gregg Barak is Professor and Chair of the Department of Criminology and Criminal Justice at Alabama State University. He received his doctorate from the University of California at Berkeley in 1974. He is the author of *In Defense of Whom? A Critique of Criminal Justice Reform* and the forthcoming *Gimme Shelter: A Social History of Homelessness in America*. Most of his publications have focused on law and order, public policy, and justice-related issues. Since 1987, he has served as book review editor for *Social Justice: A Journal of Crime, Conflict, and World Order* (formerly *Crime and Social Justice*).

Jose Maria Borrero N. practices criminal law in Cali, Colombia and has been the President of the *Fundacion para la Investigacion y Proteccion del Medio Ambiente* for the past fifteen years. He is the author of the recently published book, *Proteccion Penal De Los Derechos Ambientales* (1990).

Susan L. Caulfield is an Assistant Professor of Sociology at Western Michigan University. She received her PhD. from State University of New York at Albany in 1988. Her recent publications include "Life or Death Decisions: Prosecutorial Power Versus Equality of Justice" in the *Journal of Contemporary Criminal Justice* and "The Perpetuation of Violence Through Criminological Theory: The Ideological Role of Subculture Theory" in Richard Quinney and Harold E. Pepinsky's *Criminology as Peacemaking*.

A. Stuart Farson is the Director of Research of the Special Committee of the House of Commons on the Review of the Canadian Security Intelligence Service Act and the Security Offenses Act and a doctoral candidate in political science at the Centre of Criminology, University of Toronto. He has published several articles on security and intelligence matters, police accountability, and public complaint mechanisms. He is a founding member and a former Secretary-Treasure of the Canadian Association for Security and Intelligence Studies.

Daniel E. Georges-Abeyie is Associate Dean and Professor at the School of Criminology, Florida State University. Recent publications by Dr. Georges-Abeyie include *Criminal Justice and Blacks*, "Women as Terrorists" in Walter Laqueur and Yonah Alexander's *The Terrorism Reader*, "Political crime and Terrorism" in Graeme Newman's *Deviance and Crime*, and "Terrorism and the Liberal State" and "Toward the Development of a Terrorism Severity Index" in *The Journal of Police Studies*.

Mark S. Hamm is a former guard, teacher, and administrator of the Arizona Department of Corrections. He is currently an Associate Professor of Criminology at Indiana State University, Co-Chair of the Indiana Criminal Justice Research and Information Consortium, and a member of the Governor's Task Force on Mental Health in Criminal Justice. He is the author of *Heroin Addiction, Anomie, and Social Policy in the United States and Britain*, and an extended version of the chapter that appears in this volume.

Kayleen M. Hazlehurst has worked as a Senior Research Officer with the Australian Institute of Criminology since 1984 on aboriginal criminal justice issues. For the duration of the Inquiry by the Royal Commission into Aboriginal Deaths in Custody, she worked for the Aboriginal and Islander Legal Service, assisting in the preparation of its submission to the Inquiry. She has recently published several articles on racial tensions, policing, and aboriginal criminal justice, including the recently edited anthology, *Ivory Scales: Black Australia and the Law*.

Stuart Henry is an Associate Professor in the Department of Sociology, Anthropology, and Criminology at Eastern Michigan University. He is the author, co-author, or editor of numerous publications— *Self, Help, and Health* (1977); *The Hidden Economy* (1978); *Informal Institutions* (1981); *Private Justice* (1983); *Informal Economy* (1987); and *Degrees of Deviance* (1989).

Ronald Hinch is Associate Professor of Scoiology and Anthropology at the University of Guelph. He received his PhD. from McMaster University in Hamilton, Ontario and has taught at seven Canadian universities. He has published several articles on the pedagogy of criminology and sociology, and is currently co-authoring (with Walter Dekeseredy) *The Multidimensional Nature of Women Abuse in Canada*.

Christina Jacqueline Johns is Associate Professor in the Graduate Criminology Program at Alabama State University. She received her PhD. in Criminology from the University of Edinburgh in Edinburgh, Scotland. She has given numerous presentations about the war on drugs and its effects on Latin America, most recently at the Conference of Latin American Critical Criminologists in Bogota, Colombia. She is currently writing a book on the war on drugs and Latin America.

R. S. Ratner is Associate Professor of Sociology at the University of British Columbia. He is the co-editor (with John L. McMullan) of *State Control: Criminal Justice Politics in Canada*. He was guest editor in 1987 of the thematic issue of *Crime and Social Justice*, "Canada and the U.S.: Criminal Justice Connections." He also served as editor of issue No. 1 of the *Journal of Human Justice* on "Critical Criminology in Canada." In the Winter of 1990, he was a Visiting Fellow at the Institute of Criminology at the University of Cambridge in England.

John Wildeman is Professor of Sociology at Hofstra University. He received his PhD. from New York University. He is co-author (with Richard Quinney) of *The Problem of Crime*. He is also author of *Social Problems in America* and *Comparative Social Structures: Japan and the United States*. He specializes in issues of social control and deviance and has been the recipient of a Fulbright/Hayes lecture grant to Japan.

Index